ANNA MARIA SIGMUND

WOMEN OF THE

THIRD REICH

NDE Publishing
2000

Women of the Third Reich

by **Anna Maria Sigmund**

Translation:
NDE Publishing*

Editing:
Kathleen Harris and Penny Hozy

Desktop Publishing and Typesetting:
Natalya Romashkin and Aidyn Ismailov

Original title: **Die Frauen der Nazis**
© 1998 by Verlag Carl Ueberreuter, Vienna, Austria
© 2000 by NDE Canada Corp. for North American English Language Edition

Vladimir Mazour, President and Publisher
NDE Publishing*,15-30 Wertheim Court, Richmond Hill, Ontario
Canada   L4B 1B9   tel (905) 731-1288   fax (905) 731-5744
www.ndepublishing.com

Canadian Cataloguing-in-Publication Data

Sigmund, Anna Maria
      Women of the Third Reich

   Translation of: Die Frauen der Nazis.
   Includes bibliographical references.
   1. National socialism and women–Germany. 2. Women–Germany–History–20th century. 3. Women–Germany—Biography. 4. Fascism and women–Germany.
   I. Title.
DD245.S5413 2000   943.086'092'2   C00-900708-3
ISBN 1-55321-105-7

Printed and bound in Canada
* *NDE Canada Corp., a member of NDE Group of Companies*

TABLE OF CONTENTS

PREFACE

"They have no desire to work in an office or in Parliament. A happy home, a loving husband and a flock of happy children are closer to their hearts." These were Adolf Hitler's words. Nazi party ideologues developed the "Fuehrer's" anachronistic image into the National Socialist ideal of femininity—the tall, hard-working, Nordic blonde of cheerful disposition, keeper of hearth and home, surrounded by many children.

The fact that only a few of the wives, partners and lovers of leading Nazis lived up to these lofty ideals, was concealed from their contemporaries.

The rigorous system of censorship devised by Dr. Joseph Goebbels was able to protect the private lives of those in power from undesired scrutiny. The few rumors that existed were spread in secret, at great risk to the bearer's life. Hitler's royal retinue was an exclusive society, hermetically sealed off from the rest of the world. Hardly anything filtered through to the outer world, and the often unusual, even dramatic, fates of the women playing supporting roles to those in government remained a matter of speculation.

But how did the women in the sphere of the Nazi elite live? What role did they play in public and behind the scenes? Who were those artists, patrons and politicians Hitler counted among his "showpiece women?"

Immediately after the end of World War II, the press wrote at length about the privileged females of the Nazi state who had become subject to judicial inquiry. But many of the sensational revelations made at the time, and the passionate denials that appeared in autobiographical accounts, did not stand up under closer examination.

Only distance from the events, the current status of historical research on the Third Reich, the opening of sealed archives, and the comparison of a number of subjective and objective sources have made it possible to write the select biographies of those women who once played a significant role in National Socialist society.

Vienna, Summer of 1998
A. M. S.

HITLER AND THE "GERMAN WOMAN"

On April 3, 1923, the SPD (German Socialist Party) newspaper *Münchner Post* wrote about the "women infatuated with Hitler" and scornfully portrayed numerous patronesses and female admirers who were moved to tears by his speeches and who pawned their jewelry to lend money to the party. In retaliation for this and other similar reports, Hitler had the editorial offices of the newspaper demolished on November 8, 1923.[1]

From the outset, women proved to be among Hitler's most loyal collaborators. They set him up with contacts, provided him with money, and generally helped pave the way for him to reach the top. In 1926, the NSDAP (Nazi Party) stood on the brink of bankruptcy, and Hitler threatened to kill himself. "Don't accept bankruptcy, [but] rather [put] a bullet in my head."

"But then," he later reported, "at the last minute our dear Mrs. Bruckmann came to our aid. She arranged a meeting for me with Emil Kirdorf (a captain of industry), and we talked for four hours—Kirdorf paid all the debts and put the party back on track."[2] Elsa Bruckmann, née Princess Cantacuccene, ran a famous salon in Munich where she introduced Hitler to everyone who had power, money and influence. At his wife's request, the wealthy publisher Hugo Bruckmann paid Hitler's rent and let him have his mansion as a guest house. Elsa Bruckmann listened to Hitler's speeches there, hands folded as if in a trance.[3] Her willingness to help knew no bounds.

She wrote, "Dear Mr. Hitler, I can spare the wristwatch I am enclosing. Would you like to use it? Come by tomorrow or Thursday to have a look at the furniture, etc. you could possibly use."[4]

Hitler readily accepted it all. How he used the valuables of his admirers is documented: "As security for a loan ... Mr. Adolf Hitler deposits ... an emerald pendant with platinum and diamonds ... a diamond ring (Solitaire) ... a Venetian lace relief ... a red silk Spanish cover for a grand piano ..."[5]

Helene Bechstein, wife of the Bechstein piano maker, introduced Hitler into exclusive Berlin society. She also bought a luxury limousine for her idol. "'Wolf' [Hitler's nickname], you must have the best car there is. You deserve it.' She had in mind a Maybach," Hitler recalled. He preferred a Mercedes, and got one for the enormous sum of 26,000 marks.[6] Mrs. Bechstein had an estate on the Obersalzberg, and made it possible for Hitler to acquire his house, "Wachenfeld," there. He thanked her by awarding her the party's gold medal, which did not, however, protect her from ruthless expropriation when Bormann needed a summer residence for the Fuehrer on the Obersalzberg.

"These women were the best propagandists the party had; they persuaded their husbands to join Hitler's cause, sacrificed their spare time to their political enthusiasm ... committed themselves selflessly to the party's interests," wrote Heinrich Hoffmann, the party's photographer, in his memoirs. In Bamberg, for example, "true German" women organized tea parties to indulge their enthusiasm for Hitler and his circle.[7]

Hitler knew how to take subtle advantage of the sympathies of his female supporters. While boorish grassroots members rioted in the streets and eliminated opponents with terror and brute force, the Fuehrer mingled with the cream of high society—dominated by women—displayed his Austrian charm, kissed the ladies' hands, and opened up a new, but above all wealthy source of members for the NSDAP. Some of the less sophisticated party members, however, inaccurately assessed their leader's activities. He was even reprimanded within the party for "placing the company of beautiful women above his duties as party leader."[8]

Among the "motherly friends" of "Mr. Wolf," as Hitler coyly referred to himself, was his patroness and hiking partner Baroness Lily von Abegg, who not only donated money and art treasures to the party, but even, as the *Münchner Post* reported on April 3, 1923, her house.

In addition to the social contacts and the very generous material support, the political agitator profited most from the personality cult that his female admirers created around him. "Even the phrase 'Mein Fuehrer' was, I'm sure, coined by women," Hitler remarked with satisfaction.[9] Hitler was a master at manipulating individual men and women and using them. Absolute devotion to the Fuehrer was a condition of acceptance into the circle of the female NS (National Socialist or Nazi) elite. Hitler's charisma made people forget about the anti-woman platform—unique among Germany's parties—of the NSDAP.

Women were very welcome as regular dues-paying members, with an important proviso. "One thing must remain clear: judges, soldiers and statesmen are, and will be, only men," proclaimed Rosenberg, the Nazi theoretician.[10] "Women must be emancipated from women's emancipation" was a basic tenet of the National Socialist movement. The rise of Germany was regarded as a "male event."[11] As early as 1921, a members' meeting unanimously decided that women could never be accepted into the leadership or the executive committee of the party. After all, it was a matter of preserving nation, race and culture from downfall. And they were not about to entrust that job to women.

Hitler expressed it more simply: "A woman who sticks her nose in politics is an abomination to me. In 1924, the political women approached me: Frau von Treuenfels, Mathilde von Kemnitz [married to Ludendorff]; they wanted to become members of the Reichstag. It becomes completely unbearable if it's a question of military matters. There was not a local party group where a woman was allowed to hold even the lowest position ... I'm telling you, ninety-nine per cent of all subjects of discussion are matters for men only that [women] cannot pass judgment on ..."[12] And yet, Hitler knew that many Nazi supporters—including General Erich Ludendorff, the presidential candidate for the NSDAP— had become revolutionary politicians due to the influence of their wives. Mathilde Ludendorff, a physician, wrote inflammatory pamphlets and remained the dominant partner in her marriage.[13]

It was thanks to the political activity of Viktoria von Dirksen, wife of the future ambassador to London, that Hitler was able to address a large audience of exceedingly well-heeled people at the National Club in Berlin in 1922. It was also Mrs. Dirksen and members of the club who then arranged for the first significant contacts between Hitler and representatives of the northern states of Germany. The political salon of Viktoria von Dirksen in Berlin, with its cotierie of foreign diplomats, aristocrats and captains of industry, was an important forum for the Nazi regime for years.

In 1935, Hitler, who had an extremely elementary idea of the way British democracy worked, tried to exercise his influence on Great Britain's politics through an aristocratic English lady. He had been hoping for a long time to establish a German-British alliance. Unity Valkyrie Mitford, one of the six daughters of the eccentric Lord Redesdale, had, like her sisters, a passion for politics. While Diana sympathized with the British fascists and Jessica leaned towards Communism, Unity adored Hitler. In 1934, she moved to Munich, went to the party conventions, and finally approached her idol and spoke to him. Soon Unity was regularly seen in Hitler's company, wore the British fascist uniform, mounted swastika flags on her car and canvassed for the Nazi regime in England. But Hitler's hope of establishing direct contact with Churchill through Unity came to nothing.

Unity Mitford suffered a tragic fate. "I have two fatherlands," she said, and when one declared war on the other, she went to the English Garden in Munich, sat down on a park bench and fired a bullet into her temple. She survived the attempted suicide with the bullet stuck in her head. No German surgeon dared perform the operation to remove it, and she was sent back to England, where she lived another ten years.[14] For a long time, the Nazis' concept of the ideal woman was no more than wishful thinking and in sharp contrast to the movements and ideals of the period after World War I. Among Social Democrats and Communists, female politicians held important positions. During the Weimar Republic, women had, for the first time, exercised the right to vote. The slogans of the emancipation movements were starting to take hold. The middle class, in particular, was paying attention to the education of its daughters, believing that the future of the modern woman was in professional life.

Nazi slogans such as, "Men and women have been two separate beings since time immemorial, each with just as separate functions," and "The world of a woman is small compared to that of a man," caused outrage in many parts of Germany. The outdated and unpopular Nazi view of women had to be defended in the highest party circles. Goebbels noted in his diary; "… fierce debate on women and their role. I am a complete reactionary as far as that goes. Giving birth and rearing children are a life's work, after all. My mother is the woman I have the most respect for. And she is so far from intellect, and so close to life. Today, women have their say in everything; they just do not want to bear any children. And this is what we call emancipation. No, I am courageous enough to oppose the terror of public opinion. The discussion was heated and went on until two in the morning …"[15]

As long as the NSDAP needed the votes of women, the party saw itself obliged to soften its radical views. Hitler took prompt action.

"The Fuehrer develops completely new ideas on the position of women. They are of outstanding importance for the next election campaign, because this was where we were attacked in the first election. Woman is man's companion in sex and in work. She has always been that and always will be. Even in today's economic circumstances, she must be. In days gone by in the fields, today in an office. Man is the organizer of life, woman is his helper and his executive agent. These views are modern and lift us far above and beyond any personal resentments," Goebbels, full of enthusiasm about his leader's new versatility, wrote in his diary on March 23, 1932.

Only when the NSDAP were in power, could Dr. Goebbels proclaim hypocritically: "It was not because we did not respect women, but because we respected them too much that we kept them out of the web of intrigue of parliamentary democracy that determined politics in Germany."[16]

In 1928, Goebbels had noted in his diary:" I shall lose my mind without women around me!" One year later, it was resolutely clear that, "It is the duty of women to look beautiful and to give birth. This is not as crude and as outdated as it may sound. Among birds, the female smartens herself for the male and hatches the eggs for him. The male provides the food. At other times, he stands guard and fends off the enemy."[17]

Women retained their right to vote, however useless, in the totalitarian state that was Germany after 1933. They began to be rigorously expelled, however, from all other aspects of public life. To this end, an Act of Parliament was passed April 25, 1933, against "the overcrowding of schools and universities," which had a quota system for Jews and women—Jews were allowed to make up only 1.5 per cent of the student body and women only 10 per cent.

The Nazi view of women goes back to the social Darwinism of the 19th century, which had gained new currency in the writings of the leading nationalist and National Socialist thinkers. At the top of the list were Adolf Hitler's *Mein Kampf* and Alfred Rosenberg's *Mythos des 20. Jahrhunderts* [The Myth of the Twentieth Century]. Walther Darré, the "blood-and-earth mystic of the party," made a contribution as well, with his vision of "peasantry as the fountain of life for the Nordic race," and a "new aristocracy of blood and earth."

The Nazi state never developed an ideology for women. The "image of the German woman" developed partly on its own, based on the National Socialist world view and the practical considerations of power politics. Slogans such as, "Woman as the guardian of the race, virtue and morals," were only a front for the more pragmatic goals, such as: eliminate unemployment, increase the population for war and for settlement in the East.

Hitler knew how to simplify his ideas: "If the liberal intellectual women's movements ... were formerly developments of the mind ... our program contains only one point—the child." [18] An understandable point of view for a dictator who believed that, "If you want what's best for the German people, then ... there must be a war every fifteen to twenty years."[19]

In the *ABC of Nationalsozialism*, published in 1936, the National Socialist view of women was romantically embellished: "We want to have women again, not toys trimmed with trinkets ... The German

Enthusiastic welcome for Hitler in Klagenfurt

woman is wine. When she is in love, the earth blooms. The German woman is sunshine on the domestic hearth. You shall remain venerable, not the pleasure and plaything of foreign races. The people shall remain pure and clean—this is the Fuehrer's noble objective."[20] Women like that were hard to find, so one party member put the following advertisement in the *Münchner Neuesten Nachrichten*:

"Fifty-two-year-old pure Aryan doctor, Tannenberg fighter, wishes to settle down and, through civil marriage, have male offspring with a woman who is healthy, devout, a young virgin, modest, parsimonious, suited to hard work, thrifty, who must wear shoes with broad heels, no earrings and, if possible, with no assets. Agents declined, confidentiality assured."[21]

Women's emancipation in Germany was already highly developed and had taken root deep in the public consciousness. It was no longer possible to restrain or reverse it overnight. The "politicking woman" was not, as the National Socialists believed, merely a "post-war phenomenon." Women were working in every field and actively cultivating their image shaped by the worldly upper class of the 1920s. There were women's car races, events organized by women pilots and competitions for female parachutists—the "modern woman" was not just a common catch-phrase. Of course this new breed of woman—exemplified by Melitta

Schiller (married name Countess Stauffenberg), who had a doctorate in physics, a diploma in engineering and was a pilot—didn't know what to make of the Nazi ideal of a woman at the "spinning wheel and loom." As a pilot, Captain Schiller tested the performance of critical flight instruments in about 1,500 life-threatening nosedives. She also won the "Relilability Flight award for female amateur pilots." The second place in the competition went to an equally interesting personality—Beate Koestlin. Later, during World War II, she was a test pilot for an aircraft factory. In 1943, as a Luftwaffe captain, she was assigned to the transfer aircraft, where she flew the world's first jet fighters (the ME 262) to the front. She married her flight instructor, Hans Uhse, who died in 1944 while on a mission as flight captain. Widowed, she managed to fly out of the encircled city of Berlin with her son and his nanny at the end of April 1945. After the war, Beate Uhse started a mail order company for sex paraphernalia. Her ideas and activities contributed immensely to the loosening of attitudes toward sexuality in the climate of the 1960s.

Hitler's own view of women seems ambivalent. He would utter pithy sayings such as, "If a woman starts thinking about her existence, that's bad"—yet, at the same time, he encouraged career women. For example, he hired the architect Gerdy Troost, the owner of a large engineering and architecture company, to design the buildings on the Obersalzberg, and had Leni Riefenstahl direct films of the party rallies.

Hanna Reitsch (1912–1979) also made a name for herself in that male-dominated world, becoming one of the most celebrated test pilots of the Third Reich. Hitler himself handed her the decree, in 1937, in which she was named the first female flight captain in the world. That same year—again a first—she flew helicopters. In 1938, flying Focke helicopters in the Deutschlandhalle, she performed the first indoor flight in the world, for which she received the military pilot's medal. On November 5, 1942, Hitler awarded her the first-class Iron Cross, one of the highest German military honors, for "the unflagging commitment of her life [in] the service of the development of the German aircraft."[22] In 1943, she flew rocket-assisted planes and in 1944, she was the first to sit behind the controls of a jet plane; and on April 26, 1945, she flew to Hitler through heavy Russian anti-aircraft fire into the surrounded city of Berlin.[23]

While Hitler publicly equated women with the mentally retarded, he said in private, "Women, it is said, are not creative. But there was one

Hanna Reitsch, the famous test pilot

great woman, and it makes me angry that men are unjust here. Angelika Kauffmann was one of the greatest painters …"[24] He continued in the same vein, "What would have become of Siegfried Wagner if he had not had … Mother Cosima and his equally important partner Winifried at his side?"[25] Nothing, the simple answer must be, because Siegfried lived in the shadow of his wife. After his death, his widow Winifried, a British national, continued to reside at "Wahnfried" like an uncrowned monarch, brought up four children and managed, by herself, the internationally famous festival of Bayreuth. Hitler considered her one of his "showpiece women": "Mrs. Wagner has managed to merge Bayreuth with National Socialism—that is her great historical achievement."[26]

In the Third Reich, "ladies" were a welcome decoration at receptions at the Reich Chancellery, and as part of Hitler's entourage. Otherwise, there was only talk of "women in the fields and at the spinning wheel"—slogans that the women in the influential sphere of the Nazi elite did not apply to themselves. Lines such as, "The cooking spoon is a woman's weapon," did not pertain to them either, for most of these women had staff for this kind of work. In fact, nobody was further from the Nazi image of the ideal female than the women, spouses and mistresses of the Nazis elite. Eva Braun never thought of giving up her haute-couture clothing or her makeup; she took up body-

Hitler with Winifried Wagner and Wieland Wagner in Bayreuth (in the background, on the left: Wolfgang Wagner)

building and made movies. Margarete Himmler, a former nurse, had too much contempt for her husband to take his ideas seriously. Emmy Goering had already established herself as an actress, and Carin Goering was a textbook example of a political agitator. Henriette von Schirach advocated reviving the cultural life of Vienna. Even the lesser known, yet endlessly active, influential Nazi women were only occasionally to be found in the kitchen.

Nazi figurehead Magda Goebbels vehemently took up the fight for women's rights outside the official party platform. Women's issues were often and hotly debated in the Goebbels household. "Finally heated debate about woman, respectively her capacity; in rage, Magda gravely abusive towards me. We part in a quarrel ...," Goebbels wrote in his diary on August 15, 1931. On one occasion, even Hitler got involved in the debate. "He tells me I'm right: women have no place in public life." But Magda was not ready to admit defeat. After the couple took leave of the Fuehrer, the argument flared up again at their hotel. "But when it comes to principles, there is no quarter," Goebbels noted triumphantly on July 22, 1933.

Members of the Nazi elite hardly had the prescribed flock of children either. Only the Bormann and Goebbels families met the quota. And Gerda Bormann, wife of the powerful party secretary, was the only one inside the circle of notables who met all the criteria of the new ideal of femininity. The daughter of long-time party member Walter Buch married Martin Bormann, a convicted accomplice to murder, in a typical swastika wedding, had nine children, and clung naïvely and fanatically to her husband and to the Fuehrer. She was willing to sacrifice everything for the "cause." She carried out National Socialist meditation sessions and worked out a system that would allow her and her husband's mistresses to live together under one roof. "... put all the children together in the house on the lake and live together, and the woman who has not just had a child will always be available for you."[27]

In the beginning, the National Socialists honored the institution of marriage. It is interesting to note how often Hitler felt compelled to make excuses for not being married. As early as October 1920 he wrote to an old friend, "As for my family, for now it consists of a marvelous German shepherd. I haven't aspired to anything higher yet. The former ringleader then as today's ringleader has not been sufficiently refined for life's tender bonds just yet ..."[28] In 1928 he said, "... with my irregular life ... this is the reason that I cannot bring myself to get married ..."[29]

Marriage was encouraged not out of moral considerations, but because the National Socialists valued it as the perfect "breeding institution"—until they did a simple calculation: "Unfortunately, women outnumber men by two million. The goal will and must be for every girl to get married, but before one wastes away as an old spinster, it's better for her to have a child—even out of wedlock. Nature wants women to bear children, some women fall ill if they never give birth ... Yes, it is a thousand times better for a woman to have a child and with it some purpose for her life, rather than go grief-stricken from the world."[30]

On one occasion, Hitler talked about the issue of out-of-wedlock births at the Goebbels house in front of a large number of guests from the artistic community until three o'clock in the morning. "... Fuehrer is quite modern and without blinkers. Magda takes an absolutely reactionary point of view. Neither smart nor tactful. After the guests had left, we promptly got into another argument ...," Goebbels wrote in his diary on December 17, 1935.

Adhering to the Nazi ideology on race and on women, Himmler developed his "Fountain of Life," a breeding program for Nordic-Germanic people. "When I established the Fountain of Life, I proceeded on the assumption that first of all a pressing problem would be solved, in order to enable women of pure race who are about to bear a child out of wedlock to deliver at no cost ... I let it be known unofficially that every single woman who was alone but who wanted to have a child could turn to the Fountain of Life. The SS Reich Leader would be the godfather to such a child. Only racially sound men would be recommended as conception assistants," Heinrich Himmler confided to his doctor and masseur.[31]

The National Socialists bragged about having solved the women's problem because they were convinced they knew exactly what women wanted: "German women want mainly to be wives and mothers, not party members, as the red 'people's benefactors' try to make themselves and them believe. Women have no yearning for a factory, an office, and not [the slightest] yearning for Parliament. A snug home, a loving husband and a bunch of happy children are closer to their hearts."[32] The attempt to control present and future with reactionary methods was, however, doomed to failure.

The Nazi state's sacrifice of the economic and intellectual potential of its women citizens came back to haunt the regime, just as the backward attitude of the Third Reich toward scientific research had undesired consequences in a surprisingly short space of time.

While the leading Nazis obstructed the work of serious scientists or supported it only half-heartedly, they showed a lot of interest in obscure theories such as the *Welteislehre*, or the theory of eternal ice, developed by the Austrian engineer Hanns Hoerbiger. Meanwhile, the physicists they had driven out of the country were preparing for nuclear war. In much the same way, the idea of the "little woman at home" also backfired. While the Germans waged a petty war on lipstick and nail polish and prohibited women from smoking in public, the Allied weapons industry primarily employed women. Even when, during World War II, a shortfall of workers started to cause problems, Hitler, caught up in his own ideology, refused for a long time to use female forced labor.

Albert Speer, the minister in charge of weapons' manufacturing, complained about this: "Hitler could have had an army in mid-1941 that was twice as strong … if only he had employed the same standards for working women as Britain or the United States. About five million women would have been available to the weapons industry; and Hitler could have set up a number of additional divisions with three million soldiers …"[33] Although the theory of the ideal woman promoted by the National Socialists proved unworkable in real life, the regime continued making plans for the period following the war, plans that would have been even more radical than the Fountain of Life. It was, therefore, considered advisable to keep these plans from the public until the "final victory."

Gerda Bormann, a fanatic among the female Nazi elite, was very enthusiastic about those plans. "We should introduce a law at the end of the war like the law passed at the end of the Thirty Years' War, which allowed healthy, productive men to have two wives [marginal note by Martin Bormann: 'the Fuehrer has similar ideas'].[34] So terribly few productive men will come out of this fateful war alive, so many worthy women are destined to remain childless … We need children from these women as well!"

Martin Bormann, who, with his wife's approval, had several girlfriends besides his mistress, Manja Behrens, gladly supported that view. "Yes, absolutely, for the coming battle that will decide the fate of our nation."[35]

The ethno-biological measures being considered around 1943 seem to have originated in a chamber of horrors. It was determined that women up to the age of 35 would be obliged to conceive four children with racially pure German men. As soon as a family had reached that magic number, the husband would then have to make himself available to the program.[36]

The outcome of World War II put an end both to the Nazi breeding program and the planned "shotgun weddings." It also prevented the breakdown of monogamy that would result from the introduction and legalization of concubines.

CARIN GOERING

Nordic Idol and Cult Figure

October 21, 1888 – September 25, 1931

I n an official ceremony on June 20, 1934, the body of Carin Goering, who had died in 1931, was formally transported from Sweden to Germany. It was a unique spectacle organized by propaganda minister Joseph Goebbels, but the idea for this ceremony originated with the widower of Carin Goering, Prussian premier Hermann Goering.

For Goering, president of the Reichstag, it was a primary concern to have his beloved wife buried in the crypt that had been built for her at the Goerings' summer residence, Carinhall in Schorfheide. He also knew how to take political advantage of the funeral. Thus the date—ten days before the "Roehm Putsch," when no one actualy revolted, but the leaders of the SA (Nazi militia "Storm Troops") were murdered—had not been chosen by coincidence. It was a calculated ploy. The funeral was used as a skillful tactic by Goering and Goebbels to divert the attention of the SA leaders, who had already become suspicious. At the same time, the funeral of the revered Carin Goering, who as a heroine of early National Socialism was to be buried on German soil, provided the plausible excuse for the conspirators to gather in one place. So it was that Carin Goering, who had made so many sacrifices for the NSDAP during her lifetime, continued to serve the party three years after her death.

Her body was transported to Germany in great splendor in a zinc coffin, but without the involvement of clergy, and was reminiscent of the funeral ceremony for an Egyptian pharaoh. Joseph Goebbels, who organized everything with his customary panache, must have looked to the ancient Egyptian cult of the dead for inspiration.

First, a German torpedo-boat crew along with a group representing the Swedish National Socialists demonstrated their solidarity at the open grave in Lovö near Drottningholm. Then, in a meticulously planned funeral ritual, the coffin was loaded onto a specially decorated train that took Carin Goering's mortal remains from Sweden to Germany. In all the towns along the route to Eberswald, the train station near the destination of Carinhall, were in national mourning, with flags at half-mast and church bells ringing. Hitler Youth formed a cordon as the train passed through each station, and huge numbers of people paid their last respects to Carin Goering. For the last leg of the trip through the Schorfheide, the coffin was placed in an open vehicle, surrounded by black obelisks burning sacrificial flames, and taken to the crypt under the protection of a mounted honor guard.

The ceremony in Carinhall began with Hitler's arrival at twelve o'clock sharp. The coffin, draped in a swastika, was carried down an aisle lined with soldiers into the subterranean mausoleum to the strains of the funeral march from Wagner's *Götterdämmerung*. Carin's relatives, foreign diplomats, and all the high-ranking politicians of the Nazi regime provided an escort. At the end, Hitler and Goering descended once more into the crypt to bid the dead woman farewell.[1]

The *Völkische Frauenzeitung*, or "National Women's News," reflected on the events in June 1934. "Wherever National Socialism, [with] Germany unified under its banner, remembers its dead, let a wreath of gratitude and silent promise be laid upon Carin Goering's grave. A Germany, for which such women live, fight and die, must go on. Let the life of this Nordic woman serve us as a role model. We grow awestruck, silent before so much self-evident loyalty and inner greatness of a true woman ..."

Hermann Goering and his first wife Carin von Kantzow, née Baroness Fock, were considered the classic lovers of the Nazi era as they seemingly epitomized Dr. Goebbels's notion of the "ideal family,"—and contributed significantly to the party propaganda machine. The romance between the Nordic goddess and the Germanic flying ace from the earliest days of the NSDAP, the so-called "period of battles," was hailed as the dramatic epic of two lovers, who, with heroic commitment, paved the way for the fledgling party. The ordeals that the couple suffered while serving the party included personal injury, escape from confinement and exile, and ended with Carin's premature death in 1931, just when things were "moving forward and upward,"[2] as her sister, Fanny Countess von Wilamowitz-Moellendorf, put it. The Countess, who referred to herself as a German-Swede, published a biography of her sister in 1933.

This book, about a woman devoted to the National Socialist party from its very beginning, became a bestseller—next to Hitler's *Mein Kampf*—and went through several editions. Even though the only market for the book was Hitler's Germany, more than 900,000 copies were sold by 1943. People read it eagerly because the subject matter, allowed by Goebbels's strict censorship (Dr. Joseph Goebbels had been the minister in charge of national information policy and propaganda since May 13, 1933), provided a rare glimpse into the private life of Hermann Goering, one of the most successful fighter pilots of World War I, who went on to become Reich marshal of the Pan-German empire and commander-in-chief of the German Luftwaffe (air force). Fanny wove National Socialist legends around her sister. But what really happened?

It all began in Sweden. At the end of February 1920, Swedish globetrotter Count Eric von Rosen, Carin's brother-in-law, returned to Stockholm from his great expedition to Gran Chaco. There to his dismay, extreme weather conditions, including a blinding snowstorm, made it impossible for him to return home to Rockelstad Castle. Angry at being thwarted so close to home, the wealthy and eccentric count turned to the private airline, Svenska Lufttrafik, to charter an air taxi. Three pilots refused his requests—to them, flying in the prevailing conditions was tantamount to suicide. The fourth, however, a German with major financial problems, thought briefly of the winter coat he had just pawned and agreed, trusting in his expert skills.[3]

Hermann Goering had commanded the legendary fighter squadron Manfred Freiherr von Richthofen in World War I, and received the highest medal for bravery, "Pour le mérite." After the end of the war, the provisions of the Treaty of Versailles demanded that Germany dissolve its air force,[4] and since private air travel was also subject to severe restrictions, there was no demand for pilots. So Goering, a captain, now decommissioned and unemployed, and still suffering from an unhappy relationship with actress Käthe Dorsch, went to Scandinavia.[5] He was odd-jobbing as a salesman of flight accessories until Svenska Lufttrafik, the forerunner of SAS, hired him as chief pilot.

Goering piloted the air taxi taking Count Rosen to his castle about a hundred kilometers from Stockholm on February 20, 1920. It was a dangerous venture. Goering lost his bearings in the storm, but completed the worst flight of his life—as he would often tell people later on—when he was finally able to touch down on the ice of Lake Baven in front of the castle. With its imposing round towers, heavy brick walls and extensive park, Rockelstad today looks like a fortress and is reminiscent of the Middle Ages. The main building dates back to the 17th century. Only toward the end of the 19th century did the millionaire Count Eric Rosen realize his chivalric dreams and turn the country castle into a fortress in the style of the Wasa era. Goering was fascinated by the edifice, which brought back memories of his own childhood in the castles of Veldenstein near Nuremberg and Mauterndorf in Salzburg. Veldenstein and Mauterndorf, at that time, were owned by Baron Dr. Epenstein, his mother's doctor and lover. In 1938, Hermann Goering acquired the title to Veldenstein. The hunting lodge of Rockelstad, decorated with arms and armor, also impressed Goering. The simple lodge in the middle of the forest would give flight to his imagination for a long time to come. Eventually—when money was no longer an issue for him—he had it copied and made much larger on the Schorndorf Heath as "Carinhall."

When Goering entered the castle on February 20, 1920, a huge fire was roaring in the fireplace, and as chance would have it—as was reported later for propaganda purposes—the wrought-iron bars on which the logs were stacked, were adorned with swastikas. Mary von Rosen, wife of the globetrotter, and her daughter, also Mary, went to greet Goering at the door and bid him welcome.[6] While they were sitting in front of the

The hall in Rockelstad, where Hermann Goering and Carin von Kantzow, née Fock, met for the first time.

fireplace chatting, a young woman appeared at the top of the stairs and slowly descended the wide staircase to the hall below. She was tall and blonde, and according to contemporaries, she combined "a graceful and noble figure with a charming personality." She embraced Count von Rosen and smiled at the stranger. To Goering, who was convinced that Sweden was "home to the purest Germanic culture," she looked like a Nordic-Germanic goddess.[7] According to him, her blue eyes "struck him like lightning."

The mysterious beauty was Carin von Kantzow who was a guest at Rockelstad, keeping her sister Mary von Rosen company. At the time of their first encounter, Carin was thirty-two and Goering twenty-seven years old.

An evening filled with sentimentality and strong emotion followed. Hermann Goering relived his war memories and told them how he had ended up in Sweden. Then, Count Rosen, who loved heroic Norse sagas and venerated Romanticism, grabbed his lute and sang patriotic songs. The fun lasted until the early morning hours. Guest and host were both conservative nationalists who believed in the old-fashioned ideals of chivalry and held Nordic-Germanic culture in the highest regard. They debated and talked politics and discovered that they were kindred spirits. During that evening, Goering and Count Rosen established a lifelong friendship.

On the morning of February 21, 1920, Goering took Carl-Gustav Rosen, the son of his hosts and an airplane fanatic—who later built the Ethiopian air force and was killed while on a "mission of mercy" for the Red Cross—for a short ride in his plane. His entry in the guest book read as follows: "21. 2. 1920–Hermann Goering, commander, fighter squadron Freiherr von Richthofen." Afterwards, Carin took him around the castle and also showed him her sister's "Edelweiss Chapel." Goering then bade them farewell, but he arranged to meet Carin again. There was little doubt that this married woman and mother of an eight-year-old son[8] completely reciprocated Goering's feelings.

Carin von Kantzow was only too willing to enter into the passionate romance that was soon to develop in February of 1920.[9] After ten years of marriage, the beautiful Swede was having serious doubts about the meaning of her life with the professional soldier Nils Gustav Baron von Kantzow and longed for a knight in shining armor and for adventure. Bored, Carin complied with the well-ordered professional career of her husband but knew it held no other promise than a monotonous future of moving from one provincial garrison town to the next, a lonely and empty existence.

With her emotional nature, Carin took after her mother Huldine, née Beamish, who passed on a passion for spiritual and romantic ideas to her daughter.

Carin was the fourth of five daughters of Carl Baron von Fock, a colonel who later became regimental commander. She was born in Stockholm on October 21, 1888. Her father was from an impoverished Westphalian aristocratic family that had emigrated to Sweden in the 19th century, while her Swedish-born mother was of Irish descent.[10]

The women of the Fock family were all domineering and eccentric. But they gave themselves romantic airs that—in keeping with the spirit of the age at the turn of the century—were soulful and noble. Photos show the girls Mary, Fanny, Elsa, Carin and Lily, heads slightly bowed, in a sentimentally enraptured pose. Like their mother, they liked to avoid mundane reality. Fortunately, the family was financially well off, allowing them to turn their backs on the tedium of daily life. They lived by the bizarre philosophy of an "Edelweiss Club" founded by their grandmother. They

Carin Goering with her son Thomas from her first marriage.

used the club's own chapel to meditate and worship but also held séances there. Their enthusiasm for this was so great that Mary, after marrying the millionaire Eric Count von Rosen, created her very own Edelweiss Chapel by erecting an altar in a tower chamber of Rockelstad Castle. Carin, who was considered one of the most beautiful girls in Stockholm, was a lifelong member of the family's private religious club.

Shortly after his departure from Rockelstad, Goering wrote to Carin, "I would like to thank you from the bottom of my heart for the wonderful moments I was allowed to spend in the Edelweiss Chapel. You cannot imagine how I felt in that wonderful atmosphere. It was so peaceful and beautiful that I forgot all earthly noise, all cares fell away…"[11] These were exactly the right words to use with Carin. On February 24, she returned to Stockholm to be close to Goering, who had made a profound impression on her.

They met frequently. "He is the man of my dreams," she told her sister Fanny.[12] Later she confessed, "We are like Tristan and Isolde. We have tasted the potion of love and we are helpless, indeed ecstatically helpless under its influence."[13] Soon, Carin became the determining force in Hermann Goering's life in a relationship that was to last eleven years.

In the summer of 1920, their passion was so intense that Carin, without any consideration for her husband, son or family, traveled to Munich with her lover in order to meet Hermann's mother.

Franziska Goering was a widow with a colorful past. For years she had lived under one roof with both her husband and her lover. They all resided at Veldenstein Castle—her husband occupied the first floor, while she lived with Baron Dr. Epenstein on the second. The memory of her own behavior, however, did not stop her from severely criticizing her son for carrying on with a married woman and she demanded that he end this immoral relationship. But Hermann, who had grown up in the "ménage à trois" of his parents, was unmoved by his mother's exhortations.

The couple traveled the whole of June and July around Southern Germany, Bavaria and the Austrian Alps. Carin made no effort to hide the affair. Rather, she kept her concerned family up-to-date with letters and picture postcards and sent them photo albums illustrating her exciting adventure. Carin was a compulsive letter writer, reporting back to Sweden on every single aspect of her life. Above all, she kept her mother, to whom she was very close, informed of the eventful stages of her affair with Goering.[14]

In Hochkreuth near Bayrisch-Zell, in the mountains near the Austrian border, the couple rented an idyllic little house from a farmer named Huber that they lyrically called their "gingerbread house." The log house, which still stands today, frequently served as a residence for the couple between 1920 and 1923. Later, when the Goerings returned from exile, they lived in Berlin and did not revisit the house until 1930.

Carin cooked and corresponded directly with her husband, who was taking a course at the military academy of St. Cyr in France. To make her departure from Sweden plausible, she told him, "The air in Bavaria is better and essential to my survival." Meeting him in August 1920, Carin assured her husband that he, her mother and her son Thomas were the only people who truly mattered to her. Then she moved into a joint apartment with Goering in Stockholm, at #5 Karlvagen, and traveled with her lover to the castles of Ludwig II since the couple felt a rapport with the ideas and overall philosophy of the Bavarian king.

Upon their return, Goering urged Carin to get a divorce. At first, she refused to do so, fearing she might lose her son. Thomas often met his mother and her lover secretly after school, and would listen with interest to Uncle Hermann's stories about his days as a fighter pilot. The boy admired Goering very much. Nils von Kantzow, however, was still hoping to save his marriage, and arranged a luncheon meeting for the three of them. But it merely proved to be an embarrassment to them all.

Soon afterward, the couple retreated into the Bavarian mountains. They were not heard of until, beset with money problems, they turned to Carin's cuckolded husband. Wrongly assuming that his wife wanted to come back to him in Sweden, Nils von Kantzow promptly helped. Carin, however, pleaded the excuse of medical attention and stayed with Hermann Goering. To her parents, she wrote, "Bavaria is wonderful, a beautiful place—so rich, so warm, … so completely different from the rest of Germany. I am very happy here and feel at home. If I am home-sick for Sweden, [it is] only because I miss Mama, Nils, [my] little boy and those I love. But this painfully morbid longing means that I am sad most of the time. Oh, dear Mama, if only I were not in love with this One …"[15] Thereupon her parents tried to persuade Carin to move back to her beloved summer residence in Engsholm near Drottningholm.

But Carin filed for divorce. On December 13, 1922, the divorce was finalized. "All I can do is love her," Nils von Kantzow wrote to his parents-in-law. He was awarded custody of Thomas, but was left a broken man and became severely depressed.

In 1921, Hermann Goering enrolled at the University of Munich to study history and economics—not so much out of interest, but for lack of anything else to do. He had a vague notion of a career in politics. Goering's fate—and Carin's—was sealed the following year, however. Hermann Goering was introduced to Hitler, who immediately captivated him with slogans about saving the Fatherland from the scandalous Treaty of Versailles and the fight against Jews and Communism. Hitler, for his part, thought it opportune to recruit the decorated fighter pilot for the NSDAP for reasons of prestige and immediately entrusted Goering with the setting up and organizing of a group of rowdies that they called the Storm Troopers.[16]

"From the very first moment I saw and listened to him, I fell for him hook, line and sinker. I gave him my hand and said, 'I link my fate, for better or for worse, to yours ... through good times and bad, and ... I don't exempt my head, either.'" This was how Goering depicted his relationship to Adolf Hitler to the international military tribunal in Nuremberg in 1946.[17]

Carin Goering's experience was not so different; she merely expressed it differently. She spoke of the "sanctity of the cause" and in 1923, after Hitler's failed putsch against the Reich government and Reich President Ebert, she gushed that, "The movement that brings forth such heroes can never die." She too stressed that "Hermann and I would gladly die for it [Hitler and the party]."

Thus began the passionate self-sacrifice of Carin and Hermann Goering for the NSDAP, which would end only with their deaths.

Hitler had a rather sobering comment about the German-Swedish couple: "The men in Nordic countries are so weak-kneed that the most beautiful women there leave if they get one of our men. That's how it was with Goering and his Carin."[18]

Carin and Hermann were married in Stockholm on January 25, and in a modest ceremony in Obermenzing, their joint residence in Munich, on February 3, 1923.[19] Hermann Goering's comrades from the Richthofen squadron attended the wedding as honor guards, and Carin appeared all in white. The roses that decorated her hair were white as well, while her bridal bouquet was made up in the green and white colors of the Fock family. They spent their honeymoon in Italy, followed by a few days in Bayrisch-Zell, where Carin wrote a letter to her son.

She tried to explain the situation in terms suitable to a child. Her son by this time was eleven, but the truth did not seem to matter very much to her: "Dear Thomas. Aunt Mary [Carin's sister] has told you that I am now married to Captain Goering and that he and I live in a villa here. You know that the severe climate of Sweden is not good for my health, which is why I must remain here in the mountains. We have known Captain Goering, as you will remember, since the days in Stockholm. He was so nice and helpful to your mother when she was in a foreign country [Bavaria] all by herself. It was then that I realized that I loved him and that I wanted to marry him ... You see, my darling, he has made your mother happy, and you must not be sad. It must not ruin the love we have for each other. You know, I love you most of all ..."[20] Referring to her new husband, Carin told a girlfriend, "My God, how wonderful it is to have a husband who does not take two days to laugh at a joke."[21]

Carin's ex-husband had little choice but to provide the money for the purchase of a house with staff befitting their social position, which he had already done before the wedding. The Goerings had chosen a small, new villa at #30 Doebereinerstrasse in Obermenzing, a suburb of Munich close to Nymphenburg. They deliberately selected a place in the countryside because Carin's health did not allow her to stay in the city for too long. Angina pectoris, difficulty in breathing that led to fainting spells, asthma, severe rheumatism, latent intestinal disease and anemia were only a few of the ailments suffered by the then 35-year-old. The great distance between their new house and the city center and the poor accessibility by public transportation—before construction of the high-speed railway—did not matter. Nils von Kantzow paid for a Mercedes complete with chauffeur for his still beloved ex-wife.

The charming house full of nooks and crannies and adorned with wooden shingles, where Carin realized her dream of domestic bliss, is still standing. It has survived the intervening decades completely unchanged. With its small garden and old trees, it provides a unique contrast to the stolidity of the surrounding buildings of more recent times.

The first task Carin tackled was the furnishing of her fairytale home. She sent a detailed report to her mother. The windowpanes were painted with roses and reflected the light. The furniture, including Carin's white organ, came from Sweden. Pale pink carpets and white fur rugs covered the floors. In the den, there was a pink Smyrna carpet that accentuated the antique mahogany furniture. The bedroom walls were covered with silk wallpaper, and over the bed, there was a blue brocade canopy. Armchairs, dressing table and curtains were also in pink. Hermann Goering's study sported heavy oak furniture, and the lead-glass windows were adorned with chivalric motifs.

A hatch built into the floor of the dining room led to the actual center of the house, a vaulted cellar with an open fireplace, rustic furniture, Gobelin tapestries and fur rugs. It was Goering's way of realizing his dream of having his own castle, but for the time being on a more modest scale.[22] The subterranean, catacomb-like rooms were the ideal venue for the meetings of the first National Socialist partisans. They enjoyed meeting there, particularly because the new party member and his wife were such good hosts. Carin's sister Fanny, who also lived in Bavaria at the time, praised her for it: "… she (Carin) served home-cooked meals to many tired, harassed and hungry National Socialists. How much good her delicious and original food [did for] the Fuehrer and the personalities visiting him after hours of deliberation."[23]

Goering for his part revealed his considerable organizational talents in training the SA, turning that "seedy bunch" in a short time into a strong private army ready for action at a moment's notice. When they paraded past Hitler on April 15, 1923, Carin was completely ecstatic. She wrote to her son Thomas. "One day, you will be proud of my beloved husband who is now your second father. Today, he had his army of loyal, young Germans march past his Fuehrer, and I saw how radiant he was … he worked hard with them … so that the former riffraff … now really have become an army of light … ready to march at the command of the Fuehrer to liberate this unfortunate country … When it was all over, the Fuehrer embraced my beloved husband and told me that he could not possibly tell him what he really thought of his achivements because it would surely go to his head. I told him that I was ready to explode with pride.Then he took my hand and kissed it, and told me that this could not happen to a woman with such a pretty head on her shoulders. It may not have been the most elegant compliment I have ever been paid, but I liked it."[24]

While Carin and Hermann Goering devoted their lives to the fledgling NSDAP, Nils von Kantzow was showing the first signs of mental illness. In mid-1923, he attacked a colleague during a business trip because the colleague pitied him and insulted Goering. When he choked the man, the victim cried for help, whereupon Kantzow jumped out the window of the moving train.[25] He was dismissed from his teaching position that same year. His condition steadily worsened, and he eventually died in a state of mental derangement. But for as long as he could, he played the role of the generous benefactor. He financed Carin and Hermann Goering's luxurious household and its upkeep and sent them packages of food.

On July 15, 1923, Goering's mother died. In spite of a cold, Carin attended the funeral and came down with a severe case of pneumonia, which lasted for months. "I have a slight cold," she wrote in a letter to her son Thomas in Stockholm, "I am in bed while I am writing this letter because my beloved husband has insisted on it … He is very busy and great things are about to happen …"[26]

In fact, Hitler and the other right-wing paramilitary organizations were about to form a combat unit to be deployed in a putsch modeled on the one carried out by the Italian fascists. It happened on November 8, 1923 as Carin lay sick in bed. But her sister Fanny, who accompanied the protest march, witnessed a column of SA and shock troops set off at noon and march to the Odeon Square, sure of victory and cheered on by the crowds. Hitler, General Ludendorff and Goering were marching in the front row. But just before they got to the Feldherrnhalle [Hall of Generals], the Bavarian police opened fire. There were casualties, some fatal—the putsch had failed. Goering was shot in the hip several times. Storm Troops (SA) dragged the helpless Goering to the house of the Ballins, a Jewish family, who knew the identity of the wounded man. Nonetheless they did not hesitate to call a doctor, taking very good care of him and no doubt saving his life.[27]

Following the putsch, the NSDAP was banned, but was still able to continue counting on the complete sympathy of its members. The Goerings too remained true to their convictions and avoided political persecution by fleeing across the border to Austria. Carin's letters from exile are eloquent testimony to the agitated political mood of the time.[28]

On November 13, 1923, she wrote to her mother; "… we have gone through extraordinary hardship, but in spite of it all, it was a good time. Hermann's leg is shot to pieces; the bullet went right through, half a centimeter from the artery. There is a lot of dirt and rubble in the long channel that the bullet bored. The shot is high up in his right upper thigh, and terribly infected because the dirt etc., is trying to come out, and therefore causes a lot of pus and fever and violent pains. He has had to endure so much, my dear Hermann, [and] in spite of it all only thinks ceaselessly about me. We took the car from Munich to Garmisch (with his first bandage) to stay with some good friends in a villa there for a few days. But then people found out that we were there, and a crowd of demonstrators and supporters gathered at the villa. We thought it best, therefore, to move on, to cross the border into Austria. We took the car there, but we were arrested at the border, and [when] police officers with loaded guns took us back to Garmisch, crowds gathered, shouting "Heil Goering" from all sides, mocking and jeering the police, who were almost lynched by these excited masses. During the entire trip back, which must have been terribly difficult for him in the car, his only concern was that I might be scared or upset. Despite his emotional and physical pains, he was so kind. The authorities took his passport, and we were taken to a hospital that was surrounded by guards. Nontheless, as if by a miracle someone helped us. Hermann was carried out ... within two hours, taken across the border with a fake passport ... Mama, do not think that Hitler's cause has been lost or given up. Oh no, quite to the contrary. There is more energy than ever before. And he will be victorious, I can feel it, I know it, we have not seen the end yet ... this first failure will make the eventual victory deeper, more fitting and more serious."[29]

In Innsbruck, Hitler's numerous followers gave SA leader Goering a triumphant welcome. After being admitted to the hospital, Goering received a stream of visitors from dawn to dusk. Telegrams, flowers and cash donations arrived and were taken up. The seriously wounded Goering's condition was grave. His temperature was rising and pus was oozing out of the dirty wounds. He had to undergo surgery on his right hip and leg. To relieve the terrible pain, the doctors in Innsbruck frequently gave him morphine, which led to a morphine addiction that would stay with him for the rest of his life. It was not until shortly before he died, as an American prisoner of war, that he was cured of it.

Carin almost never left his side. When Communists threw rocks at her and broke one of her toes on the way to the hospital, she moved into her husband's hospital room. By Christmas of 1923, Goering had recovered enough to be able to exchange his sickbed for a grand suite at the best hotel in Innsbruck, the Tirolerhof.

"We are now living here so well in this hotel, the best in Innsbruck; the owner is a 'Hitler man' and is letting us stay at cost. We have a large bedroom with a bath and even a large, comfortable living room. The food is very good. We eat à la carte, and everything we order is subject to a thirty percent discount. The waiters are Storm Troopers and idolize Hermann: ... They told us not to worry about the bills until we got everything sorted out again. They would take it as an insult. Even if we could never pay, it would not matter at all, it would be only a minor sacrifice they would gladly make for Hermann. At any rate, the hotel will donate all the money to the Hitler movement. Isn't that great? ..." This is how Carin described the new circumstances in a letter to her mother on February 20, 1924.

On Christmas Eve, the Storm Troopers of Innsbruck gave Hermann and Carin Goering a small decorated Christmas tree. The candles had been symbolically adorned with black, white and red ribbons. Goering was limping along on his crutches and, in view of his condition, the couple agreed not to exchange gifts. On New Year's Eve, according to Carin, the management invited "everyone who wanted to gather and join in a toast and a salute to Hitler and Goering" to the dining room, where they celebrated in high spirits under the German flag.

Their daily routine was otherwise pretty dismal. Carin's health left much to be desired. She was sick most of the time, often laid up in bed. She was not cut out for the life of a political activist on the run. At times she would faint and have to be revived with camphor injections. After three interns had diagnosed an untreatable heart condition and given her only a short time to live, Carin cherished no illusions.

On the portable typewriter that Goering had given her for her birthday, she put down her observations about winter in Innsbruck at that time. To her, the town seemed like a "plate brimming over with whipped cream," she wrote to Nils von Kantzow. She collected foreign newspaper reports about the secret activities of the now outlawed NSDAP that relatives had mailed her and sent them to Hitler. A return to Munich was a very remote possibility. Both Hermann and Carin were wanted by the police, posters with their pictures hung everywhere, and they would face immediate arrest if they tried to cross the border. Goering finally considered giving himself up to the police. He contacted the party's lawyer, Dr. Roder, who was commuting back and forth between Innsbruck and Munich, to ask the Fuehrer for his permission to do so. Hitler refused. There was no hoped-for amnesty either.

"Our villa in Munich has been seized, our accounts frozen, the car [a Mercedes] confiscated ... they have now issued a warrant for my arrest, as well ...," reported Carin to her mother. But she was not discouraged by the events, she went on: "Still, everything is falling into place for Hitler and his work is progressing better than even before ..." Full of pride, she also sent letters back home to Sweden, even writing about minor achievements of party comrades. Whenever there was a setback, she would console her family who, as she knew, completely shared her views. In the case of her sister Fanny, she expressed her sympathies to a degree that might best be described as fanatical. Even Goering said, "She is too National Socialist for my taste!" But Carin's political commitment also helped keep her mind off her own suffering. In addition to cardiac troubles, she also suffered from severe rheumatism.

On February 22, 1924, Hermann Goering explained the situation in a letter to his mother-in-law and made plans for his and Carin's future. "During the trial [of Hitler and the leaders of the putsch, from February 26 to April 1, 1924], I will stay here. Then, if all hope of returning is lost for the time being, we will take a ship to Sweden via Italy. After all, staying there is cheaper and [it is] much more beautiful than here in Austria … maybe I can even find something to do until the situation in Germany allows me to return. I will only return to a national Germany, not to this Jewish republic. I will always be ready to fight again for the freedom of my fatherland …"[30]

Carin shared Goering's anti-Semitism. In one of her letters to her sister Lily, she wrote about the situation of her former chauffeur Schellshorn: "He is out of a job now, penniless. A Jew offered him a job as a chauffeur at his castle, but he rejected the offer saying, 'Anyone who has ever been privileged enough to serve Hitler or Goering must feel mortally insulted to be offered work by a Semite. It is a thousand times better to die of hunger than to work for a Jew.' Strong, zealous, isn't he? But how proud, and wonderful from a poor man like him … tell Mama and Papa."

On February 26, 1924, the trial of Hitler began in Munich, and Dr. Roder kept the Goerings fully informed. On that same day, Carin wrote: "I am tremendously excited, my thoughts are mostly with Hitler. May God help him. I must write to my mother—it will help me cope with my restlessness …" Carin's fears proved to be unfounded. In the presentation of the facts, the banknote theft and the killing of the four police officers committed by the National Socialists while marching on the Feldherrenhalle were suppressed. The Bavarian court was very lenient and sentenced Hitler to five years' confinement in Landsberg fortress. But he would only have to serve six months; for the remainder there would be a period of probation. What Hitler, an Austrian citizen, had feared the most—being deported—did not happen.[31]

In April of 1924, soon after the verdict was announced, Carin went to Munich to raise money on Goering's behalf. General Ludendorff, was the first to whom she turned for help. When she asked him to help Goering, who had "made so many sacrifices for his Fatherland," Ludendorff replied that the fatherland demanded sacrifice without pay.

Carin then went to see Hitler in Landsberg. She did not get any money from him either, but he did favor her—as he did many of his 500-odd visitors—with a photograph showing himself at the entrance to the Landsberg fortress and bearing the handwritten inscription: "To the esteemed wife of my SA Commander, Mrs. Carin Goering, in memory of her visit to the Landsberg fortress on April 15, 1924." Hitler had a mission for Goering. He was to go to Italy, contact Mussolini and ask him for financial support for the NSDAP.

The Fuehrer's wish was the Goerings' command, and they immediately set off for Italy with the meager remains of their assets. The house in Munich had already been sold. Mussolini, however, would not meet with Goering, nor did he lift a finger to save the NSDAP. After the failure of the mission, the disappointed, exhausted and, by now, destitute couple traveled through Austria, Czechoslovakia and Poland—bypassing Germany-to reach Sweden. There Carin, who was dying, and Hermann, addicted to morphine, sought help from the Fock family. They rented a small apartment at #23 Odengatan and Goering started looking for a job. But after an attempted jump out of a window in front of his parents-in-law, he could no longer keep his illness a secret.

In this condition, Goering turned to the orthopedic surgeon, Dr. Nils Silfverskiöld, who was related by marriage to the Rosen family. The doctor explained to him that he could not help, gave him no morphine and suggested withdrawal treatment.[32] Carin's father, Colonel von Fock, assumed the costs, and Goering had himself admitted to three different sanitariums, one after the other, in order to be cured of his addiction. At the Aspuddens Sanitarium, however, he suffered such severe withdrawal symptoms that he broke into the dispensary and threatened the staff. As recorded in his case history, he was then given morphine because "she [Carin] was afraid that the captain might kill someone in his rage."[33] With the consent of his wife, Goering, who had been placed in a straitjacket, was taken to the Katarina Hospital and from there to the Langbro Psychiatric Clinic. In his case history, he is described as a "Jew-hater and brutal hysteric, [a] man of poor character, malicious to others, but sentimental when it comes to his own family."[34] On October 7, 1925, he was given a clean bill of health and released.[35] Goering soon suffered a relapse, however, but managed to hide his addiction well with a cunning that confirmed his clinical portrait. Only his wife Carin, whose heart condition was rapidly worsening, saw through him.

When Goering returned to Germany alone in 1927 in order to renew his contacts with Hitler and try a comeback in the NSDAP party—which had already canceled his membership—his wife, who had stayed behind in Stockholm, wrote to him: "In such cases, truth is the only right thing, and you have a right to hear it because you love me and you have always done everything for me. Therefore, you must also know that I am not afraid to die ... The only wish I have is that His will be done, because I know that His will is the best for everyone. And, my love, if there is no God, then death will be only like resting, like sleeping forever—and everything will be forgotten. But I believe firmly that we shall see each other again up there. Of course, I would rather live on so as not to cause you any grief, and for Thomas's sake, but because I love you and Thomas more than anything else, I want to—yes, I really want to—stay with both of you ... The health of my beloved husband is my greatest concern. In fact, his health is much more at risk than mine. My love, I am thinking about you all the time. You are everything I have, and I am asking you to do everything in your power to free yourself, before it is too late. I fully understand that you cannot stop immediately, now that so much depends on you and now that you are harassed and hunted by so many. But try to keep it to a minimum ... Take long breaks, as many as possible. You must suffer and be uncomfortable, but please do it for me, because my love for you knows no bounds ... Being a morphine addict is comparable to committing suicide—each day, you are losing a little of your body and your soul ... You are possessed by an evil spirit and an evil force, and your body is slowly wasting away ... Save yourself and, thus, me too!"[36]

Fanny von Wilamowitz did not mention Goering's addiction to morphine in her biography of Carin Goering. On the contrary, she turned the reader's attention to Carin's loyalty to the party. She related fabricated anecdotes about Hitler and described in great detail Goering's successful comeback in the party and his political successes. When Hitler nominated his comrade-in-arms as the NSDAP's leading candidate in the elections to the Reichstag in May 1928, Goering brought his sick wife to Berlin. She was to share in his triumph. Carin bore the strain of the long trip, arriving three days before the election, and immediately wrote to her mother from Goering's small apartment at #16 Berchtesgadener Strasse. "The trip went well, but was exhausting ... In Berlin, Hermann met me at the train station ... then [brought me] here in his car, where Hermann has an enormous room, a corner room with a beautiful sunny balcony and blooming lilac. I took a bath, then rest-ed for an hour ... then a three-hour car trip, on a racetrack for cars, we were going a hundred and fifteen kilometers an hour! All of Berlin is in an election mood; the election will be on Sunday. They have already started to shoot and kill each other. Every day Communists with their red flags with burning Bibles on them march through the city, and they always clash with Hitler followers with equally red flags adorned with swastikas. This results in fighting—people are killed or injured ..."[37] On May 21, Carin sent her mother a telegram. "Hermann elected yesterday. Mother, you understand. Yours, Carin."[38]

Carin Goering attended the opening of the new Reichstag to which the NSDAP sent eleven members. The party had won 2.8 percent of the valid votes. Carin considered herself a highly established National Socialist and remarked on the strength of the Communists—"some completely criminal types"—and that many members (with the exception of Hitler's party) were obviously Jewish. In the fall of 1928, the Goerings, whose financial troubles were now a thing of the past, flew to Zurich. They rented a large apartment at #7 Badensche Strasse when they returned to Berlin.

When Carin and Hermann Goering had their picture taken in Munich by NSDAP "court photographer" Heinrich Hoffmann, they were introduced to his daughter Henriette, and invited the young girl to Berlin. Henriette had this to say about her visit to the Goerings' apartment on Badensche Strasse: "... and although it was a small apartment, Goering often invited guests, princes of Prussia, princes of Hesse, friends from Sweden ... captains of industry who had taken an interest in the member of the Reichstag ... Carin was unusually appealing and Hermann was a born host. He prepared mayonnaise and put the beer on ice. I was allowed to stay up until the last guest had left, for I slept on the couch ..."[39]

Although she was already dying, Carin continued to be a tireless propagandist in Berlin society, canvassing for new party members. "... but I see that it is good and that the circle around us is growing wider and wider and that we have won a lot of support for Hitler and his cause. August-Wilhelm [von Hohenzollern], like the Wieds [Princes of Wied], brings us into contact with a lot of interesting people."[40]

Sometimes, relatives from Sweden would visit. One such visitor, Carin's unmarried sister Elsa, was surprised at the Nazi milieu. "You know, Carin and Hermann invited us to an event at the Sports Palace. We had hardly walked a few steps when a crowd of young people raised their hands and shouted wildly. I was looking around me, completely puzzled, and asked, 'What's happening here? Who's coming? Is it royalty?' And to my surprise, it was Hermann they were paying tribute to. He seems to be quite popular down there ..."[41]

Memories of the confiscation of their house in Munich were still fresh, and Reichstag member Goering also constantly had to fear prosecution or lawsuits for damages because of his numerous criminal activities on behalf of the NSDAP. With that in mind, the retired captain and his wife went to see a notary public on October 2, 1930, and applied to "exclude the administration and usufruct of the husband and to have this fact entered in the matrimonial property register."[42] The assets brought into the marriage by the wife were listed, and included the entire valuable inventory of the apartment, consisting of the study, parlor, dining room, bedroom, guestroom and maid's room. Even in those days, Goering's passion for collecting Persian and Chinese carpets, antique furniture, oil paintings and miniatures was evident. Carin's harmonium, vacuum cleaner and aluminum pots were also included in the inventory in order to protect them from any court-imposed attachment. On October 13, 1930, the ailing Carin once again attended the opening of the Reichstag in Berlin. This time, the NSDAP sent 107 delegates in brown shirts to the Reichstag.

The Goerings had a very busy social life. Crown Prince Wilhelm, August-Wilhelm von Hohenzollern (also known as "Auwi") and his brother Eitel-Friedrich, Viktor Prince of Wied and his wife Marie Elisabeth, Frau von Dirksen and Fritz Thyssen were among their guests, as were the party leaders. Carin Goering was so weak that most of the time she had to receive her guests while lying on a sofa. If the lady of the house was particularly ill, then, as Carin mentioned in a letter to her mother on January 4, 1931, the guests were served only simple foods such as pea soup with pork and Swedish apple pie in vanilla sauce.

At Christmas 1930, Carin's condition took another turn for the worse, and she knew her life was coming to an end. "... I fell ill on Christmas Eve. I ran a fever of 39.5 degrees Celsius. The day was spent decorating the tree, organizing things, wrapping the presents, and at eight o'clock, Goebbels came by to celebrate Christmas with us. He brought such charming and thoughtful gifts for all of us ... The candles on the

Christmas tree were alight, and the presents were handed out. Then I got the shivers. They were so strong that I fell off the sofa ..."

Goering's morphine addiction was already an open secret. "Frau v. D. (Victoria von Dirksen) tells me that G. has again succumbed to morphine. This is terrible. One cannot even be angry with him anymore because his restlessness is just a result of his condition. I will look after him a bit ...," Goebbels wrote in his diary on January 4, 1931.[43] A short time later, on February 20, he complained: "... he [Goering] suffers from megalomania. It all stems from his morphine addiction ... an uninhibited opportunist ... he must be institutionalized first of all. He must not be allowed to perish like that ..." On January 29, 1931, Goebbels had already noted: "... Goering tells me that his wife is seriously ill and on the verge of death ..." In mid-February he noticed that Carin's condition had improved. "... at Goering's for coffee—Carin the beautiful is still in bed. She looks good and is genuinely happy to see me. I have a lot of respect for her."

While Goering was spending a great deal of time on the road as a speaker for the National Socialist party, his wife checked into various sanitariums, such as the one in Kreuth in Bavaria. While in Kreuth, she spent most of her time sewing, designing colorful outfits for Hermann and reading. Whenever she was in Berlin, according to contemporaries, she would have a very positive influence on Hermann. In her presence, he was usually calm and understanding, even though he had a tendency toward harsh language.

In July 1931, Hitler gave his loyal henchman a new Mercedes as compensation for the one confiscated in November, 1923. The couple was flattered by this "proof of the care and kindness of the Fuehrer." They immediately took a vacation, setting off in the new car on a sightseeing tour through Germany and Austria, with the final destination being Sweden. Carin was so weak that, to conserve her strength, she hardly ever left the car and even took her meals sitting in the car. They passed through Dresden, where they met Hitler. According to Fanny Wilamowitz, Carin, upon seeing Hitler, exclaimed, "When all of Germany comes to see what we have in Hitler, then, a new era will begin!"

Six days after her arrival in Sweden on September 25, 1931, Carin's mother, Huldine von Fock, died quite unexpectedly following a short illness. The shock was too much for Carin Goering. In the absence of her husband, who had returned to Germany, she died of a heart attack on October 17, 1931. After lying in state in the Edelweiss Chapel, she was buried on her forty-third birthday in the small cemetery of Lovö near Drottningholm, the summer residence of the Fock family.

Goebbels described the inconsolable widower from the point of view of a party comrade. "His features have become set since, in the middle of his biggest battle, his beloved wife was taken from his side. But he never wavered even once. Seriously and firmly he went his way, an imperturbable shield-bearer to the Fuehrer. This upright soldier with a child's heart …"[44]

Hermann Goering continued to stay in touch with the family of his late wife in Sweden. On special occasions he would send them exquisite arrangements of red and white flowers—always in the shape of a swastika. In 1932, he was invited to the wedding of Brigitta von Rosen where he proposed a toast to the new Germany and to the NSDAP.[45]

After the National Socialists took power, Carin, the Swede who had followed her husband Hermann Goering to a foreign country, shared his enthusiasm for Hitler and National Socialism and who supported him from beginning to end, became a cult figure of the regime. Her role was to be honored upon achievement of the "final victory" as part of a comprehensive documentation of the history of the Third Reich. But it never came to that, and, apart from Fanny Wilamowitz's tales, National Socialists were left with only a draft by Goering's personal biographer Erich Gritzbach.[46]

The big, efficient propaganda machine of the Nazi regime put the love story between the German pilot and the Swedish aristocrat to good use as well. It provided those heroic and romantic elements that were never considered by the official press which dealt primarily in diatribe and demagoguery. The romance of Carin and Hermann Goering served to establish a new type of reportage, in which the Nazi elite took the place of the crowned monarchs of the past. One of these publications, dripping with sentimentality, was called "Das Hohelied der Liebe: Deutsches Werden" [Song of Love: The Rise of Germany].[47] It was supposed to sway a politically uninterested readership on the level of Hedwig Courts-Mahler toward the ideas of the NSDAP and, at the same time, fill the void left by the vanished tabloids. The story of Carin and Hermann Goering filled a gap in the cleverly woven web of total indoctrination of the population.

The Nordic beauty was Goering's great love.

Carin Goering viewed National Socialism as a substitute religion, similar to her grandmother's "Edelweiss Club." For Carin, this movement seemed to combine all that was good, ideal and noble. But she worshipped Hitler like a Messiah and, in her exalted infatuation, believed that he would free Germany from the yoke of the vanquishing Allied powers and lead it into a glorious future. "The individual is so powerless in view of all this. The one and only person in whom I place all my hope is Hitler, once he takes the helm of this sinking ship ...," she wrote to her mother on January 4, 1931.[48]

Hitler, to her, was a "genius in love with the truth." She admired his "chivalric" struggle and his "decency." In spite of all the setbacks, she never doubted that the movement would one day win. She was a perfect example of the National Socialist whose blind enthusiasm stunted all capacity for independent thought.

In October, 1933, during the trial over the Reichstag fire, Goering visited the grave of his dead wife in Sweden and laid an arrangement of green leaves in the shape of a swastika. On November 8, someone trampled the flowers and left an inscription in Swedish on the swastika-adorned headstone. "We, a few Swedes, feel insulted by the desecration of this grave by the German Goering. May his former wife rest in peace, but may he spare us German propaganda on her grave."[49] This prompted Goering to have an underground mausoleum built on his splendid new estate of Carinhall, surrounded by the idyllic forests and lakes of the Schorfheide, and to have Carin's remains transported there.

But the crypt of Carinhall would not be Carin Goering's final resting place. When the Red Army was approaching the Schorfheide in the spring of 1945, Goering ordered his summer residence to be blown up. Carin's mausoleum was also destroyed, after her remains had been taken out of the coffin and buried in the forest nearby. In May, 1945, soldiers of the Red Army looking for Goering's hidden treasures ransacked the property and desecrated Carin's new grave. The local forester retrieved the body, had it interred and then informed the family. Meanwhile East Germany had been taken over by the Communists, and the Communist authorities would never have approved the Fock family's request to return Carin's remains to Sweden. At this point, Fanny Wilamowitz turned to the Swedish pastor in Berlin, Heribert Jansson, for help. Together they hatched a plan that would make any mystery writer proud. First of all, Jansson had the forester secretly open the grave, place Carin's remains in a bag and bring them indirectly to Berlin. Then Jansson had the corpse cremated under a different name—the paperwork was also falsified—at the crematorium of Wilmersdorf on February 3, 1951.

Shortly thereafter, Jansson traveled to Sweden with the urn in his luggage. After a brief stopover in Hamburg, he found his car had been broken into and all his belongings stolen. The thieves had left behind only the "worthless" urn. So he managed to deliver it to the Fock family, along with the receipt for the cremation. After a memorial service that only the family attended, Carin Goering, née Fock, was buried in her original grave in the cemetery of Lovö. It was her fifth burial.[50]

EMMY GOERING

The "Grand Lady"

March 24, 1893 (?) – June 8, 1973

"**G**rand Lady," borrowed from the medieval knight's homage to his lady, was the romantic title given to the second wife of the Prussian premier and subsequent Reich marshal Hermann Goering soon after their wedding. The chivalric title was met with mockery, especially among the artists who had known Emmy Sonnemann when she was still a little provincial stage actress. Helene von Weinmann, the Viennise opera singer, said of her sarcastically, "My God, Emmy is such a showoff. I knew her before she was a 'grand lady' and could be 'had' for a cup of coffee and 2.50 schillings." Such an insult to Goering's wife had terrible repurcussions under the Nazi regime.

On a tip from a trustworthy National Socialist and informer, Mrs.

Weinmann was immediately arrested for insulting the "First Lady of the Reich" and severely abused during the interrogation. She was sentenced to three years in prison, which she served in full at the penitentiary of Stadelheim. In 1943, fatally ill, she was released.[1]

Although there were many documents and letters addressed to the "Grand Lady," Emmy Goering stated for the record after the end of the Third Reich that neither she nor her husband had ever desired that form of address, and she believed that this title had been a spontaneous creation by the people.[2] It is not clear who gave her the designation. But the term was reintroduced by Heinrich Himmler, who was planning special Nazi schools for "tall, strong, superior, biologically and intellectually select women." The graduates of these schools were to be awarded the title "Grand Lady."

Emma Johanna Henny (Emmy) Sonnemann was "officially" born in Hamburg on March 24, 1894, but more likely in 1893 or even before that. Her father, a prosperous businessman, had a successful chocolate factory.[3] "He had [a] really cheerful disposition and was tall, blond, and blue-eyed, and above all full of a real north German sense of humor. A man fit as a fiddle until his death in his eighty-second year!" Emmy, who bore a strong resemblance to her father, wrote in her memoirs. [4]

Her parents' fifth child, Emmy grew up sheltered and wanting for nothing. After reading Shakespeare's *The Merchant of Venice* when she was twelve, she developed a passionate and all-consuming interest in the theater. However, his daughter's ambitious plans for an acting career met with violent resistance from her father: "You are supposed to get married and make a man happy!" But her mother, who, as a young woman had dreamed of being an actress herself and hoped now to see her own dreams realized through her daughter, promised Emmy support—on one condition. First, Emmy had to learn housekeeping. By coincidence, her mother read in the *Hamburger Fremdenblatt* in the spring of 1911 that the director of the Thalia Theater in Hamburg, Leopold Jessner, was planning to open an acting school and that he would give two scholarships to exceptionally gifted students. "If you were to be admitted on this scholarship, then even your father would allow you to become an actress," Emmy Goering recalled her mother telling her.[5] The young girl learned the part of Gretchen in Goethe's *Faust*, auditioned, was accepted and began the longed-for acting career as a scholarship student. At the age of eighteen she had her first engagement in the provinces, at the municipal theater of Aussig. On her next stint, in Munich, she met a young actor colleague, Karl Koestlin. The two were engaged in the summer of 1915 and, in the middle of World War I, on January 13, 1916, they were married in Trieste. At the end of the war and in the period after the collapse of the Austro-Hungarian empire, Emmy played at the Wiener Volksbühne (Vienna Public Theater). After that, she accepted engagements in Stuttgart and Wiesbaden. Her marriage, entered into during the chaos of the war, did not stand the test of peace-time and soon existed only on paper. The couple went their separate ways, and at the early 1920s obtained a divorce.

In 1922, Emmy Sonnemann applied to the artistic director of the German National Theater in Weimar, Dr. Franz Ulbrich, for the role of a "youthful heroine," and was invited for a guest performance as Thekla in Schiller's *Piccolomini*. She was successful, received a long-term con-tract and moved to Weimar. For the next ten years, Emmy Sonnemann lived in the city of Goethe, and concentrated on her career. She played Gretchen in *Faust*, the queen in *Don Carlos*, Emilia Galotti and Agnes Bernauer in the plays of the same name. She was given the leading female parts of the classical repertoire, but also performed in plays by Hermann Bahr, Oscar Wilde and Henrik Ibsen. She led a disciplined life—rehearsals in the morning, lunch at the "Goldener Anker," a socia-ble chat with colleagues at the "Kaiser Café" in the afternoon and final-ly—the high point of her day—the evening performance.

As she approached her thirty-eighth year, the actress realized that she had reached the pinnacle of her career, if she had not already passed it. At any rate, she expected no more major challenges in the future.

But she was very much mistaken. Weimar, the capital of Thuringia between 1920 and 1940, was not only a city of theaters, but also a stronghold of the National Socialist movement, which had held its party congress in the "city of Goethe" in 1926. Top Nazi politicians were always certain of an enthusiastic welcome. Treated like celebrities, they enjoyed showing up for such events, and did so frequently.

At the beginning of 1932, Emmy Sonnemann met Hermann Goering when, as part of Hitler's entourage after a political event, he went to the Kaiser Café where the theater people met. Although he was regarded at that time as the second most powerful man in the Nazi hierarchy, Emmy, as she wrote in her memoirs, initially confused him with Goebbels.

In the spring of the same year, they met again by accident in Weimar and went for a walk in Belvedere Park. Emmy, who had lost her mother only a short time before, was impressed with the loving manner in which Goering spoke of his wife, who had died in 1931. Emmy's sympathy struck a chord with the widower, and he gave her a picture of his late wife to express his gratitude. Talking about Carin Goering, whom Emmy had seen once but never spoken to, they quickly grew closer and Emmy told a girlfriend: "I am happy to have met a man, Hermann, who meets my expectations ..."[6] When, a short time later, Goering took a trip to Capri, Italy, he sent Emmy Sonnemann a telegram in which he expressed his affection for her. The die was cast. At a National Socialist party event in Weimar where Goering was one of the speakers, the politician and the actress had a defining conversation. "He walked home with me, and [in] that short [time], my future was decided," Emmy Goering wrote in her memoirs.[7]

The frequent contacts between the actress and Goering, who became president of the Reichstag after the elections on July 31, 1932, were the main topic of daily conversation in provincial Weimar. Emmy Sonnemann's numerous visits to Goering's apartment in Berlin did not go unnoticed either. Goering's fondness for luxury was public knowledge by then. He had completely remodeled Carin's cozy apartment on Badenschen Strasse by August 1932. By taking down walls and through other alterations, the comfortable five-room apartment had become a luxury suite that covered an entire floor. The gigantic rooms were filled with Gothic candlesticks as tall as a man, valuable statues of the Madonna and antique furniture. Goering often showed guests a Gobelin tapestry with red embroidered castles that hung in his living room, and would tell them, "These are the castles and fortresses of my ancestors!"

Because of his tendency to boast, friends—with the exception of Emmy Sonnemann—also knew about Goering's addiction to morphine.[8] Whenever Emmy was at Carinhall, Goering's summer residence, she was introduced to guests as Goering's private secretary. But the pair, both almost forty years old, never fooled anyone.

Emmy Sonnemann was a tall blonde with a statuesque figure. To Goering, she represented—as did the late Carin—the typical "Germanic-Nordic woman," who would be the perfect soulmate and a quiet comfort to the widower. Their relationship was overshadowed for a long time by the ghost of Carin which would continue to haunt the couple in the future. The actress soon realized that she could win Goering's affection only slowly and through his late wife. She was clever enough not to compete with a dead woman. She accepted the fact that Goering's emotional obsession with Carin was constantly taking on new, more bizarre forms.

In his new Berlin apartment at #34 Kaiserdamm, Goering had a room that was dedicated solely to the memory of Carin, with her furniture, her white harmonium and personal effects. Goering was the only one allowed into this sanctuary, in which everything had to remain unchanged. Numerous pictures of his late wife hung on the walls at Carinhall, and the yachts moored at the boathouse on the nearby lake were called Carin I and Carin II. It was not until 1936 that a modest hunting lodge would become "Emmyhall."[9]

At the end of 1932, Goering celebrated Christmas with Emmy, then went off to Sweden with her gift in his bag in order to celebrate New Year's Eve with the Rosen family at Rockelstad Castle. To Emmy, he wrote, "Your radio is just now playing music from the Swedish radio station ... I really enjoy your gift ... people here have the nicest things to say about you, and now, my love, let me express my deepest gratitude to you for your love, your sacrifices and everything you have done for me. May the next year be another good year for us."[10]

When Hitler became Reich chancellor on January 30, 1933, and Goering, as one of three National Socialists, was given a position in the coalition government for his contribution over the years, Emmy Sonnemann rushed to Berlin to share in this triumph. She stood at a window of Hitler's apartment at the Kaiserhof Hotel and watched the torchlight procession with which the NSDAP celebrated Hitler's appointment. For the actress, it was like being present at the birth of the New Germany when Goering, on the Reich Chancellery balcony directly opposite, proclaimed Hitler as the "young Fuehrer of Germany."[11] Goering had given Emmy a gun, just in case the Communists attempted a last-minute disruption.

On February 27, 1933, the Reichstag in Berlin was ablaze. Goering, who had already been planning a strike against the Communists, exploited the fire as a welcome pretext to brutally settle scores with his political opponents. For a long time, it was suspected that Goering had orchestrated the burning of the Reichstag in order to discredit the political left, especially the Communists. Emmy Goering never believed it and cited a telephone conversation on the day of the disaster as proof of his innocence: "The family pictures! Why did I put my most valuable possessions there, that are so dear to me?" Goering shouted at her over the phone. Emmy knew that he was talking about the photos of his late wife, which he would never have sacrificed. These specious arguments sounded ridiculous and trivial, but were completely in character for the unscrupulous politician but sentimental family man. More recent research, however, has exonerated Goering as a possible arsonist.[12]

On April 11, 1933, Goering was appointed premier of Prussia, which was to have positive effects on Emmy's career. At Goering's behest she was called to the renowned Schauspieltheater in Berlin to play the female lead in *Schlageter*. This political drama, hastily written by Hanns Johst in 1933, served to glorify Nazi supporter Albert Leo Schlageter, who had been executed by the French for his participation in acts of sabotage against the occupation forces in the Ruhr area in May 1923. The Nazis had declared him a martyr and worshipped him as the first to "witness the rebirth of the German nation with his own blood."

Few considered Emmy Sonnemann a gifted artist, but she certainly had some talent. She had been a successful actress for twenty years, even without Goering's patronage. The Deutsches Nationaltheater in Weimar, the state theater of Thuringia and the venue of the festival of the German Goethe Society, had an excellent reputation. But Emmy Goering at forty, could never have made the big leap from the provinces to Berlin without the help of her powerful friend.

The actress expected her career to reach new heights following her engagement in Berlin. She was contracted by the Reich Chamber of Culture, as documented by State Commissioner Hinkel[13] in September 1933, to play the part of Hedwig in the 1934 film version of Schiller's *Wilhelm Tell*.

In February 1935, during a weekend stay in Weimar, Hermann Goering suggested to Emmy Sonnemann that she marry him: "Shall we get married at Easter? The Fuehrer will be our witness." That was Goering's marriage proposal. Emmy enthusiastically agreed. On March 15, Goering announced his engagement at a small party of forty to which he had invited the ambassadors of France, Japan and Hungary. Goering explained the romantic union to Lady Phipps, wife of the British ambassador: "I am only marrying her because the Fuehrer has asked me to do so. He says there are too many bachelors among us party big shots."[14]

A description of Goering from those days by the American ambassador-at-large William C. Bullitt reads as follows: "He has the usual proportions of a German tenor. His derriere has a diameter of at least a yard … in order to make his shoulders as wide as his hips, he wears two-inch pads on both sides …, he obviously always has a cosmetologist with him, as his fingers, about as thick as they are long, have pointed and carefully enameled nails … and his complexion gives evidence of daily care …"[15] At the end of 1933, Goering weighed 140 kilograms, and continued to gain weight. His vanity, the flamboyant clothes he wore in private—some of them designed by his late wife—and his taste for luxury and for showing off were well known at the time.

Among the "Upper Ten Thousand," the millionaires and aristocrats, Goering was considered the most important member of the Nazi movement. He was also the man whom Hitler admired because of his Draconian measures. Emmy Sonnemann had known Goering for a year when, prior to the Reichstag elections on March 5, 1933, he ordered the construction of two concentration camps—Oranienburg-Sachsenhausen and Papenburg—which were under the strict supervision of his ministry. Emmy defended Goering in her memoirs. "There were already concentration camps in Germany at that time … it is correct that Hermann Goering built the first ones while he was still head of the Prussian police. But they were not intended for Jews, but for Communist enemies of the state … nobody knows as well as I do that Hermann's conception of these institutions corresponded to a re-education plan. When he learned that one of the interned Communists had been beaten and severely injured by the guards, he went into a terrible rage …"[16] In truth, Goering's infamous order to shoot on February 17, 1933, instructed the Prussian police force to counter political opponents with all means of force.

It was also Goering who, on April 26, 1933, founded the secret police, or Gestapo, which was ordered in June 1934 to arrest or kill the old leaders of the SA.[17] Emmy could have read about Goering's true motives in 1933 in foreign newspapers to which her lover freely gave interviews. In Sweden, for example, he said, "I will never allow the police to become a security force for Jewish department stores. It is not the job of the police to protect swindlers, frauds, usurers and traitors. Do not cry so much for justice [for the Jews] because there could be a kind of justice coming that is written in the stars, and not in your lawbooks, and it could spell the end for you."[18]

Goering's second wedding was markedly different from his first. On April 10, 1935, when the forty-two-year-old Hermann Goering married the forty-one-year-old Emmy Sonnemann, eight bands played in front of his official residence in Berlin. The day was declared a holiday, and work ceased. Even for his stag party, a thousand invited guests had assembled at the state opera to see a gala performance of Richard Strauss's *The Egyptian Helena*, and afterward indulged at four sumptuous champagne buffets. On the wedding day, every house was flying the flag, and thirty thousand soldiers lined the streets as honor guards for the bride and groom as they made their way to the Reich Chancellery in an open car decorated with tulips and daffodils through rejoicing crowds. Hitler welcomed the bride with white orchids and assured her that she could turn to him in time of personal trouble. What was more, he promised to grant her every wish—no matter how unusual. The civil ceremony was held at City Hall. Then they went to the cathedral while Goering's pilot friends from his World War I squadron thundered by overhead, and practical jokers released two storks.

The correspondent for the Associated Press, Louis Lochner, who attended the wedding, wrote in a letter on April 20, 1935 that, " … one had the feeling as if the emperor were getting married."[19] He shared this view with the British ambassador, Sir Eric Phipps: "Visitors to Berlin these days could believe that the monarchy had been restored and that they had landed in the middle of preparations for a royal wedding."[20]

Although Emmy Sonnemann had been divorced, it was not a problem for her to have a church wedding. The wedding was conducted by the Protestant Reich bishop Müller, who also willingly yielded to the groom's wish for a sermon not longer than five minutes. For the wedding reception at the sumptuous Kaiserhof opposite the Reich Chancellery, three hundred and twenty relatives and friends were invited, among them Prince Philipp of Hesse, August Wilhelm of Prussia, Winifred Wagner, the actress Käthe Dorsch, the Swedish count Eric Rosen, a brother-in-law from Goering's first marriage, and society journalists from around the world. The bride wore very expensive jewelry, as she had done the evening before at the opera performace. Emmy wrote in her memoirs: " … Hermann gave me a very beautiful zircon set. To his deep disappointment, I was not as happy with it as he had hoped. Unlike him, jewelry has never meant much to me ..." Emmy Goering also claimed as a defence strategy at her denazification trial on July 20, 1948, that any luxury had only been pursued for the sake of her husband, but the prosecutor disproved her claim, reminding her of October, 1940, when she was in Vienna by herself. "... on the occasion of an opera performance, the person concerned entered the Vienna State Opera in a white ermine coat with most expensive jewelry, and [shocked] the audience."

The day after the wedding—as was the custom at royal courts—the press was freely invited to view the wedding presents, which had been put on display in two heavily guarded rooms of the premier's residence. Goering modestly claimed that they were "gifts from my people." Directors of the state museums had plundered their most valuable collections, and mayors their city coffers. Following an unmistakable hint, German clubs and institutions had given just as generously as foreign potentates. The senate of Hamburg, for example, had given the couple a boat made of solid silver that Emmy had admired as a child in her hometown, and King Boris of Bulgaria gave Mrs. Goering a sapphire bracelet.

While the muzzled German press of 1935 reported the wedding of the Prussian minister and the actress Sonnemann in favorable language, Klaus Mann, son of the "notorious writer and half-Jew Thomas Mann," who had emigrated in 1933, wrote an open letter to his artistic colleague. "... now, you have indeed lifted yourself high above the artistic circles, where there was so much friendly gossip about you. Heavens, now, my dear First Lady, you have really made it ... And what guests you had at your wedding: all former comrades-in-arms, those that your fast-moving husband had not ordered killed yet were among them: fellow-combatants Kerrl and Streicher vied with each other in harmless banter. Grace was said by Müller, who has his colleagues beaten up in their parishes. At the provincial theaters where you appeared, there was never so much to laugh at. I never had the opportunity to see you perform there ... Are not the slain from the concentration camps, those tortured to death and shot when they tried to escape, those that committed suicide stepping through the luxurious hangings? Is not a bloody head appearing? ..."[21]

Shortly after the wedding, Emmy Goering gave up her career at the request of her husband and left the stage where she had appeared for twenty-three years without interruption. Her last engagement had been

In 1935, Emmy Goering gave her farewell performance as "Minna von Barnhelm" at the Berlin State Theater.

at the Berlin State Theater, where she acted under the direction of Gustaf Gründgens. Playing the role of Lessing's Minna von Barnhelm, she took her leave from the world of theater in order to play a leading part in Goering's life, which itself did not lack for theatrical effects.

It was a step that she never regretted. She had risen to become "First Lady" of the German state, had a loving, faithful husband, who would later prove himself a caring father, shared a happy marrige, and "overlooked everything else," as Klaus Mann had accused. The former actress and now "First Lady" managed the most popular salon in Berlin for diplomats and politicians and took on some of Hitler's social obligations. Emmy Goering did not have the close relationship to Hitler that other wives of top Nazi leaders could boast. She never met Eva Braun in person, even though the Goerings had a house on the Obersalzberg, as private contacts were rare. Her admiration for the Fuehrer had its limits. The somewhat cool distance in their relationship became quite obvious at public events. On November 8, 1935, in memory of the failed putsch of 1923, Goethe's *Egmont* was performed in the presence of the entire party leadership. "Mrs. Goering is like a queen. The Fuehrer sits quite modestly next to her. On the train [Hitler's train to Munich], he later [tells me] how much he suffered" Goebbels wrote in his diary.[22]

Interestingly enough, persistent rumors soon surfaced, especially among artists, about Emmy's "not quite Aryan" origins. In September, 1935, the Reich justice ministry issued a circular stating that certain people had made "vicious remarks about the wife of the premier, in particular spreading lies about her allegedly non-Aryan origin and an alleged earlier marriage to a non-Aryan."[23] Possibly as a precaution, Emmy's first husband was not mentioned in the Nazi Gotha, the family tree of famous Germans published in 1936 by Baron von Dungern. Klaus Mann, too, referred to this in his open letter: "Your gossipy former colleagues, say that you are non-Aryan ..."[24] Goering reacted promptly, demanding total respect for his wife and threatening to hunt down ruthlessly anyone who engaged in "malicious slander." One alleged slanderer of Emmy Goering was sentenced to five months in jail, which prompted her husband to respond, "Five years would have been more commensurate with the crime."

When Goering had to answer to the international military court in Nuremberg after the war, the prosecutors proposed to "wear him down by interrogating him about the former intimate relationship of his wife with a Jewish actor."[25]

But there were also rumors and jokes about the rotund premier, and Guertner, the minister of justice, suspected that those "irresponsible rumors about Goering's private and family life may be due to the systematic smear campaign of certain groups hostile to the state." The British ambassador sent a telegram to London in 1936, summarizing the rumors. " ... he, as I have been told, cannot beget children."[26]

Therefore the surprise was all the greater when Emmy Goering became pregnant at the age of forty-four. On June 2, 1938, she gave birth to a baby girl, Edda, who, it was believed, was named after Mussolini's daughter. Later, Emmy said that her daughter had been named for a friend of hers. At any rate, the Reich marshal had become a father for the first time at the age of forty-five. The couple received over 628,000 congratulatory telegrams from around the world. Fuehrer and Reich Chancellor Adolf Hitler became Edda's godfather, sharing the responsibility with the Air Force, which wanted to place the child under its protection. In the setting of a grand ceremony at Carinhall on November 4, 1938, Edda received a Christian baptism, to the chagrin of the party leadership.

Hundreds of thousands of postcards showing the proud father with little Edda were printed and distributed, but could not silence the popu-

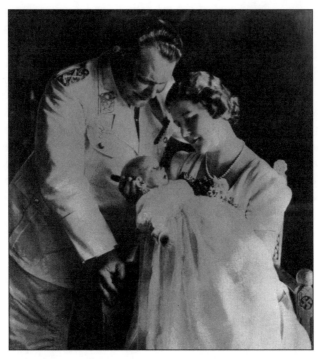

The couple with their daughter Edda, born on June 2, 1938.

lar jokes. "What does Edda stand for?" someone asked maliciously. The answer was: "Ewiger Dank dem Adjutanten" (Eternally grateful to my aide-de-camp). The cabaret performer Werner Finck took the subject further and suggested that the child should really be called Hamlet: To be or not to be. Goering did not find it funny and had Finck sent to a concentration camp. Later, as Edda grew to resemble Goering, people gradually lost interest in the paternity subject.

Wagonloads of presents arrived at Carinhall for Edda's baptism. Thousands of officers and soldiers of the Air Force donated cash, which was then used to build "Edda House" in the orchard of Carinhall. It was about the size of a small castle and had its own theater, where the children's ballet group of the Berlin State Opera danced for the infant. The City Council of Cologne, however, rashly gave Edda the most precious gift—*The Madonna and Child* by Lucas Cranach, a famous painting from the treasures of the Wallraf-Richartz Museum in Cologne, about which a bitter legal dispute would erupt after 1945.[27]

For the proud parents, Edda was the "sunshine in their lives." They went to great lengths in caring for their daughter and showered her with every luxury imaginable. On her fourth birthday, they presented her, dressed in a red hussar's uniform and black riding boots, on the terrace of her dollhouse.

Emmy Goering and her husband indulged in the lifestyle of the ruling princes of the 18th century. The "Sun King of the Third Reich" had built himself a splendid residence worth millions in the north of Berlin in the Schorfheide. Carinhall was equipped with a movie theater, a gymnasium, a Russian steam bath and a giant reception area on the scale of the nave of a church. The whole estate was more luxurious by far than the residences of all of the other Nazi bosses, none of whom renounced luxury. Resentful, Hitler said, "My mountain farm, of course, is no match for that. Maybe it can serve as a summer house."[28]

Emmy Goering got to see her husband, as the "Reich Master of the Hunt" in his leather hunting outfit with bow and arrow, occupy himself with his oversized model railroad, or play around for relaxation in his "diamond basket." Emmy Goering hosted many parties. The most splendid of all was the annual summer party at the premier's residence in Berlin. On this occasion, spotlights on the roofs of the neighboring houses lit up the park, where the ballet of the Berlin Opera was dancing. The swimming pool was covered with blossoming white water lilies. The master of the house and his wife—both in their best finery and diamonds—received the guests wearing ornate Renaissance costumes, specially created for the occasion. The food was served on long banquet tables beneath high trees. A high screen divider was then removed, revealing to the incredulous audience a backdrop created personally by Goering: a reconstruction of the Viennese Prater, an amusement park, complete with slides, shooting galleries, old-fashioned merry-go-rounds and Grinzing wine bars, where young actresses, wearing costumes from the film *Der Kongress tanzt* (The Congress Dances), welcomed the guests.

Among the guests Emmy Goering received at Carinhall were Prince Paul of Yugoslavia, King Boris of Bulgaria, the Swedish Crown Prince Gustav Adolf, the Hungarian Vice-Regent Horthy, King George of Greece, the Duke of Windsor, Charles Lindbergh and Sven Hedin.

Money was not an issue with the Goerings. The tobacco company Reemtsma alone donated one million Reich marks every year—osten-

Foreign visitors admire Little Edda

sibly for "cultural purposes, nature conservation and hunting"—unofficially, however, for Goerings private purse.[29] The German automotive industry for its part provided one and a half million marks just for the motorized yacht Carin II.

Emmy's life at Goering's side was certainly very exciting. One of the eccentricities of her husband, who, incidentally, was growing fatter and fatter, involved keeping lions at his residences. The Berlin Zoo provided the lion cubs, which stayed in the Goering's household for about fifteen months, where the predators were allowed to roam freely. Once they reached a dangerous size, they had to go back to the zoo. Over the years, the Goerings raised seven lions. In 1936, when the elite of Italian society, among them Mussolini's sons Vittorio and Bruno, in Germany for the Olympic Games, were at Carinhall having tea with the Goerings, a door opened and in came a lion. The guests, rigid with fear, fell silent until Emmy shooed the pet away. She herself once talked about keeping the lions: "Once we had to move into the residence of the president of the Reichstag for a short while because our house at Leipziger Platz was being renovated. We had taken a lion with us and put it in the basement. Suddenly, at night, we were awakened because the door to our bedroom was opening. Our lion stood before us. It had used its paws to push the handles on eight doors between the basement and the bedroom to find us. The lion was so excited to have found us, we just could not bring ourselves to take it back down to the basement. So, we kept him with us for the night..."[30]

As one of the greatest art thieves of the 20th century, Goering shamelessly enriched himself and picked up jewels, furniture and paintings from all over Europe. He kept notes on works of art that he liked in order to confiscate them: "Check tapestry at the Reichstag to see whether suitable as curtain for the movie screen or for reception hall ..."[31] His wife could not see anything wrong with that, either.

Unlike Heinrich Himmler or Joseph Goebbels, Hermann Goering was popular. Emmy, too, was liked by many, mainly because she never appeared in public with political demands. The Jewish journalist Bella Fromm, who was not given to any misconceptions about Goering's character, found Emmy very pleasant. "... she is not a schemer. She is a compassionate, motherly woman, a Valkyrie type. Tall and strong, yet gentle and graceful. Her beautiful blonde hair frames her brow in a wide plait. Her big blue eyes are gentle and cheerful ... Emmy is a nice person ..."[32]

Her relatives saw her in a similar light. Emmy's great-niece said of her that Aunt Emmy had been naïve, good-natured and trusting. She did not want to hurt anyone and thought the best of everyone.[33] Emmy Goering's nature and character were clearly revealed in the cross-examination conducted by the Nuremberg prosecutor Dr. Kempner on September 2, 1948. The subject was Paul "Pilli" Koerner, Goering's state secretary in charge of the administration of the four-year plan. Emmy Goering wanted to exonerate him. "Is it correct that your late husband ... could rely on Koerner, or did he have to check on him constantly?" Kempner asked. "No, he didn't need to do that. Koerner was an absolutely reliable person," Emmy assured him. "He was not a puppet as some people want to make him out to be, is that correct?" "Certainly not," Emmy answered candidly. "And you would not say anything bad about Pilli Koerner?" "No, certainly not. I cannot say anything [bad] about Pilli Koerner." On the basis of this cross-examination, Paul Koerner was sentenced to fifteen years in prison.[34]

Emmy Goering always emphasized, especially after the end of the Nazi regime, that she was not a "political person." She claimed that her husband had mentioned politics in a conversation with her only once. This conversation was supposed to have taken place at the beginning of

January in 1941—prior to her departure to take a cure in Bad Gastein- when Goering, quite upset, informed her that Hitler was considering attacking Russia.

In 1948, Emmy Goering's role in the Third Reich came under the microscope. "... The person concerned was admitted in this way as a party member in 1938," the indictment in her denazification trial reads, "when Hitler called her by phone at Christmas 1938 to tell her that she had been awarded a membership.[35] She had received the membership number of a comrade who had died in 1932.[36] The per- son concerned was a member of the Nazi sorority and the Reich Theater Chamber. She does not deny that she always shared the phi- losophy of her husband, even though she was never politically active herself."[37]

Emmy Goering was not involved in Goering's political career in any way. His role as minister of finance—Goering was responsible for the imple- mentation of the four-year plan—was only of interest to her because the position required travel abroad, in the form of official state visits. The Goerings went to Libya on April 7, 1939, in order to pay a visit to Italo Balbo, the governor-general of the Italian colony. They were welcomed with Oriental pomp, went riding on camels, visited the Roman excava- tions and enjoyed luxurious parties at the governor's palace. Afterward, they traveled to Italy on a state visit and were personally greeted at the Termini train station in Rome by Mussolini.

After the war, Emmy Goering claimed that neither she nor her husband had ever heard of death camps for Jews or political opponents. "... as I see it, these camps still served for political-re-education. And that was Hermann's original idea ... I cannot imagine that he [Goering] knew anything about the extent of the horrible events going on at one camp outside Germany—the one near Auschwitz ..."[38]

In fact, Emmy Goering had many Jewish friends from artistic circles with whom she made a particular point of maintaining contact even after her marriage. She visited them or invited them to her home. One example was her former teacher Jessner. Many of those who survived the Nazi regime due to her intervention put themselves at her dispos- al as witnesses for her defense in 1948. The fact that so many of her colleagues needed help and had disappeared or emigrated, had never given Emmy pause to think. While she angered Hitler with her constant

"Jew saving," which he refused to discuss with her, Emmy did occasionally find support from her husband. Goering, who was in charge of the four-year plan, had issued a "decree for the elimination of Jews from the German economy" on November 12, 1938, and had even personally worked out large-scale plans for their deportation and extermination, but was open to reason in extenuating circumstances. During the denazification trial of Emmy Goering, it was said that, "… the party concerned, on a number of occasions, stood up for former (Jewish) colleagues, who had turned to her in an emergency. But there can be no question of anti-National-Socialist motives …"

With the conclusion of the Munich Agreement in September 1938, it was evident that Hitler did not share Goering's hopes of maintaining peace, and in 1939, when Prague was occupied, Goering was no longer involved in the decision-making process. In 1941, Emmy Goering was elevated to the status of wife of "Reich Marshall of the Pan-German Empire," but Goering's star was already fading. After the failure of his economic plan and the breakdown of the Air Force, for which he was responsible, in the battle for England and at Stalingrad, Goering's power and influence swiftly disappeared. More and more often, the couple retreated to Carinhall or Veldenstein, giving the impression that the dramatic events unfolding around them no longer concerned them. In the course of the war, the glittering parties also gradually came to an end.

Toward the end of the war, on January 31, 1945, as the battle lines moved closer to the Schorfheide and Carinhall, Emmy Goering took her daughter Edda and left for Bavaria. She headed for the Obersalzberg, which had been spared any bombing up to that point. There the Goerings had a house near Hitler's, which gradually filled in 1945 with Goering's numerous female relatives who, like Emmy, wanted to get away from the horrors of the war.

In April, Goering's art treasures worth two hundred million Reich marks arrived in Bavaria. A special train transported a thousand paintings, eighty sculptures and sixty Gobelin tapestries to Berchtesgaden so that they could be buried in a mineshaft on Untersberg Mountain. Goering went to see Hitler at the bunker of the Reich Chancellery on April 20, 1945, to wish him well on his birthday, and then had his beloved Carinhall blown up. That accomplished, he headed for Obersalzberg, with a huge baggage train, in order to "attend to most urgent matters."

Although he had long been on the political scrap heap, Goering was still waiting for a chance to return to power, and pounced on the opportunity that seemed to present itself to him on April 23, 1945. Acting upon the false report that the Fuehrer had collapsed, he contacted the Fuehrer's headquarters by radio, offering to take over as Hitler's successor. The reply from the bunker in the Berlin Reich Chancellery came quickly. Goering was accused of high treason, and with his family arrested by an SS commando team and interned in the air-raid shelter at Hitler's mountain farm.[39] "Before the collapse, my husband, our child and myself were arrested by Adolf Hitler on April 25, 1945, and sentenced to die ...," Emmy Goering wrote about that time.[40] When an aide-de-camp tried to organize some beds for Emmy and her child, who had been arrested in their nightgowns and were freezing, an SS officer threatened to shoot them on the spot. While bombers of the Royal Air Force razed their villa to the ground, the Goerings were held prisoner in the dark, ice-cold limestone shafts for several days. After Hitler's suicide, they were transferred to Mauterndorf Castle, which Goering had inherited from the property of his Jewish godfather.

May 7, 1945, when Goering was arrested by the Americans, was the last time Emmy Goering would see her husband as a free man. For her part, she and her daughter, her maid and Goering's nurse managed to make their way to Veldenstein castle near Nuremberg. There they found accommodation, but discovered that looters had been busy, removing the entire contents in twelve transport trucks. On October 25, 1945, Emmy Goering, too, was arrested. Edda was taken to some local farmers to be cared for. Later, the seven-year-old girl was sent to her mother at the Straubing prison.

Emmy Goering describes that time: "I was under house arrest [in Veldenstein] for five months. Then, as a witness in the Nuremberg trials, I spent five months in prison in Straubing together with my child, then was released from Straubing prison on February 19, 1946, ..."[41]

While Goering was held at the military prison in Nuremberg, where he had to stand trial as one of the top war criminals before the international military court of justice (November 14, 1945 to October 1, 1946), Emmy Goering and her daughter had found refuge in a hunting lodge that was part of the Veldenstein estate, in Sackdilling near Neuhaus in the Upper Palatinate, about thirty kilometers from Nuremberg. Her lawyer, Dr. Erich Ebermayer, described it as follows: "... the party concerned spent the last winter with her eight-year-old daughter Edda, sharing with two other people two rooms, the toilet in the kitchen, two hours away from the nearest settlement. They had no water and almost no heating."[42]

From Sackdilling, Emmy Goering requested that the military court in Nuremberg allow her to visit her husband. "… I have not seen him [Goering] for one and a half years, and I miss him so much, that I do not know what to do anymore. If only I could see him for a few minutes and hold his hand … My husband is very worried about our daughter and me because we are without help and protection …"[43]

It was not until September 12, 1946, during the final phase of the trial against the top war criminals, that Emmy was allowed to see her husband in prison. "They cannot possibly hang him," she later said to Henriette von Schirach, "Just imagine that, Hermann hanging from the gallows. Surely they are deceiving us …"[44]

In the two weeks leading up to the announcement of the verdict, the wives of the accused were allowed to visit over a period of eight days— a half hour each day. Emma and her daughter went to the visitors' cell at the Nuremberg prison several times. Goering was always chained to his guard, and the couple had to talk through a wall of glass and a close-meshed grille. Edda would recite short poems, and her parents would chat desperately about something trivial.

On October 7, 1946, Emmy Goering bade farewell to her husband, who had been sentenced to die by hanging. "You can face death with a clear conscience now," she answered, after he had asked her whether she wished him to make a plea for clemency. "You have done all you could here in Nuremberg, for your comrades and for Germany … I will always remember that you gave your life for Germany." Goering, however, consoled his wife, "There is one thing you can count on—they will not hang me."[45]

The meaning of that statement became dramatically clear when Goering committed suicide by swallowing a poison pill on October 15, 1946, the night before his scheduled execution by hanging. Who had smuggled the ampule of potassium cyanide into his cell and where Goering had hidden it in spite of constant observation has never been determined. It was assumed that a young American guard officer had given it to Goering,[46] but Emmy Goering was also among the suspects.

She openly admitted that she had known about the poison, which Goering had kept in his cell for some time.[47]

On May 29, 1947, Minister Dr. Loritz issued warrants for the arrest of Goering's widow and the wives of all those convicted at Nuremberg. She was alleged to have benefited greatly from the National Socialist dictatorship and was to be prevented from fleeing to the British zone in order to avoid a trial. Emmy Goering was sent to the Göggingen internment and labor camp near Augsburg, which consisted of five low barracks and housed a thousand women. The camp was left over from the Nazi era and had been constructed as a camp for Russian female workers.

"... [D]uring her incarceration, she looked like one of those abducted Teutonic women that we used to see in pictures in our school readers. Her blond hair tightly plaited, rage in her face," wrote Henriette von Schirach, also interned in Göggingen.[48] One of the two lawyers for Emmy Goering, Dr. Strobl, likened his client's internment to the witch hunts of the Middle Ages, while the second, Dr. Ebermayer, had already appealed the arrest warrant in June, 1947.

On October 31, 1947, Emmy Goering wrote a letter to the minister in charge: "May I present my case to you and request your assistance? I was taken, on an arrest warrant issued by former minister Loritz, to the women's camp Göggingen on May 28, 1947. I had been at home with a severe sciatic condition and phlebitis in the right arm when I was arrested. I have been suffering from sciatic attacks for thirty-five years. I was receiving treatment from a doctor, who strongly objected to my removal ... All the same, at midnight I was strapped onto a stretcher and brought here during a seven-hour trip for allegedly trying to flee to the British zone ... I have been bedridden for five months, [in constant] pain ... I am fifty-four years old and I have had to endure a lot in the last few years ... Mr. Minister, you are perhaps familiar with my files. I was completely unpolitical. I helped those who were persecuted for racist or political reasons when and where I could—there are enough affidavits to this effect. My only fault is that I am Hermann Goering's wife. You cannot possibly punish a woman for loving her husband and being happily married to him. From the bottom of my heart, Mr. Minister, I am asking you to help me so that I can be assigned a date for my denazification trial as quickly as possible. If this should not be possible in the immediate future, I would like to ask you to release me from prison until that date. If you are not authorized to grant such a request, could you arrange for a suspension of detention [during] the coming harshest winter months? If I have to lie in these wooden barracks in the winter, I will suffer permanent, severe damage and my health will be completely ruined."[49]

After interrogating numerous witnesses—twenty-one depositions were submitted in the trial—the prosecutor Julius Herf brought official charges before the denazification court of the labor and internment camp in Garmisch-Partenkirchen on July 20, 1948. At the same time, he moved that Emmy Goering be considered a principal defendant. "She does not deny that, as Goering's wife, she always shared the views of [her husband], even though she was not politically active. If the party concerned was an ardent supporter of National Socialism and a person who benefited greatly from her connection to the dictatorship, she is, ... a major offender ... As Hermann Goering's wife, she not only shared in a large number of personal honors, but also the exceedingly luxurious lifestyle of her husband, which clearly went far beyond the usual living standard of a Prussian premier and left every customary measure far behind ... The defendant received an 'honorarium' from the NSDAP, which she claims she used for charitable purposes ..."

Emmy Goering's theater engagement in Berlin in 1933 was also mentioned. "According to the findings of the Commission for Artists, the defendant's call to the Berlin State Theater immediately after the takeover was solely due to her relationship with Goering, for she did not have the qualifications to justify her engagement. She was even paid two and-a-half times more than for previous engagements.[50] The president of the German Stage Actors Cooperative, Emil Otto, shares this view. Only the artistic director of the Prussian State Theater, Gustaf Grüdgens [who was her colleague in 1933], felt that the engagement was not politically motivated."[51]

Emmy Goering found many people—apart from her official defense lawyers—who were willing to stand up for her. Thus, in addition to Gustaf Grüdgens, 15 other witnesses testified on her behalf. The most forceful was the Berlin garrison priest Jentsch. "She helped everyone, she covered for many Jewish and half-Jewish members [of the parish]." He called Emmy Goering a "religious fighter."[52]

Emmy Goering was found to be a beneficiary of the Nazi regime (Group II). The court ordered that thirty percent of her assets be confiscated and sentenced her to one year in a labor camp, which she was considered to have already served. The court also imposed a five-year prohibition on her engaging in any profession or work. The accused was immediately released.

The verdict caused quite a stir and was hotly debated. The *Donau-kurier*, of July 27, 1948, called it the "verdict of the dying denazification," while the *Südost-Kurier* of August 28, 1948 commented on her testimony with the words, a "good, innocent heart."

On July 28, 1948, three hundred Stuttgart women gathered in a determined protest against the sentence passed on Emmy Goering by the denazification court in Garmisch-Partenkirchen. They said it was a "slap in the face for the German people." The indignant women demanded an appeal of the verdict, classification in the group of major offenders, a longer prison term, and confiscation of all the assets that Emmy had acquired as a result of her position in the Third Reich.[53]

In 1949, Emmy Goering was involved in a tough battle over a number of valuable possessions.[54] She accordingly had many of these declared the property of her then ten-year-old daughter Edda. For the record of the general prosecutor, Dr. Auerbach, who had been entrusted with returning to their rightful owners works of art that had been given to the Goerings more or less voluntarily, Emmy Goering said, "These things were given [to Edda] by my husband, various godfathers and godmothers. I really do not know who gave what."

Among the "things" were Cranach's painting *The Madonna and Child* (1518), which the City of Cologne had taken from one of its museums and given to the child at her birth, as well as Cranach's world-famous *Rest on the Flight into Egypt*, fifteenth-century Madonna statues from southern Germany, gold cutlery, Japanese mats and much, much more. The general prosecutor rudely replied to Emmy Goering's testimony by saying that the "'product' [Edda] of the Reich marshal had merely received the gifts and favors of powerful potentates so as to put them in good standing with her illustrious father."[55] He brought a motion to open a denazification trial against Edda, a minor, in order to secure the works of art for the restitution fund.

The dispute over Edda's christening gifts went on for decades because not only the city of Cologne but also the Federal Republic of Germany, the Free State of Bavaria and eventually Edda Goering herself asserted their rights. The regional court of Cologne decided in favor of the city of Cologne, and the painting would have been returned to its original home if Edda Goering, who was in law school, had not appealed the decision. The Higher Regional Court in Cologne, which now had to deal with the christening gift, dismissed the property suit brought by the city of Cologne. It came to the conclusion that Goering had not exerted any pressure and that the Nazi lord mayor had on the contrary tried to curry favor for the city of Cologne by giving away the Cranach painting. Immoral, "repugnant selfishness" of the ostentatious lord of Carinhall could, at least in this case, not be proven.

Edda's victory was short-lived. The painting was returned to Cologne following a decision by the Supreme Court. In 1954, the State of Bavaria was ordered to return the 150,000 marks' worth of jewelry (according to Edda Goering, the value was much lower) it had confiscated and that had been given to the baby during her father's glory days.[56]

After her release from the Göggingen women's camp, Emmy Goering stayed in Sackdilling with her daughter for a while. Later, she moved with Edda to Munich, where they lived a sheltered life in a small apartment. Edda Goering first went to law school, then changed her plans and began training as an assistant medical technician. She did not marry, choosing instead to take care of her mother.

In 1967, when the true nature of the Third Reich had long been exposed, the full extent of Nazi crimes revealed and the more than fifty million dead from World War II constant reminders, Emmy Goering wrote her memoirs, *An der Seite meines Mannes* (By My Husband's Side). Her legal counsel, lawyer and writer Dr. Erich Ebermayer, and Alfred Muhr acted as ghostwriters, but neither is mentioned anywhere in the book.[57]

Her motive for writing her memoirs is explained in Emmy Goering's preface: "I feel it my duty to say what is necessary to correct the untruth and errors about my husband, who was attacked from so many sides after the fall of the regime, since I knew his nature and character better than anyone else."

In his wife's book, Goering is portrayed as the epitome of virtue. "He, who was always there for others ... he was very generous, bringing ... love, kindness, ... joy, help ..." His addiction to morphine is not mentioned in this "whitewash of the Reich marshall," neither are his corruption, brutality and many art thefts. Life in National Socialist Germany appears as an idyll in a circle dance of kind-hearted people.

Anxious not to depart from the purported line of "unpolitical woman," Emmy Goering claimed that her political knowledge stemmed from conversations she had with surviving confidants of her husband only after the war. But then she goes on to discuss naively the mistakes made by the German war leaders, the debacle at Dunkirk and the battle for England, whereby Hermann Goering always appears in a favorable light.

The essence of her life, according to Emmy Goering, reveals itself in her conclusion: "Today, looking back, I feel as if I had never really been alive, except for the years that began in the spring of 1932 and ended in the fall of 1946 ... fourteen years for an entire lifetime! I was happy and expected my fellow human beings to be compassionate ..."

The German news magazine *Der Spiegel* shrugged off Emmy Goering's memoirs in an article entitled "Too much Heart." [58] In March 1973, the German weekly newspaper *Die Zeit* reported that Emmy Goering, living on her "social security pension," celebrated her eightieth birthday at the Four Seasons Hotel in Munich.[59] Thomas von Kantzow, Carin Goering's son, organized the party.

Emmy Goering died in Munich on June 8, 1973.

MAGDA GOEBBELS

The First Lady of the Third Reich

November 11, 1901 – May 1, 1945

M agda Behrend Ritschel Friedlaender Quandt Goebbels, the First Lady of the Third Reich, is without a doubt the most dazzling personality among the women of the Nazi elite. Her volatile life is reminiscent of a Greek tragedy. As the wife of the infamous National Socialist propaganda minister, Dr. Joseph Goebbels, she is known to history as the "devil's spouse." She shared his life and supported his ideas for fifteen years.

Magda Goebbels was born on November 11, 1901, the illegitimate daughter of twenty-year-old Auguste Behrend. A short time later, Auguste married Magda's biological father, wealthy builder and chartered engineer Dr. Oskar Ritschel. When Magda was three years old, her parents divorced and not long afterward, her mother married a well-to-do leather manufacturer named Friedlaender. Magda, who would later marry a fanatical anti-Semite, loved and cared very much for her Jewish stepfather. Her father and stepfather came to know and respect each other and competed with each to provide an education for the young Magda.[1] At the age of five, she moved in with her father, Dr. Ritschel, in Brussels and the Friedlaenders followed. With no siblings and always in adult company, Magda soon became a well-mannered and precocious child. Her mother was totally absorbed by the social life of Brussels and had no time for her little daughter so Magda was sent to the Ursuline Convent in Vilvorde for her education. She spent eight years in the strict world of the convent, going home only on school holidays. However, her two fathers continued vying with each other to spoil her, taking Magda on trips and catering to her every whim.

In 1914, after the invasion of Belgium by the Germans, Magda fled Brussels and returned to Berlin, where her stepfather soon re-established himself in business. The teenager was grateful for his kindness and attention and showed her appreciation by taking his name, even though her mother had divorced him.

During the four war years, Magda attended a public high school in Berlin and regularly visited her real father, who had settled in his home town of Bad Godesberg. Dr. Ritschel was proud of his pretty blonde daughter's ability, quick wit and intelligence.

He treated her as an equal, teaching her about Buddhism, and taking pleasure in the passion with which Magda studied the philosophy of non-violence.[2] He had no idea of the depth of his daughter's capacity for enthusiasm and how easily she was able to adapt her ideals to suit the circumstances. She would later turn away from Buddhism, becoming a fervent Zionist, who would soon after turn into a fanatical National Socialist.

In March, 1919, Magda completed the matriculation examination and enrolled in the exclusive and expensive girls' college, Holzhausen in Goslar. There she outshone all the other girls of her own age, being well-educated, much more sophisticated and more attractive than the others. She suffered from neither shyness nor an inferiority complex. The assertiveness with which Magda Goebbels, as a "woman of the world," would later impress many National Socialists, was already apparent.

As a college student returning after summer vacation in 1920, she shared a compartment on the train with a very proper and distinguished thirty-eight-year-old man. He was Gunther Quandt, head of a business empire and one of the richest men in Germany. He stopped reading his papers and turned his attention to the eighteen-year-old girl. Their lively conversation, and Magda's sympathetic and flattering interest in his work was all it took for Quandt, who had recently lost his wife, to fall in love with the attractive girl.

Everything proceeded like a romance novel, when, after only a few months, the student became engaged to the multi-millionaire. At the behest of her future husband, Magda converted from Catholicism to Protestantism. She also exchanged the name Friedlaender for the name of her real father before she and Quandt married on January 4, 1921 in Bad Godesberg.

The problems were inevitable. While the groom was thirty-nine years old, the bride was not yet nineteen. Quandt's two sons were only slightly younger than their stepmother. In November 1921, Harald, the only child of the marriage, was born. For the twenty-year-old Magda, the swift transition from college life to the head of a large household with a number of staff was almost overwhelming. Reality proved to be a bitter disappointment. Magda's dreams of appearing in public at her millionaire husband's side did not materialize. The high living that the sociable and highly emotional young woman had expected, with splendid receptions, glorious dinners, cocktail parties and stylish public appearances failed to materialize. Her initial elation at the luxurious residences of the Quandt family, the villa on the Frankenallee in Berlin, the estate in Neu-Babelsberg and the Severin property near Parchim in Mecklenburg, soon faded.

The conservative, humorless and small-minded Quandt found his fulfillment in his work. He had little interest in cultural life and even less free time, which he liked to spend in solitary meditation. Magda already had two father figures in her life, and she did not want a third. She despised her distant husband because he lived his life by a rigid timetable, and had the effrontery to try and educate her. He gave her a notebook, in which she had to account for how she spent her modest allowance.

It was a work-filled life in a gilded cage. Quandt had taken in the three children of a business partner who had died in an accident, leaving his young wife in charge of a total of six children. In addition, the arch-conservative Quandt family coldly rejected her. Considering Quandt's quick remarriage—barely at the end of the mourning period for his first wife—a sacrilege, they kept her memory alive. At every opportunity, they would draw comparisons that were always to Magda's disadvantage. Only her sister-in-law, Eleonore Quandt, or "Ello," who was the same age as Magda, became a friend and remained Magda's closest confidante for twenty-five years.[3]

Gunther Quandt and his young wife were worlds apart. But the millionaire liked to take Magda along on business trips to the United States and South America to impress business partners, and that apparently kept the marriage alive. Magda sparkled in the exclusive salons of New York society with her charm and elegance; Mr. Hoover, nephew of the American president and one of the richest men in the United States, admitted to being smitten with her.

Back at home, there was no longer any need to keep up the appearance of harmony in public and the differences between the two became glaringly evident. Magda plunged into an affair with a friend whom she had met at a student ball and with whom she had kept in touch.

The affair was later considered so distasteful that the true identity of her lover was concealed in the early biographies of Joseph Goebbels—he was simply referred to as a "student named Hans."

The extremes that characterized her life led Magda to Chaim Vitaly Arlosoroff, a Zionist. Curt Riess, one of Goebbels's biographers, knew him personally. "... Magda's affair with a student, a Jew, by the way, whom I knew—there are such coincidences—because he attended the same school as I did ... "[4] Chaim Vitaly Arlosoroff (1899–1933) was Russian by birth, the son of Jewish parents and grandson of a rabbi. In 1905, the family had fled to Germany before a wave of anti-Semitic pogroms. In Berlin, Chaim attended—with Riess—the Werner-von-Siemens High School. After matriculation, he studied economics and philosophy. A fervent Zionist and strong supporter of the teachings of Theodor Herzl, Chaim went to Palestine in 1923 and devoted himself to establishing the Mapai Party with Weizmann, who would later become president.[5]

Later trips for the world Zionist organization brought him back to Berlin, where Chaim Vitaly renewed his passing acquaintanceship with the, by then, Magda Quandt. The bored millionaire's wife turned out to be an interested listener to his dreams of a state of Israel. Their discussions about the future of the Jews in Palestine soon led to a torrid love affair that probably began at the end of 1928, lasted at least until the spring of 1932, and eventually ended in violence.

Magda had been attracted to the much older Quandt because of his wealth and position as a captain of industry. But she was in love with the young, fanatical and charismatic Arlosoroff.

Bella Fromm, a journalist who knew Magda well, speculated on the course Magda's life might have been taken without Goebbels. She sees her, "...in a kibbutz in Palestine, standing guard with a rifle hanging from her shoulder, a passage from the Old Testament on her lips."[6]

Arlosoroff fought for the political interests of the Jewish community and was among the leaders of the delegation to the Zionist world congress in London. With his assassination in Tel Aviv in June 1933—the assassin was probably a supporter of the revisionists, who opposed the socialists—he became a figure that Jews in Palestine could identify with. He is considered one of the founding fathers of Israel.[7]

Magda's affair with Arlosoroff brought an abrupt end to her marriage. Her betrayed husband was so enraged that he hardly gave her time to pack her suitcases. After nine years of marriage, he threw her onto the street, forbidding his staff to allow Magda back into the house. Magda moved in with her mother and started planning her future. Her infidelity put her in an unfavorable position—she was considered the guilty party.

Some old love letters from Gunther Quandt's youth, which she had found in a desk of the Babelsberg house, solved Magda's problems of alimony and a settlement. The Quandt family was afraid of a scandal, and Gunther Quandt paid up promptly: fifty thousand marks for a new apartment, four thousand marks as a monthly allowance, twenty thousand marks for any medical emergencies. She was also given custody of their son Harald.

Magda Quandt, now financially comfortable and a free woman, rented a big, beautiful apartment in Berlin at #2 Reichskanzlerplatz. When Mr. Hoover, the besotted American multi-millionaire, heard of the couple's separation, he crossed the Atlantic to propose marriage to Magda. To his great surprise, she turned him down. But since Magda had a predilection for melodramatic scenes, it became an evening of heated discussion in the tense atmosphere of the Wannsee golf club. On his way back to Berlin, the irritated Hoover instructed his chauffeur to drive quickly. The car rolled over, and while the American escaped the wreck uninjured, Magda had to be admitted to the Westend Hospital with broken bones and a double skull fracture.

A dramatic turning point in Magda Quandt's life was soon to come. Toward the end of summer of 1930, the young and social divorcée, who had never shown much interest in politics, out of boredom and curiosity joined a crowd of excited people who were streaming by the thousands into the Berlin Sports Palace—a building that held fifteen thousand people—for a party conference of the NSDAP. Since the successful appearance there in September, 1928, of Dr. Joseph Goebbels, a Nazi Gauleiter (local official) in Berlin, the building had been used several times for National Socialist rallies. The elections to the Reichstag in September, 1930 that would provide the NSDAP with their breakthrough, were around the corner. The crowd was exuberant and fired up.

The speaker that evening was once again Dr. Goebbels. Wearing a black leather jacket, riding breeches and high boots, he limped through an honor guard of "brownshirts," their arms raised in the Nazi salute to the frantic cheers of his supporters.

The thirty-five-year-old Dr. Joseph Goebbels was a short man with a small torso and a head that was too big for his body. He had black hair and brown eyes. Due to an inflammation of the bone-marrow when he was a child, Goebbels had a clubfoot, which necessitated a dragging gait. Throughout his life, the stunted foot had to be kept in an orthopedic brace and dragged along behind him. His appearance, in stark contrast to the ideal of the tall, blond and blue-eyed Germanic warrier that he espoused, earned him the nickname *Schrumpfgermane*, or "shrunken German."

But the *Schrumpfgerm*ane was a highly talented and feared demagogue who "made history in the streets."[8] With his powerful contingent of loyal bodyguards, he organized riots, gunfights and brawls. Using unprecendented agitation and brutal violence, Goebbels managed, within three years, to raise the vote count for the NSDAP in Berlin from one hundred to one hundred thousand.[9] Next to Hitler, Goebbels was considered the most powerful personality in the National Socialist leadership.

The man Magda Quandt would soon worship like a god was full of sentimental enthusiasm, yet at the same time he was cynical, malicious, vengeful and totally lacking in compassion. The many facets of his contradictory character easily united a missionary zeal, feelings of inferiority, the desire for salvation and the will to destroy. His well-tuned rhetoric was breathtaking, and his propaganda was inspired.

Goebbels was loyal only to Hitler, whom he idolized. Many people felt uncomfortable around him, others avoided him. Contemporaries verified both the repulsive and fascinating effect Goebbels had on them. For Magda the latter was true. "The National Socialist ideology captured her imagination in a way she had never experienced before, but, it became mixed it up with the remnants of the Zionist teachings her old friend Arlosoroff had injected her with ...," wrote the journalist Bella Fromm, in her diaries.

The Nazi scene in Berlin, full of fanaticism, brutality and tumult fascinated the cultivated Magda. Here was the "real life" she had wanted so much.

So Magda set the course for her future. Under the influence of Goebbels's speech, Mrs. Quandt signed up as a member of the local NSDAP group in Berlin-Westend, where the presence of the well-known young society woman was noted with some interest. On their advice, she read Hitler's *Mein Kampf* as well as Rosenberg's *The Myth of the Twentieth Century*.

She soon became leader of the local Nazi women's group. But close contact with ordinary people was not to Magda Quandt's liking. She did not care for the grassroots members, and quickly recognized that her talents were not in demand there. But rather than turn her back on the National Socialists, she tried to work her way into the hierarchy and reported to #10 Hedemannstrasse, seat of the party leadership at that time, as a volunteer. They assigned her to the office of the deputy provincial administrator. Not long afterward, she met Goebbels.

On November 7, 1930, Goebbels wrote in his diary: "A beautiful woman called Quandt is setting up a private archive for me."[10] The multilingual

Magda conscientiously gathered all the national and international newspaper reports about Goebbels, and engaged in the exchange of ideas with her boss. "Yesterday afternoon, the beautiful Mrs. Quandt, came over and helped me sort through the material ...," he wrote in his diary. Goebbels confided everything to his diaries—his social life, political events, the milestones of his career and his many love affairs.

On December 5, 1930, Magda Quandt saw her much admired boss in full action. The occasion was the acclaimed premiere of the moving anti-war film, *All Quiet on the Western Front*, based on the book by Erich Maria Remarque, that shattered the mystique of heroic sacrific and condemned the meaningless deaths at the front. Stefan Zweig described the situation: "The Nationalists in Germany are desperate. Remarque's book ... six hundred thousand copies in twelve weeks, and approaching a million, has devastated them. This simple and truthful book has done more than all the pacifist propaganda of the past ten years ..." Remarque unmasked the false bravado of the "thunderbolts of steel," exposing them to ridicule and making himself the mortal enemy of the National Socialists. "Down with the filthy movie," Goebbels wrote for the magazine *Angriff* (Attack). Then he readied himself for the premiere. He bought up tickets and disrupted the show—with stink bombs and white mice—and threatened the audience. Six days later, the film was withdrawn from the cinema "because of its damage to Germany's reputation."

Four weeks later Goebbels, accompanied by Magda Quandt, traveled to a party congress in Weimar. There he ran into the first love of his life, who hung eagerly on every word of his anti-Semitic speech. Goebbels introduced the two women. On January 23, he wrote in his diary: "I met Anka. She is very sad. Over and done with! Finally! Finally! I cannot stand her and her awful lack of discipline anymore ..." He had known Anka Stahlherm since 1918 when he was a student of German literature. Back then, he had followed her faithfully from university to university. He had made many sacrifices just to be near Anka, and studied at five different universities. In love, he wrote her sentimental poems and bore her mood swings without complaint. The fact that her mother was Jewish did not bother Goebbels. Anka, for her part, calmly accepted Goebbels's hatred of Jews as an unavoidable part of his makeup. Surprisingly, his radical anti-Semitism was not the reason for the end of the youthful love affair. Anka married someone else. They remained friends, and when the couple was divorced, Goebbels came to Anka's aid. "And I can sense how much I loved this woman and still do!" he confided to his diary in 1928. It was not until 1933, when Goebbels had become propaganda minister, that he started to distance himself from Anka.[11]

Changes of heart and contradictions in behavior are to be seen in both Magda Quandt's and Joseph Goebbels's attitudes toward Judaism. Jews had played a decisive role in the lives of both. Both experienced their first great love with people of Jewish descent. When they met in 1930, neither was yet free of that previous relationship. Magda Quandt loved Chaim Arlosoroff and was steeped in Zionist thought, while Joseph Goebbels adored Anka Stahlherm and suffered her mood swings.

In 1932, Goebbels summarized his ideas in the essay, "The Jews Are Guilty!" and set in motion an enormous propaganda machine for his dogmatic campaign against Judaism. In 1936, while still having tea with Anka from time to time, he came to the conclusion that "this Jewish plague has to be eradicated!" as he noted in his diary on November 6. Magda approved of all this, as "part of the National Socialist philosophy." On February 1, 1931, Goebbels's relationship with his archivist entered a new phase: "Yesterday afternoon, Mrs. Quandt came over to do some work. She is, indeed, a fabulous woman, and I am already wishing she loved me." It happened on February 15, 1931. "Magda Quandt comes over in the evening. And stays for a very long time. And blossoms into a fascinating blonde sweetness. How are you my Queen?"

Goebbels kept a meticulous, numbered record of his sexual encounters. This first intimate meeting with Magda, for example, was assigned the number one (1). Then he went on about more trivial matters. "... with Onak through the zoo. The disgusting monkeys! What a way from that primeval creature to Nordic man!"[12] The following entry is from March 10: "... she (Magda) gets here late (2, 3)." Only five days later, the notorious womanizer had already started thinking about monogamy: "I will refrain from affairs and turn my full attention to only one ... she has an intelligent, realistic sense of life and her thoughts and actions are generous. A little more education for me and for her, and we will be a perfect match (4, 5)." On March 26, 1931, he wrote, "Love, now, love (8, 9)."

On April 2, 1931, the SA Storm Troops rebelled against Goebbels, attempting to unseat him and occupy the regional office in Berlin.

Goebbels quickly left for Munich to seek Hitler's help. Magda followed him. "She came in from Berlin and is waiting for me at the hotel. She is quite devastated. But that is good! She is loyal to me and is standing by me." Goebbels had found his soulmate.

But Magda hesitated for some time, not quite sure if she should end her ongoing intimate relationship with Arlosoroff. Far from keeping her thoughts from Goebbels, she shared carefully considered glimpses into her past to make him jealous. Goebbels, as Nazi Gauleiter (local official) in Berlin, must surely have known the identity of his rival. After all, he had at his disposal the means to have people shadowed. On April 12, events took a dramatic turn. Goebbels wrote, "I call this morning. No answer. Then, finally, she calls: The man she loved before me has shot her in her apartment and severely wounded her. Now she's completely gone. I can tell by her voice that I am going to lose her …"

Those plaintive words are typical of the overblown emotional tone of their conversations, but do not correspond to the truth. Arlosoroff had, in fact, visited his unfaithful lover, demanded an explanation and fired a shot during the violent argument that followed—but the bullet only hit a doorjamb. Nobody was injured. It was the end of Magda's Zionist adventure, which would be the wellspring of a calculated, thrilling melodrama, with quarrels and stormy reconciliations with Goebbels for a long time to come.

"A little argument with Magda. She is somewhat heartless when she speaks about her past. She has not really broken with it yet …," Goebbels wrote on July 23, 1931. And on July 26: "Magda is bewitchingly wild. She loves as only a great woman can love …" The following day he confessed: "My confidence in her has been shattered. She has been in love too many times and only told me fragments of the story. And now I lie awake until the early morning hours, feeling the whip of jealousy …"

Goebbels was in love with Magda, but also cherished his freedom. "Eros speaks too strongly in me." It would therefore follow that this affair, too, should go the way of all the others before. Hitler's intervention prevented this.

The thrill of being involved with two men at the same time had always exercised a great attraction for Magda. Such "double partnerships" run through her life like a red thread. After the Quandt and Arlosoroff relationship came Arlosoroff and Goebbels, followed by Goebbels and Hitler—although the latter would remain platonic. For a while, there was even the triad of Hanke–Goebbels–Hitler! Otto Wagener's memoirs of Hitler—he was part of Hitler's inner circle between 1929 and 1933—provide information about Hitler's role in Magda's life. Wagener, while a prisoner-of-war in England, feverishly wrote them in blue ink in thirty-six notebooks.[13] According to him, Hitler soon realized that Magda Quandt could be of some use to the NSDAP. Having her at Goebbels's side would add prestige to the party. Manipulating Joseph Goebbels was always child's play for Hitler. He also won Magda Quandt's enthusiastic cooperation, with great psychological subtlety, through a simple trick. He told Dr. Wagener in private; "This woman could be of vital importance in my life, even without my being married to her. In my work, she could be the counterbalance to my one-sided male instincts … too bad that she is not married."[14] Wagener passed on the confidential words of his "Fuehrer" just as confidentially to Magda.

This deliberate indiscretion triggered a storm of emotions in Mrs. Quandt. She interpreted Hitler's message as a sign of the Fuehrer's secret love for her, which he could not publicly announce due to political constraints. But she accepted Hitler's offer and put her life—with Goebbels as the intermediary—at the Fuehrer's disposal. A short time later, party comrades learned that the Gauleiter had become engaged.

Magda's fervent, uncritical enthusiasm for National Socialism and her adulation of Hitler surpassed even that of her fiancé. This is quite remarkable considering that Goebbels had written in 1926: "Adolf Hitler, I love you because you are great and simple at the same time … I bow before the greater one, the political genius …"

The competition to get close to and receive the approval of their idol was also the bond that kept Magda and Goebbels together. Each was beholden to Hitler in one way or another. In the end, Magda preferred to die for Hitler rather than for Goebbels. But Goebbels had recognized in Magda a suitable means for strengthening his own position with the Fuehrer.

Dr. Joseph Goebbels and Magda Quandt were married on December 19, 1931. Dr. Wagener had the impression that three people were made happy that day. The wedding was held at Severin, the Quandt

Dr. Joseph Goebbels and Magda Quandt get married in December 1931
(right: Harald, Magda Quandt's son from her first marriage; behind: Adolf Hitler)

farm. Nobody thought it necessary to inform the absent owner. National Socialist administrator Walter Granzow organized the event, Hitler was the witness, and eleven-year-old Harald Quandt attended the ceremony wearing the uniform of the Hitler Youth. Shortly after, the Catholic Goebbels was excommunicated from his church for marrying a Protestant without dispensation. The witness Hitler, also a Catholic, received only a warning.[15]

The actress and film director Leni Riefenstahl claimed in her memoirs, written half a century later, that Magda Goebbels had confided in her the real reasons for her marriage. "To my surprise, I received an invitation for a Sunday outing to Heiligendamm ... In the first car, sat Hitler, Goebbels, the photographer Heinrich Hoffmann and Brückner [Hitler's aide-de-camp]. Mrs. Goebbels and I [were] in the second. After exchanging trivialities, Magda told me, 'I do love my husband, but my love for Hitler is even stronger; for him, I would give my life ... Only when I realized that Hitler can never love any other woman but Geli, his niece, whose death he will never overcome, [and loves] as he always says, only Germany, I agreed to marry Dr. Goebbels because I can now be close to the Fuehrer.'" Riefenstahl has Magda Goebbels claiming that she divorced Quandt for Hitler.[16]

By remarrying, Magda lost both custody of her son Harald and her generous alimony. Harald moved in with his father, but visited his mother every day, quickly becaming friends with Goebbels and fully integrating into his mother's new family. Even the loss of the monthly support payments was easy enough to live with when Hitler doubled Goebbels's salary.

Hardest to take was the separation from her closest relatives. Magda's Jewish stepfather was deeply disappointed and refused to have anything further to do with her. He never spoke to his adopted daughter again. Her father also voiced disapproval of his son-in-law and broke with Magda after receiving an uncivil letter from Goebbels. Only her mother stood by her, even though Goebbels forced her to drop the name Friedlaender and go by her maiden name of Behrend. She lived in the Goebbels household and helped Magda raise her rapidly expanding brood of children.

In the spring of 1932, Joseph Goebbels gave up his bachelor's residence in Steglitz and moved into Magda's upper middle-class apartment on the Reichskanzlerplatz, which became Hitler's private headquarters. Internal party meetings were regularly held in Magda Goebbels's drawing room. Nothing was too much for the tireless, charming hostess, who was almost constantly pregnant. She cooked the Fuehrer his favorite vegetarian meals and opened her home to Goering, Roehm, Himmler and other party bigwigs.

"Since the poisoning of Roehm [while eating at the Kaiserhof, Berlin hotel], Hitler was convinced that the staff at the hotel had been infiltrated by Communists. Magda Goebbels immediately made herself popular by preparing small vegetarian dishes that were sent to the hotel early in the morning in thermos containers ...," wrote Hanfstaengl, the foreign press officer, in his memoirs.[17]

He also described how the Goebbels were courting Hitler. "Usually they would take me along as 'minstrel' [Hanfstaengl was an excellent pianist]. Goebbels was jealous and had recordings made of Hitler's speeches to play them at the reception ..." Hanfstaengl also witnessed the "continuous effort of the Goebbels couple to provide female company for the Fuehrer." Hitler had a luxurious suite at the elegant Kaiserhof Hotel, where, during Bismarck's time, the Prussian country aristocracy spent the winter, but he dropped by the Goebbels's apartment almost everyday. He always brought friends and, being a night person, stayed until the early hours of the morning. Hitler also spent a lot of time at the Goebbels's weekend cottage in Caputh on Lake Schielow. "In Caputh—Magda is happy—Hitler stayed until midnight ...," Goebbels wrote in his diary on June 20, 1932.

There is no doubt that Magda, by her husband's side, enjoyed the frantic pace of the "time of battle," as the Nazis called the period leading up to the takeover of power. She traveled with him from city to city, witnessing his party congresses and becoming intoxicated by the tense, violent atmosphere which prevailed in those packed halls whenever Goebbels unleashed his eloquent demagoguery. It was a strangely stilted speech pattern with the stress falling on the final syllables. "Gelsenkirchen before 15,000 [supporters], Essen before 15,000, Dortmund before 30,000," Goebbels noted.

At the beginning of August, the Fuehrer invited the couple to Bavaria. "Trip from Berlin to the Tegernsee—Mrs. Hanfstaengl, Harald. Magda [in the advanced stages of pregnancy] was throwing up all night ...," Goebbels wrote in his diary. Nevertheless, Magda was overjoyed because they felt they were "at the gates of power" and night after night discussed with Hitler on the Obersalzberg the "problems of seizing power." The couple's primary concern, of course, was the distribution of positions. Goebbels already saw himself as Prussian Reich minister for cultural affairs and education.

Germany in 1932 still enjoyed freedom of the press. Goebbels took full advantage of that by publishing his diatribes, but was, however, exceedingly sensitive whenever he or his wife were attacked. Then he would respond with tried and true Nazi methods. "An editor ... in a popular newspaper ... attacked and insulted my wife in the most dreadful way imaginable. An SS member went to his place and beat him with his horsewhip until he fell to the floor, covered in blood: then he dropped his business card on the table and left the newsroom without being stopped by any of the press reptiles present ...," Goebbels described the incident in his own words.

On December 23, 1932, Magda suffered a miscarriage and was admitted to the clinic of her gynecologist Professor Dr. Stoeckel—who respected and admired his most congenial patient. Goebbels and Magda's son Harald visited her daily and organized a little Christmas party at the hospital. Hitler sent a telegram with best wishes for a speedy recovery. On December 29, Goebbels traveled to Berchtesgaden, with Magda due to join him later for the obligatory New Year's Eve party on the Obersalzberg. When her condition rapidly worsened, Goebbels returned to Berlin on New Year's Day 1933. "Oh heaven, I implore you, please do not take her from me. I am nothing without her ...," he wrote in his diary.

Magda was in critical condition for a long time. Her husband, however, according to his own reports, buried himself in work in order "to seek oblivion," and spent his time developing a simple but effective strategy for the imminent elections to the state parliament of Lippe, the smallest state in the German Reich. While the other parties did not pay much attention to the local election, the NSDAP did its utmost. Goebbels sent hordes of propaganda workers to win over the people. In the election on January 15, 1933, the NSDAP won almost forty percent of the votes. The National Socialists celebrated this as the "miracle of Lippe" and were able to divert attention from their losses in the previous Reichstag elections.

Magda was released from the clinic on February 1, 1933. The day before, Hitler was appointed Reich Chancellor—reason enough to throw a party for some close friends. "Epp, Esser, Amann, Mrs. Raubal are here. Hanfstaengl is playing ...," Goebbels noted in his diary. At ten o'clock, Hitler read his proclamation to the people. After that, as Goebbels wrote enthusiastically, "He is with us."

As wife of the Gauleiter and head of propaganda in Berlin, Magda developed an unprecedented political ambition, and was therefore very hurt to learn that Hitler's first cabinet would not have a place for her husband. "Magda is very unhappy. Because I am not advancing. I have been overlooked ... Magda is still crying," Goebbels wrote in his diary on February 3. But after he orchestrated a masterful piece of political agitation on the occasion of the Reichstag election in March 1933, Hitler rewarded Goebbels by creating for him the ministry of public information and propaganda. Ecstatic, the new minister vowed that, with the education of the German people placed in his hands, he would "work on the people until they have succumbed to National Socialism".[18]

Goebbels renovated Palace Leopold on the Wilhelmsplatz public square for himself and his family. Designed by Karl Friedrich Schinkel,

The Yugoslavian Prince and Princess Regent at the Goebbels's

it sat in the middle of a beautiful park. Goebbels had it remodeled for 3.2 million Reich marks for use in his "important ambassadorial duties." Most of the interior furnishings came from museums and public collections. The den was done all in red. The lady of the house received crystal, china, silver, glasses and linen for several hundred people. The state paid for everything.

Magda had six children during her marriage to Goebbels. Helga was born in September, 1932, Hilde in April, 1934, Helmuth in October, 1935, Holde in February, 1937, Hedda in May, 1938 and Heide in October, 1940. She also had two miscarriages. All of her children were good-looking and intelligent, except for Helmuth, who appeared slow and had a learning disability. That all of her children's names started with "H" was one of Magda's whims. Even her son Harald from her marriage to Quandt had a name starting with "H." Magda had seven children in all, along with three documented miscarriages and several additional ones that cannot be verified—in nineteen years.

For the large flock of children that she "gave to the Fuehrer," Magda Goebbels became in 1938 the first to receive the "Honor Cross of the German Mother." This decoration, created by Adolf Hitler, looked remarkably like a military medal. Apart from having to give live birth to a certain number of children (four for a bronze medal, six for silver and eight for gold), the mothers also had to meet racial, political and physical criteria. They had to be "of German blood, genetically sound and deserving."[19]

Magda played the role of a "Nazi woman" quite well, as a mother at her husband's side and by "exercising her influence in the household." The only time she addressed the public was on the first Mother's Day of the dictatorship, on May 14, 1933, when she gave a speech about "The German Mother." Her husband noted proudly in his diary: "Magda is speaking on the radio today ..." Following her speech, a journalist from the British newspaper *Daily Mail* visited the "ideal German woman" in order to learn more about the status of women under the National Socialists. Mrs. Goebbels explained to her that reports published in Britain saying that women in Germany were being driven out of their professions were greatly exaggerated. German women were excluded from only three professions: the military—like everywhere else in the world—government office and the law. If a German girl had to choose between marriage and a profession, she would always be encouraged to marry, for this was without doubt the best choice for a woman. "I am trying," Mrs. Goebbels concluded the interview, "to make the German woman more beautiful."[20]

Magda, well-groomed and wearing makeup, in becoming hats and elegantly dressed, set a good example. But she was hardly able to refine the homely profile of the ideal National Socialist woman. In mid-1933, Magda Goebbels became interested in the "fashion office," which she wanted to run. Her husband, however, disapproved of the idea. On July 20, 1933, the couple got into an argument on that issue. The following day, Mrs. Goebbels refused to join her husband on a trip to Bayreuth to attend a performance of Wagner's *Meistersinger*. "I am going by myself ... If Magda does not change, I shall have to act accordingly ...," Goebbels wrote in his diary the next day, enraged. But the Fuehrer intervened. "Yesterday: lunch with Hitler. He is appalled that Magda has not come with me. I tell him the whole story. He immediately sends a plane to Berlin to pick her up. She comes gladly ... After the first act [of the *Meistersinger*], Magda arrives. Brilliant with beauty ... very subdued mood ... in the night, some coffee. He [Hitler] makes peace between Magda and me. He is a true friend."

The Goebbels's life together started out very well. Ernst Hanfstaengl summarized the relationship as follows: "Magda called out for her 'angel' and the devil himself appeared." According to Hanfstaengl,

Magda later got a taste of Goebbels's psychological makeup. "After showing a private film in his home, Goebbels slipped and almost fell. Magda just managed to grab hold of him. After the initial shock, he grabbed her by the neck, forced her down on the floor and hissed at her with a crazy laugh, 'Yes, that would have suited you, standing there as my savior.'"[21]

After Goebbels had settled into his role as propaganda minister, the private lifestyle of the family became quite luxurious. In 1936 they moved into a magnificent brick villa expropriated from a Jewish family on the Wannsee on Peninsula Schwanenwerder .[22] Of the purchase price of three hundred and fifty thousand Reich marks, eighty thousand were an advance payment from the Nazi publisher Max Amann for the posthumous publication of Goebbels's diaries, which the latter kept with increasing intensity; Magda Goebbels contributed a hundred thousand from the compensation she had received from Quandt; Hitler gave them seventy thousand for "all the years of hospitality in the Goebbels house"; and the couple took out a mortgage for a hundred thousand. Later the minister expanded his holdings by forcing another Jewish neighbor to sell his property. There he built his "castle," which nobody, not even Magda, was allowed to enter. He used it for work and for his trysts. The minister considered Mercedes sports cars, motorboats and a yacht fair compensation to him and his family for the "many things they had had to do without ... Cannot go to a bar, restaurant, variety show, cannot go for a walk and I cannot spend time with my family ...," the minister complained. But whenever Goebbels did find time, he enjoyed reading to Magda and the children.

Mit fremden Federn (Borrowed Plumes) was his favorite book, from which he drew inspiration and which he almost learned by heart, feeling that he and Robert Neumann, with his satirical style and his biting sarcasm, were kindred spirits. But this did not stop the propaganda minister from putting the works of the Austrian author of Jewish descent, who emigrated to England in 1934, on the list of banned books and having them burned in public.

To celebrate the Olympic games in Berlin in 1936, Magda and Joseph Goebbels had a reception for more than three thousand guests on Peacock Island in the River Havel. The fantastic ball was a great social success, the elegance and refinement of which were marred only by the heavy drinking of the party comrades from the "time of battle."

The Goebbels family had a country house, a "simple log cabin on a quiet lake"— castle Lanke on the Bogensee, an estate of the old Prussian aristocracy owned by the coal industrialists Friedlaender-Fuld, distant relatives of Magda's stepfather. The city had acquired the "Aryanized" property at a favorable price, then, with a little pressure given it to province administrator and honorary citizen Dr. Goebbels. Developing the estate into a property with five buildings started with five hundred thousand Reich marks, which Goebbels was able to raise himself. But eventually, the reconstruction cost more than two million, but since the owner was also the head of the nationalized film industry, Ufa paid for it, and for the annual operating costs of eighty thousand Reich marks. The main building alone had twenty-one rooms and a private cinema—just like the mountain villa "Berghof" of his beloved Fuehrer— a modern air-conditioning system, forced-air heating, numerous bathrooms and, just as in Hitler's private residence, electrically controlled windows.

Birthdays were always a big affair at the Goebbels's house. When Magda turned thirty-five, her husband wrote in his diary: "Magda got plenty of presents. She is so volatile. Sometimes nice, sometimes angry ... in the evening, big reception ... the Fuehrer is here." For her husband's thirty-ninth birthday, Magda organized a party. "Celebrated with Magda and the children. It is so nice and heart-warming. The children recite poems. Then, we watch a film of them, they are so lovely, just as they are. We are all very happy ... more and more guests arriving ... And then the Fuehrer arrives. He is quite touched ... he talks to me in a very nice and confidential manner ... at home for dinner ... piles of letters, flowers and presents ... then out here to the Bogensee ... I am so excited [Magda had had some alterations done] ... the house has become wonderful ...," Goebbels wrote on October 30, 1936.

Above all, however, Magda enjoyed public appearances at Hitler's side. "The Fuehrer and Reich Chancellor requests the honor of your presence," was the text of the invitations to receptions and dinners, which were held at the new Reich Chancellery in Berlin built by Albert Speer. Magda Goebbels, who shared her role as "First Lady" of the Third Reich with Emmy Goering, performed her duties as hostess with enthusiasm. She stood out with her quick mind and fine style at the "première cour du monde," as the French ambassador François Poncet called the residence of the dictator before the outbreak of World War II. Magda also attended all the tea parties Hitler organized for selected

The Goebbels family. Standing behind: Harald Quandt,
Magda's son from her first marriage.

actors and artists. In the fall of 1935, however, she disappeared for a
while when Hitler temporarily banished her for her malicious criticism
of Eva Braun.

Minister Goebbels never left his work "at the office," often using his private life as the setting for his propaganda. Thus, the couple and their
well-mannered children played the perfect family for the German people.
"Uncle Fuehrer" also took part, and the illustrated magazines showed
touching photos of Hitler as a friend of children. But the idyll was decep-
tive. Presiding over the Reich chamber of cultural affairs created in 1935,
Goebbels controlled all of Germany's cultural life. He controlled theater,
film, radio and the press. He built and destoyed careers, and took full
advantage of his position for amorous adventures.

Magda knew everything and she tolerated a lot of it—until her husband
met Lida Baarova in 1936 and fell madly in love with her. "Afternoon: a
number of people over for tea. Ello [Quandt, who was a constant
guest], Baarova, Fröhlich [Baarova's fiancé] ...," was Goebbels's harm-

less entry in his diary on November 30, 1936. It was in the suggestive film *Stunde der Versuchung* [Hour of Temptation] that he first noticed the Czech actress. Soon he was courting her with all the means at his disposal. The twenty-two-year-old actress did not hold out for long. She left her fiancé, the actor Gustav Fröhlich, and began an affair with the powerful minister. Fully confident of himself and his position, Goebbels did not keep the affair secret and openly dated her. Soon he was trying to arrange a threesome, but his wife threatened to divorce him. "She is so harsh, so mean," he complained.

Magda Goebbels was unwilling to compromise because she thought she had the upper hand. In fact, she had begun an affair with Karl Hanke, state secretary to Goebbels. In him she had found a willing ally, who not only vehemently stood up for her, but was also grimly determined to deprive his boss of position, wife and girlfriend with some documents he had collected.[23] As the betrayed and angry wife, Magda, providing him with lots of evidence— copies of love letters and a list of Goebbels's mistresses—fled in spectacular fashion to the Fuehrer at the Berghof. But she had miscalculated. Her attempt at extortion, like the one that had once brought such good results with Guenther Quandt, went nowhere in the Nazi milieu.

Hitler was enraged. The loose lifestyle of his subordinates, about which his rivals kept him constantly informed, usually did not bother him. But now, political interests were at stake. A divorce of the propaganda minister from the best-known recipient of the state "Mother's Cross" could not be tolerated. Even the timing of Goebbels's affair with Baarova was bad. A relationship with a Czech woman at the moment when Hitler was planning to invade the girl's country, was more than inopportune. To top it all off, people were still talking about the scandalous marriage of the Reich war minister, Field Marshal von Blomberg, to a former prostitute.

Pushed too far, the Fuehrer laid down the law. He forbade all contact between Goebbels and Baarova and ordered Goebbels and Magda to continue to live together peacefully. Goebbels obeyed: "Life is so hard and cruel." The First Lady of the Reich also felt a blast of the ice-cold force behind the glittering façade of the Third Reich. She became acutely aware of the superior power to which she had surrendered herself. She had to go on playing the role she had once chosen, like it or not. Leaving the Nazi hierarchy and going back to an ordinary life—as

Magda had planned—was not an option. A guest appearance in a leading role in the Third Reich could not be canceled on a whim and a wish.

Lida Baarova was deported to Prague. She recalls it differently: "I had had it up to here and wanted to get out of Germany."[24] The career of the very successful actress came to an abrupt end and her life changed dramatically. At the end of the war, Lida Baarova was jailed in Prague for a year and-a-half for collaborating with the Germans. In 1946, she married the Communist minister of the interior, with whom she fled to Austria. For some time, she made films in Italy and Spain and also performed at German theaters. She wrote her memoirs, in which she did not mention the affair with the Reich propaganda minister. Even in old age, she clung to this version: "We had no affair."[25]

In 1938, Joseph Goebbels had fallen out of favor, but he knew a sure way to put his superior into a sympathetic mood again. On November 9, 1938, he staged the so-called "Reichskristallnacht," (The Night of Broken Glass) with grievances directed from above against the Jews.

Over the following years, the anti-Semitism of the propaganda minister, who prescribed the "Star of David" armband for Jews, reviving the medieval obligation of the Jews to identify themselves, and who commissioned the malicious and inflammatory film, *Der ewige Jude* (The Eternal Jew), became more and more radical. When asked about this by her best friend, Ello Quandt, Magda replied, "Joseph tells me it all comes down to reasons of state. The Third Reich has an anti-Semitic policy now, he says, and it is his duty to fight them in the press and on the radio. It is the Fuehrer's wish, and Joseph must obey."[26]

When, in 1942, "the final solution to the Jewish problem" appeared on the agenda, Magda complained to her friend, "It is horrible what he tells me now. I just cannot bear it any longer … You cannot even imagine the terrible burdens he puts on my shoulders, and there is no one to whom I can open my heart. I am not allowed to speak to anyone about this. I gave him my word …"[27]

Just as Goebbels had orchestrated riots in the early years of the NSDAP, he created the scenario of total war. In contrast to the Fuehrer, who addressed "his people" less and less frequently during the war, and to the party leadership, which gradually retreated, Goebbels and his wife never shied away from public appearances. While the propaganda minister was surveying the bomb damage, Magda effectively worked the public relations machinery of wartime daily life. She had herself drafted and took on a factory job at Telefunken. Every day she would take the streetcar to work, and at home, she would demand food stamps from her guests.

When the Reich was clearly in decline and the Fuehrer's other henchmen had already left Berlin out of fear for their own lives, Joseph and Magda Goebbels were readying themselves for the operatic production of the end of the world. On April 22, 1945, Hitler permitted his propaganda minister and "Reich officer in charge of total war" to move into the shelter of the Reich Chancellery. On the same day, the Fuehrer issued his notorious summons to the people: "Remember: anyone who propagates, or even approves of, measures that are intended to weaken our ability to resist is a traitor! He will be shot or hanged instantly!"[28]

Goebbels explained that "the invasion by the Mongols will be stopped at our city walls. I, and my co-workers, will of course remain in Berlin. My wife and children are also here and will stay." That was a change of heart, for as late as March 28 he had written in his diary that his wife was preparing the children for an evacuation to Schwanenwerder.

Magda and her children went to the Fuehrer's headquarters in Berlin, and moved into four chambers in the front shelter. Meals were served in the wide hallway. Goebbels stayed in the lower level main bunker next to Hitler and Eva Braun.[29] While Goebbels wrote in his diaries as if possessed, his wife read to the children, played with them and appeared remarkably calm. The young captain, Gerhard Boldt, on duty in the shelter, recalled: "Mrs. Goebbels never showed any signs that she was afraid for her life. Full of life and elegance, she would usually come up the spiral staircase, taking two steps at a time. She always smiled at everyone … maybe her admirable strength of character was inspired by her fanatical belief in Hitler."[30]

She never shed any tears for her own or her children's fate. But when, on April 27, Hitler removed his gold party badge from his lapel and pinned it on the "First Lady of the Reich," Magda was moved to tears. She wrote: "Last night the Fuehrer gave me his gold party badge. I am proud and happy. May God give me enough strength to fulfill my last, the most difficult, task. We have only one more goal: loyalty to the

Fuehrer unto death. To end our lives with him is a favor of fate that we never dared to hope for."

On April 28, Magda wrote a letter to Harald Quandt, her son from her first marriage. She did not know that he had been captured by the Russians. It is a horrible testimony to the fanaticism of a mother who has decided to kill her own children.

"My dear son! We, Papa, your six siblings and I, have been in the Fuehrer's bunker for six days now. Our purpose is to bring our National Socialist lives to the only possible, honorable conclusion. I do not know if you will receive this letter ... You must know that I have stayed with Papa against his will, that the Fuehrer wanted to help me escape last Sunday. You know your mother—we are of the same blood, there was no doubt in my mind. Our wonderful idea has perished—and with it everything beautiful, admirable, noble and good I have known in my life. The world that is coming after the Fuehrer and National Socialism will be a world not worth living in, and therefore I have brought the children here with me. They are too good for that world to come. The merciful Lord will understand me if I personally give them release. You will live on, and I have only one request of you: never forget that you are a German, never do anything dishonorable, and take care that through your life our death has not been in vain.

"The children are marvelous. Without any assistance, they know how to help themselves in these primitive conditions. Whether they sleep on the floor, whether they can wash themselves, whether they have something to eat—never a word of complaint or tears. The detonations shake the bunker. The bigger ones protect the smaller ones and their presence here is a blessing, if it only makes the Fuehrer smile every now and then ..."

Then the First Lady of the National Socialist regime advised her son: "Be loyal. True to yourself, true to the people and true to your country. In each and every respect! ... Be proud of us and try to remember us happily, proudly. Everyone has to die sooner or later, and is it not better to have lived a short, yet honorable and brave, life than to live a long life full of humiliation and in abject conditions? The letter is to go out— Hanna Reitsch will take it along. She is going to fly out again! I embrace you with the most heartfelt and motherly love. My beloved son, live for Germany! Your mother."[31]

Joseph Goebbels also wrote a letter to his stepson, telling him that he would "set an example of loyalty." Harald should be proud to be a member of such a family. One day the hour would come, "in which we will stand before the world again, clean and immaculate. As clean and immaculate as our belief and our goal have always been."[32]

The letters were entrusted to pilot Hanna Reitsch, who managed to fly out of the besieged city.

On April 30, 1945, when Hitler and Eva Braun, now married, took their leave in order to commit suicide, Magda Goebbels, cried out in shock, "My Fuehrer, do not leave us; we will all perish miserably without you!" Traudl Junge, Hitler's secretary, was just giving food to the Goebbels children when she heard a shot coming from Hitler's den.

With regard to Magda Goebbels's intentions, there are conflicting reports. Albert Speer believed that, "… she found the idea that her children had to die unbearable, but she submitted, it seemed, to her husband's decision."[33] Two close co-workers of the propaganda minister, however, claimed they had overheard Goebbels suggest to his wife that she flee to the West since they had nothing to fear from the British.

On May 1, 1945, Joseph and Magda Goebbels had decided to commit suicide. All the efforts of Hitler's secretaries and Liesl Ostertag, Eva Braun's maid, to persuade the couple to entrust the children to their care were in vain. They told the couple they would take the boy and the girls to Bavaria and hide them there. The Goebbels refused. Rochus Misch, the radio operator, described the ghastly scene: "There was a drama in the shelter when we heard: 'The children will stay!' Women, kitchen and office staff all came and begged Mrs. Goebbels on their knees for the children. Then there was Hanna Reitsch, the pilot. She wanted to fly the children out of Berlin. Mrs. Goebbels declined. Then came the day when Mrs. Goebbels was in my room, preparing the children for death. She put them in white dresses and combed their hair. Goebbels was not there. Doctor Stumpfegger went over to them, and Doctor Neumann said to me, 'They will get some lemonade to drink, and then, it will be over.'"

Dr. Stumpfegger, however, whom Goebbels had asked for a fast-acting, painless poison for Helga, Holde, Hilde, Heide, Hedda and Helmuth, refused. They might have been given a sleep-inducing drug, followed by a lethal injection, administered by a doctor who had found refuge in the coal cellar of the Reich Chancellery.

At around seven-thirty in the evening, Goebbels gave the order that his body and that of his wife be cremated after their death but before that, to fire another bullet into them to ensure they were dead. At eight-thirty, the couple said goodbye.

Goebbels was, as always, carefully dressed in hat and gloves. He extended his arm to his deathly pale wife, and they both walked upstairs. With a smile, Goebbels commented that, this way, they would eliminate the laborious task of carrying out the corpses. Goebbels shot himself. Magda took poison.

LENI RIEFENSTAHL

The Amazon Queen

Born on August 22, 1902

*T*riumph des Willens (Triumph of the Will), a documentary film directed by Leni Riefenstahl on the NSDAP Nuremberg rally in 1934, made her internationally known. That title could have served equally well as the motto for her life. Even as a child, born in Berlin on August 22, 1902 to a businessman and his wife, Leni Riefenstahl exhibited an iron will, tenacity, burning ambition, and a multitude of interests. Leni's hyper-activity frequently got on her parents' nerves. Her curiosity and volubility were so overwhelming that fellow passengers in the streetcar would ask her parents to silence their high-strung, talkative daughter. Even as a four-year-old, she was interested in theater and dance. Her powerful need for attention quickly became evident. At the Berlin zoo, she would perform rollerskating stunts that attracted quite a crowd, and ended only when the police stepped in.

Leni graduated from the Kollmorgen high school with excellent grades. She was top of her class in mathematics, physical education and drawing. Her one bad grade was for her behavior, the result of—among other things—her climb onto the school roof one day to raise the national flag, hoping to get the students a day off.

The strong-willed Leni's demands for training as a dancer were emphatically rejected by her equally strong-willed father. Supported by her mother, Leni secretly took dancing classes without his permission. Her part in a performance put on by the dance school, which her father learned about by chance, created a crisis in the Riefenstahl marriage, in which Alfred Riefenstahl threatened to divorce his wife. Later he grew resigned and, while predicting a grim future for her, enrolled his daughter in the ballet school of Eugenie Eduardowa. This once famous Russian prima ballerina from St. Petersburg instructed the nineteen-year-old Leni in classical ballet. Normally, such training would have begun at the age of six. Leni became her best and most ambitious student, but paid a high price for it—breaking her ankle three times in a row. But that didn't discourage her, and Leni would never shy away from risk, deprivation or danger.

On October 23, 1923, Leni Riefenstahl gave her first public solo dance performance in Munich. Her mother designed and sewed the imaginative costumes, while Leni put together the dance program. It consisted of ten numbers and made demands on the young artist to the point of exhaustion. The reviews were enthusiastic. In Berlin, her performance of "Eros," "Fire," "Devotion" and "Release," made her a star. Max Reinhardt engaged her at his Deutsches Theater, and guest appearances in European capitals followed. Her success was great, but short-lived. During a performance in front of three thousand people in Prague in 1925, Leni injured her knee and had to cancel the planned tour. All the doctors she consulted told her to ease up, prescribed crutches and warned her to be patient.

As a diversion, she limped into a movie theater to watch *Berg des Schicksals* (Mountain of Destiny), with Luis Trenker, and was spellbound. After six more visits to the film and a visit to the mountain at Guglia di Brenta, her mind was made up: she wanted to act in a mountain film. Through her network of friends, Leni actually managed to meet the director of the film and to win him over completely. Dr. Arnold Fanck, a geologist by profession, was the founder of the Freiburger

Mountain and Sport Film company. He was considered a pioneer in the field of alpine documentary film, and created a genre aptly called "mountain films." His revolutionary photography and clever editing caused quite a stir.[1]

Dr. Fanck allowed himself to be persuaded by Leni's beauty and eloquence, as well as her success as a dancer, and hired her as an actress to work alongside the renowned Trenker. The fact that Leni had a slight squint was considered romantic at the time and was not considered a problem. The film was to be called *Der Heilige Berg* (The Holy Mountain), and contained dance sequences. But the project was still up in the air because Leni Riefenstahl could barely walk, let alone dance— a torn meniscus, accompanied by cartilaginous growth, had been diagnosed. The dancer decided to have an operation, but it was not a routine procedure in 1925. Hospitalized for three months, she risked ending up with a stiff knee. But Leni's indestructible optimism was rewarded. The operation was successful and Arnold Fanck began preparing her for the role while she was still recovering in hospital.[2]

The film was not shot in a studio, but on location in the Swiss mountains, at the lake on the Lenzerheide and in Heligoland. Riefenstahl had to learn how to ski for the film, and again she broke her ankle. While the leading actress was laid up with her leg in a cast, the costly scenery—fifteen-metre-high ice structures—melted away. One disaster followed another. Two other actors and a cameraman were injured and had to be transported to a hospital in Cortina. *The Holy Mountain* appeared doomed. Depressed, the director went to Berlin to report to Ufa, the studio that was funding the movie.

On her own initiative and at her own expense, Leni picked up the camera, took 600 metres of nature shots, and saved the film. Ufa provided more money and the team proceeded to Heligoland. There, Leni danced on slippery rocks in the wild surf while a violinist on the cliffs played Beethoven's *Fifth Symphony*.

Between scenes, Dr. Fanck showed his leading actress the secrets of directing films. She learned from him the techniques she would ultimately develop to perfection.

"He taught me the importance of filming everything equally well: people, animals, clouds, water, ice ... with each shot, he said, it was a matter of exceeding the average, departing from the routine, seeing everything as far as possible from a fresh angle. He let me look through the camera and select shots. I became familiar with negative and positive prints, working with different focal distances, and the effects of lenses and color filters. I felt that film could be a [metier] for me, [a] new [dimension]. At the same time I realized that, in movies, you cannot do it alone, that here everything can only be developed in teamwork," Leni Riefenstahl wrote about her time as director's apprentice.[3] In Freiburg, the actress worked in a photographic processing laboratory where she was trained in processing, printing and—above all—editing film.

The première of the film, which included Leni Riefenstahl dancing to Franz Schubert's *The Unfinished Symphony*, took place at the Ufa Film Palace on December 14, 1926. The press praised both the romantic drama set in the Alps and the actors. "Leni Riefenstahl dances perfectly beautifully to the rhythm of the sea. She gives expression, with constant harmony, to both terrible and beautiful events," the critic for the *Neue Preußische Kreuzzeitung* wrote for his newspaper on December 16, 1926. "Everything in this film is mighty—the mountains, the people … only the young at heart, the wonderfully naïve, can imagine life, love and loyalty in that way. In each word, each step, [is] the Grail motif—in the eyes of [these simple] people, in their thoughts, emotions …," gushed the *Berliner Lokalanzeiger* about the bucolic film on December 18. One newspaper, however, evaluated the movie based on criteria more in keeping with today's taste. *Der Montag Morgen* wrote on December 20: "If only it were just boring, one could resign [oneself] and accept [it]. But this film is not only stupid, but hypocritical … bombastic nature worship, unbearable large-scale hypocrisy—sentimental trash." Admirers denounced these reviews as distortions by a press "spellbound by capitalism and sinning against the spiritual revival of the people."[4]

The film launched Leni Riefenstahl's acting career. In 1927 she appeared in *Der Große Sprung* (The Big Jump). In 1928 she left the alpine world to play Mary Vetsera dying with crown prince Rudolf in the unsuccessful *Tragedy in the House of Hapsburg*. But she returned in 1929 in *White Hell of Pitz Palu*, directed by the famous Georg Wilhelm Papst, with Arnold Fanck directing the exterior shots. In 1930, Leni took voice-training and easily mastered the transition from silent films to sound in *Storms over Mont Blanc*, in which she was required to cross a deep glacial crevice on a shaky ladder.[5]

In 1931 Riefenstahl founded a film production company and started to produce and direct her own projects. She directed *The Blue Light—A Mountain Legend from the Dolomites* in which she played a peasant girl named Jutta. The film won the first-time producer a silver medal at the Biennale in Venice in 1932, and ran for fourteen months in Paris and sixteen in London.

When Leni Riefenstahl toured Germany with the film, she heard, apparently for the first time, of the impact of a politician named Adolf Hitler. In order to get a closer look at him, she attended an appearance by Hitler at the Berlin Sports Palace. Riefenstahl was so overwhelmed that she wrote him a letter, addressed to "Brown House, Munich," even though she was in the middle of intensive preparations for a trip to Greenland:

"Dear Mister Hitler, recently I attended my first political rally... I have to admit that you, and the enthusiasm of the audience, impressed me. I would really like to meet you in person ..."[6]

To her great surprise, Riefenstahl received a reply in the mail. The Nazi politician and the filmmaker met for the first time. She was amazed at the difference between the political agitator and the private Hitler with his friendly congeniality and great charisma. During a walk along a North Sea beach, Hitler inquired about Leni's work and her plans.

Immediately after, Riefenstahl set out on a fact-finding expedition to Greenland, where the film *SOS Iceberg* was made. The actress played daredevil pilot Hella, in search of her husband who had disappeared on the ice. Renowned pilot Ernst Udet (who later appeared in *The Devil's General*) provided breathtaking stunts: "He flies his plane through ice [passes], makes a steep ascent up the rock faces, only to let himself suddenly fall again ... at one point, I [hold my] breath... that is when he tries to fly between the steep sky-scraping towers of an iceberg, but then suddenly realizes that his wingspan is too wide. Then at the last second, he inclines the plane and [darts] between the ice towers like a flash of lightning gone mad, then turns the plane around hard ... After that shot ... we finished," Leni Riefenstahl vividly described the dangerous shoot in Greenland.[7] In her memoirs, written in 1987, she expanded the story by describing Udet's exit from the burning plane.

Riefenstahl returned to Germany at the end of 1932 and became a frequent guest at parties and other events sponsored by highly placed

The actress and director in the garden of her Berlin home; with Goebbels and Hitler.

NSDAP functionaries. She attended Goering's reception in honor of the Italian aviation minister Balbo, enjoying it tremendously. "Magda and L. Riefenstahl were flirting with Balbo," Goebbels noted in his diary at the time.[8] While the filmmaker's social activities are verifiable through witnesses and documents, we know about her relationship with Hitler only through her own accounts. She describes how she ran into Brückner, Hitler's aide-de-camp, by chance on her way home from a concert in Berlin on December 8, 1932. He took her to see Hitler. "He gave me his hand, then he walked up and down the room. His face was pale, his hair hung down over his forehead, which was covered with beads of sweat. Then he burst out, 'Those traitors, those cowards—and shortly before the final victory at that—those idiots—we have fought, toiled, for thirteen years and given everything … and now, with the goal within reach, this betrayal!'[9] Then he looked at me, held my hand and said, 'Thank you for coming.' Without having said a single word, I left the room."[10]

The story not only sounds apocryphal—it is. Hitler hardly ever discussed politics with women. In fact, on December 8, 1932, he spent the whole evening at Goebbels's house.[11] Many other encounters with Hitler where Riefenstahl claims to have provoked the Fuehrer with such direct questions as, "Do you believe in God?" or "You do have racial prejudices, don't you?" leave an impression of unreality.[12]

A fan of Luis Trenker, Hitler had seen *The Holy Mountain*, in which Riefenstahl had co-starred.[13] *The Blue Light*, Riefenstahl's own production, appealed to Hitler, because of its depiction of the people. "Riefenstahl is doing the right thing; she selects her peasant actors herself in the villages," Hitler observed appreciatively.[14] He had recognized the director's considerable ability in her first movie, and had already thought about how her talents might be used for the party. Dr. Goebbels, propaganda minister for the NSDAP, had the artist's political affiliations checked out.

Goebbels wrote in his diary on May 17, 1933, "In the morning, Leni Riefenstahl. She speaks about her plans. I suggest a Hitler film to her. She is enthusiastic." The film never materialized, and the question of what Leni Riefenstahl would have done remains a matter for speculation. Hitler and Goebbels were actually pursuing quite different plans. On May 26, they invited the artist for a weekend on the Baltic Sea. "Yesterday a great trip to Heiligendamm. Picnic a failure. Marvellous sea. Boss (Hitler) also here. Leni Riefenstahl, too, ... with the boss until late at night," Goebbels wrote in his diary that same night. Apparently the director's attitude was convincing and they proposed a film project to her. "Talked to Miss Riefenstahl about a new film. She is the only one of all the stars who understands us," Goebbels noted on June 12, 1933.

Two days later, they reached an agreement. "Riefenstahl talked with Hitler. She is going to start work on the movie." Her first commission for the NSDAP, a film of the [fifth] Reich party congress, was called *Sieg des Glaubens* (Victory of Faith). Riefenstahl was not pressured into making the picture. It was produced by the film department of the Reich ministry of propaganda, and Riefenstahl called it "a reflection of the military review of the movement in the year of victory." It was presented to great acclaim on December 1, 1933.[15]

In her memoirs, Leni Riefenstahl often mentions bitterly that Goebbels hated her, interfered with her work and sexually harassed her. Goebbels seems to have been unaware of that, and there is no sign of animosity

"Artistic presentation of the Muremberg Reich party rally [as a] film"—that was Hitler's order to Leni Riefenstahl

in the daily entries in his diary. "In the evening, with Magda and Leni Riefenstahl at 'Butterfly.' Then we chat at the 'Traube' (a restaurant)," Joseph Goebbels writes in his diary on May 17, 1933.

The NSDAP approached Riefenstahl again the following year. "Artistic presentation of the Nuremberg Reich party rally [September 4–10, 1934] [as a] film, that's the assignment the Fuehrer has given me for the second time."[16] Leni Riefenstahl wrote.

She renamed her film company "Reichsparteitagfilm," or "Reich Party Congress Film," and made the film because "my inner readiness for this task overcomes all doubt, all scruples, all inhibitions."[17] A documentary film without a plot which was to last for two hours posed problems for the director that could only be solved using artistic and technical innovations. Assured of full artistic licence, Riefenstahl decided to make the movie in the style of a newsreel and to break up the monotony of endlessly marching troops with every conceivable device. Working conditions were not ideal, and only two weeks were at her disposal for all the preparations for shooting. In addition, the organizers of the congress were only grudgingly willing to assist her. Many party comrades considered the presence of cameramen on the Luitpoldshain in Nuremberg sacrilegious, and they obstructed the director and her crew whenever they could. The four newsreel teams present—Alfa, Tobis-Melo, Fox and Paramount—also had their own agendas and were competing with the Reich Party Congress film company.

Leni Riefenstahl's leadership style and her total lack of compromise in artistic matters made her many enemies. But with photographic equipment flown in from Hollywood, she triumphed over her opponents, defused all their animosity, and with a team of one hundred and twenty co-workers, made movie history. The director's creative ideas and her willingness to experiment technically were inexhaustible and yielded revolutionary results. Generations of filmmakers have drawn on Riefenstahl for inspiration. The special effects that she created are today considered standard practice by all documentary filmmakers. For example, small elevators were mounted on flagpoles—some thirty-eight meters high—in order to capture expanding panoramic shots, a unique concept. Cameramen practiced rollerskating to get better moving shots with hand-held cameras. The arrival of Hitler's plane was filmed from rooftops. For semi-circular pan shots, the cameramen stretched from fire ladders to get close to the crowds from above. Tracks were laid around the podium to obtain special optical effects from a variety of camera angles during Hitler's two-hour speech and attenuate repetitive or monotonous sequences. All the secondary locations of the congress—the city of Nuremberg, the tent camps of the Hitler Youth, and the campfires of the SA—were also included.

Cameramen crouched in holes in the ground for five hours to film non-stop the hundreds of thousands of people marching mechanically in columns across the Nuremberg Luitspoldshain. They saluted their Fuehrer who, standing stiffly, acknowledged their tributes and, like a high priest, performed pseudo-religious, well-calculated rituals such as the consecration of flags and standards. It was a grand spectacle in true Hollywood style, and Joseph Goebbels, the organizer of the congress, was completely satisfied. The many diplomats and guests of honour—who completely filled a special train—were impressed as well. The director compiled a pictorial record of the filmmaking in a journal, which was published by the National Socialist publishing house "Eher" and in which she lauded both the movie and herself.[18] There were sixteen pictures of Hitler in the publication, but thirty-seven of Riefenstahl. These show the director working with fanatical enthusiasm, contradicting her later claims that she had been forced to make the film.

Her efforts resulted in impressively persuasive images that made commentary superfluous. A unique document of the times, for which Hitler chose the title *Triumph of the Will*, shows the NSDAP in action. It served both as a calling card and propaganda for the Third Reich, and unleashed enthusiasm in people inside and outside Germany. Leni Riefenstahl became internationally known. At the World Exhibition in Paris in 1937, she was honored for her achievements, and the French prime minister, Edouard Daladier, personally presented her with a gold medal.

It is interesting to note that the party congress film gave equal time to the German Armed Forces, or Wehrmacht, that first appeared in Nuremberg in 1935 ("the brown army marches"), and the delegations of Nazi women's associations. While the women didn't complain, the generals did. They suspected that they had been left out of the movie on purpose by the party leaders because they were still in the process of development and were ill-equipped. Riefenstahl was asked to redress the omission. In 1935 she directed a short film about the German army produced by the NSDAP. Called *Tag der Freiheit* (Day of Freedom), it was shot in just two days and contained scenes of military exercises. Ufa showed it as a supplement to the feature film. It presented the army in action and served as propaganda. The film's first public showing took place at the Reich Chancellery in Berlin in the presence of Hitler, high-ranking officers and two hundred guests.

Shortly after, the organizing committee for the eleventh Olympic Summer Games, to be held in Berlin between August 1 and 16, 1936, asked Leni Riefenstahl to make a movie about the Games. She was reluctant, aware of the difficulties of such a project. She remembered that the film made by her mentor Arnold Fanck of the Olympic Winter Games in St. Moritz in 1928 had been a total flop. She thought long and hard, developed and discarded many ideas and concluded that simply recording a hundred competitions would be boring. Instead, she would make a film about the Olympic ideal.

"Suddenly I saw the ruins of the ancient Olympic sites rise slowly from the mists of time, and the Greek temples and sculptures take shape, Achilles and Aphrodite, Medusa and Zeus ... then Myron's, the discus thrower, appeared. I dreamed how he was transformed into a real person of flesh and blood, and in slow motion began to swing the discus— the statues were transformed into Greek temple dancers, who dissolved into flames, the Olympic Fire in which the torch is lit and carried from

The director during shooting of her Olympia film at the stadium, 1936

the temple of Zeus to the modern Berlin of 1936—[became] a bridge from antiquity to the present day," Leni Riefenstahl wrote about her vision of the prologue to the Olympic film.

Her ideas were received with enthusiasm. Only the planned production schedule of three years was hard for the Olympic committee to accept. They argued that the appeal of the subject was its topicality. Years after the Games, they said, no one would be interested in seeing it anymore, so financing it would be a risky affair. Leni Riefenstahl overcame all resistance. That same year, 1935, she had the "Olympia" film listed in the commercial register (Leni Riefenstahl and her brother were named as partners). The project was funded by the Film Credit Bank, in effect the Reich ministry of propaganda, which controlled and monitored all film production during the Nazi period.

"Miss Riefenstahl is being hysterical with me. No one can work with such [a] crazy woman. Now she wants an additional half a million for her film [to] make [a copy] of it. Yet her operation stinks as never before. I keep it cool. She weeps. This is women's last weapon, but it will no longer get her anywhere with me. Let her work and get some order in her affairs," Dr. Joseph Goebbels, the propaganda minister, wrote in 1936 about one of the many arguments involving money that he had with the director during the production of *Olympia*.

The two-part opus consisted of "Festival of Nations" and "Festival of Beauty." After the completion of shooting, Riefenstahl went into isolation and edited a work of art from 400 kilometers of film. On November 24, 1937, she showed it at a private screening.

"In the evening with Magda and Mrs. von Arent at Leni Riefenstahl's. Saw parts of the "Olympia" film. Indescribably good. Wonderfully photographed and presented. Quite a great achievement. In some parts deeply moving. That Leni is really very talented. I am excited. And Leni very happy ... chatted with the ladies for a long time," Goebbels, whom Riefenstahl considered an enemy, wrote in his diary. Only two days later, he shared his enthusiasm with the Fuehrer.[19]

"In the evening, dinner for the Hungarians with the Fuehrer. I tell the Fuehrer about Leni Riefenstahl's "Olympia" film. He is very pleased that the film has come out so well. We want to do something to show Leni our appreciation. She deserves it. She has gone without glory and recognition for so long."[20]

The première of *Olympia* coincided with the invasion of Austria by the German army. The story behind the postponement of the film's release is one of Leni Riefenstahl's Hitler anecdotes. "I was so desperate that I got the crazy idea to meet with Hitler somewhere or other on his trip through Austria and ask him for his help in ensuring the film could be released in the spring. I took the train to Innsbruck. What I experienced in Tyrol may sound incredible today ... The people of Innsbruck were behaving as if in a frenzy. As if in religious ecstasy, arms and hands were extended toward Hitler ... I stood at the barrier erected around the Tiroler Hof hotel for a long time ..."[21]

In fact, Hitler never went to Tyrol on his trip through Austria. He traveled via Passau and Linz to Vienna, where he took a plane and returned to Germany. But Leni Riefenstahl tells us that Hitler's aide-de-camp just happened to spot her in front of the Tiroler Hof and took her to see Hitler—as in her earlier Berlin anecdote—with whom she then arranged a new date for the première of her film. *Olympia* premiered on April 20, 1938, the Fuehrer's birthday.

In 1939, Riefenstahl received a gold medal from the International Olympic Committee for her achievement. On her subsequent European tour promoting *Gods of the Stadium*, the foreign language version of *Olympia*, Leni Riefenstahl rushed from one première to the next. She was at the apex of her career. But a private trip to the United States in 1938 brought her back to reality after her heady European success. Arriving in New York, she was immediately attacked as "Hitler's mistress." She was seen as a representative of the Nazi regime and confronted with the anti-Semitic excesses of "Kristallnacht." Her acclaimed film, *Olympia*, was boycotted, and former colleagues who had emigrated to the United States and were working in Hollywood, did not want to see her. Disappointed, she returned to Germany, where she related her experiences to Goebbels, the instigator of "Kristallnacht," over dinner. "In the evening Riefenstahl tells me about her trip to America," Goebbels noted in his diary on February 5, 1939. "She tells me everything that happened, and it does not sound very promising. There is nothing more there for us. The Jews reign with terror and boycott. But how much longer?"

The outbreak of World War II represents a break in the career of the filmmaker. Leni Riefenstahl was looking for something new to do and with the approval of Hitler and the high command of the army, she and some of her experienced cameramen underwent training as front-line reporters. Her first confrontation with the horrible reality of the blitzkrieg in Poland, where she witnessed the massacre of the civilian population, was enough to scare Riefenstahl away from the theater of war—forever.

The film industry of the Third Reich received special support during the war when many propaganda and documentary films were produced. The demand for light entertainment to maintain the morale of the people was equally great. The famous documentary filmmaker was expected to contribute to the abundant program proposed by the Reich Chamber of Cultural Affairs. They suggested that she make a film about the "Siegfried line." Her refusal was met with displeasure and there were no further offers. Riefenstahl was put on ice, so she turned her attention to a project she had been toying with for a long time—*Tiefland* (Lowland), adapted from the opera by Eugene d'Albert. She worked on the project from 1939 to 1945 to the exclusion of everything else. The ministry of propaganda monitored and tolerated the director, but gave her no support of any kind. "Leni Riefenstahl has problems with her new film. But I do not want to get too involved," Goebbels wrote in his diary in March, 1940. The project seemed doomed from the start. The war forced Reifenstahl to relocate the shoot from the Pyrenees to the Karawanken Mountains. The Spanish parts were played by gypsies, who had been found in a camp near Salzburg. The farmers cast as extras shaved off their beards in a misguided attempt to beautify themselves, and the tame wolf that had a major role in the film died. Officialdom interfered with the work on *Lowland* in every way possible. For example, the replica of the Alhambra of Granada, painstakingly reconstructed in the studios in Babelsberg, was torn down because it was said that the studio space was needed for an important film. This was *Ohm Krüger*, and was produced to entertain and motivate the troops at the front.

Riefenstahl had already been working on the film for a year when Germany's successful blitzkrieg on the Western front forced the surrender of France. The director, who still admired Hitler, sent him a personal telegram congratulating him on the German army's entry into Paris.

"Adolf Hitler—Fuehrer Headquarters. With indescribable joy, deeply moved and full of gratitude, we now bear witness to your, my Fuehrer, and the Germans' great victory—the entry of German troops into Paris. You achieve feats that have been unimaginable so far, unprecedented in the history of mankind. How can I thank you? Expressing congratulations is much too little to show you the emotions that move me. Leni Riefenstahl."[22] Later the director explained that with this, she wanted to express her joy at the coming peace.

On March 21, 1944, Leni Riefenstahl, then forty-two years old, got married. All of her previous love affairs had ended unhappily. Her four-year engagement to Peter Jacob, a captain of the "Gebirgsjäger" (mountain infantry), had been stormy because Jacob was a notorious womanizer. He would periodically disappear with other women. These dalliances were not concealed from Riefenstahl, and her decision to marry Jacob was accompanied by serious doubts. After the wedding in Kitzbùhel, Hitler received the couple on the Obersalzberg. It was her last meeting with the Fuehrer.

After the war ended, Leni Riefenstahl was arrested and made to explain her career during the Third Reich in numerous interrogations. She was accused of engaging in propaganda for Hitler and the NSDAP. As documentarist of the movement, it was claimed she had used her considerable talent to idealize Nazi party ideology.

The minutes of the interview at the interrogation center of the Seventh US Army on May 30, 1945, reproduce the director's defense as follows:

"Like the press all over the world, she, too, claims to have viewed the Olympic Games as symbol of youth, strength and beauty. She says she never received any directives and that she was free to choose her own team. The film was not censored and did not give preference to any one race or nation. The American blacks were treated with the appropriate respect and Jesse Owens, the famous black runner, got a special place in the book that accompanied the film. If her statements are truthful," the report summarizes, "then she has never realized and even now does not realize that her art gave expression to a terrible regime and that she contributed to its glorification.'"[23]

Even afterwards, Leni Riefenstahl would emphasize again and again that she only filmed "what was there" at that time. Riefenstahl had to go through denazification tribunals and trials. Her initially considerable assets were seized, and strangers took over her villa in Berlin. The artist moved into a small attic apartment in Munich, taking in her widowed mother, to whom she had always been close. The problem marriage to Peter Jacob did not survive the burdens of the post-war years, and they were divorced.

Contrary to oft-repeated reports, Leni Riefenstahl was not barred from pursuing her career. In 1948, she was classified in Villingen as a "sympathizer" and as "not directly involved," for she had neither been a member of the NSDAP nor of any of its organizations. She got off with a mild punishment, while her colleague, Heinrich Hoffmann, photographer to the Fuehrer and preeminent Reich photojournalist, was sentenced to four years in jail and barred from professional activity for five years. In his case, too, it was a question of whether he had just been a press photographer or an eager propagandist.[24] Heinrich Hoffmann handed over his voluminous archives in good order and was never heard from again after serving his sentence.

Leni Riefenstahl, however, pursuant to the decision of the denazification court, planned a new career. But she hadn't counted on public opinion, which condemned her as Hitler's mistress, Goebbels's girlfriend and a Nazi sympathizer. Luis Trenker, her former colleague, exploited the situation and forged a diary of Eva Braun—widely circulated until it was confiscated—which described wild orgies on the

Obersalzberg and mentioned Leni Riefenstahl dancing naked in front of Hitler.[25]

Riefenstahl filed more than fifty lawsuits in an attempt to salvage her reputation and recover the rights to her films, illegal copies of which were being sold without restriction.

After a long odyssey, *Lowland* had its première in Stuttgart in February, 1954. The timing was inopportune and the film was not successful. It quickly disappeared from theaters when a rumor circulated that the gypsies acting in the film had been inhabitants of   concentration camps.

Looking back, it is clear that Leni Riefenstahl's career as a director really ended in 1938 with her great film *Olympia*. She was considered an outlaw and experienced public rejection, but refused to face up to it. She continued to work tirelessly but failed to complete even one of the eleven film projects she started between 1950 and 1964. It was a life between "fame and shame," as she put it. Ironically, in 1959 at the Biennale in Venice, there was an acclaimed retrospective of all Riefenstahl's films, but not a single producer could be found for her current work.

At the age of sixty she started over again. She turned to photography and shot a series of pictures on the Nuba tribe in Sudan, largely unknown at the time. While preparing for the expedition, she met a young cameraman who joined her. Their harmonious friendship would soon evolve into deep affection. In Horst Ketter, forty years her junior, Leni Riefenstahl had not only found an excellent co-worker, but a companion with whom she has since shared all the ups and downs of her eventful life.

Riefenstahl's extensive reportage on the Nuba tribe appeared in two volumes and was a sensational, worldwide success.[26] Her photo documents were praised as a "visual feast, overwhelmingly fascinating." The masks, ritual fighting and love dances were seen as "probably the last testimony of a natural tribe threatened by industrial civilization." At the same time, comparisons were noted between the body cult of the beautiful Nuba and the fine bodies of the athletes at the 1936 Olympic Games. The debate about Leni Riefenstahl's role during the Nazi regime flared up once again. Some said that she had revived the art form of her Nazi years, that is, "the glorification of the beauty of barbarity." But in 1975, the Art Directors Club declared her books to be the best photographic work of the year. At the age of seventy-two, Leni Riefenstahl discovered yet another metier. She developed a passion for underwater sports, learned to dive and shot breathtaking photos of marine animal and plant life.[27]

At the age of eighty, Riefenstahl decided it was time to write her memoirs. She devoted five years to the task and filled over nine hundred pages with the exciting story of her life. The book became a bestseller and was translated into many languages.

In 1995, on the initiative of Princess Alessandra Borghese, the city of Milan organized an exhibition of Leni Riefenstahl's complete works. In 1997, Rome also decided to honor the artist at the famous Palazzo delle Esposizioni. It concluded with the three-hour-long critical documentary called *The Wonderful, Horrible Life of Leni Riefenstahl*—a compilation of documents and interviews with Leni Riefenstahl produced by Ray Müller.[28] In it, Riefenstahl openly discusses her life. She describes what an overwhelming impression Hitler's personality had made on her and talks about how he, like a protector, had shielded her against the jealous intrigues of the party. She also speaks about the influence of the famous Russian director Sergei Eisenstein on her work. She sees herself as a non-political person and says she would have liked to film the Communist party conventions, if someone had only commissioned her to do so.

The controversy that still surrounded Riefenstahl and her work in 1997 is apparent in the positive and negative reactions of the press and public to her appearance in Rome. The Roman organizers stressed that it was "unfair to shun such an important artist forever." The liberal newspaper *Corriere della Sera*, however, wrote that, "It would have been better if the havoc-wreaking 'vestal virgin' of the Third Reich had been left at home," and it suggested that she visit the ghetto from which more than a thousand Jews had been deported. In response, the liberal left weekly *L'Espresso* offered Riefenstahl movies on video as a gratuity.

Meanwhile, Leni Riefenstahl, considered one of the most interesting women of the century, can look back on a life of almost a hundred years full of highs and lows. Her film of the Nazi Party Congress is considered the "best propaganda film of all time," and *Olympia* ranks among the ten best movies in the world. More than a hundred dissertations analyze her artistic work. The women's movement has claimed her as their idol. At the age of 96, Riefenstahl was working on an underwater film with her partner. The film museum in Potsdam organized an exhibition on her life and work in 1999. In the spring of 2000, the legendary Riefenstahl, 97, survived a helicopter crash in Khartoum, while shooting scenes for a film depicting her life story.

GERTRUD SCHOLTZ-KLINK

The Party Comrade

Born on February 9, 1902

With her braided hair crowning her head, wearing a white high-necked blouse and severe blue dress, and smiling modestly, the National Socialist Reich women's leader, Gertrud Scholtz-Klink was the Party's female paragon whose image appeared on millions of postcards. Scholtz-Klink, the epitome of ideal womanhood as defined by the NSDAP, was the mother of a large family that, to the outside world, appeared perfect. Her background was also exemplary.

Gertrud Emma Treusch was born on February 9, 1902, the daughter of a civil servant in the town of Adelsheim in Baden. She attended high school in Baden, but dropped out of school during World War I in order to, in her own words, "devote herself completely to the war effort." She worked at train stations and in the households of officers' families.[1] At the age of nineteen she married Eugen Klink, a school teacher, who was an NSDAP sympathizer. Klink urged his wife to do practical community work for the party, including cooking, minding the children of working female party members and participating in sewing shops. But Gertrud, who was inspired by National Socialist propaganda, soon outgrew these simple auxiliary tasks. Hitler made her feel such "confidence in myself, faith in the future and courage"[2] that she joined the NSDAP with her husband, on March 1, 1930. Her fervent recruitment of female members soon attracted attention.[3]

Eugen Klink, who had been made district leader, suffered a heart attack that year during an NSDAP rally and died. Gertrud, as she recalled later, filled the void by becoming "leader of the regional women's association" in Baden, and began to appear as a speaker at party events. Four small children at home—a fifth had died—could not keep the widow from her intense political activity and, in fiery speeches, Klink called upon women to withdraw from public life and embrace traditional female values. Under Klink's leadership, the National Socialist women's organization of Baden "achieved very gratifying results for the families of those that died in action, the wounded and the indigent of the party," as the regional leader of Baden, Robert Wagner approvingly remarked.[4]

In 1932, Gertrud Klink married a country physician, Dr. Guenther Scholtz. In 1933, the regional women's leader, who now went by the name Scholtz-Klink, was summoned to the Ministry of the Interior by Wagner, in whom she had found a patron, to be "advisor on women's associations."

She used the opportunity to dissolve all the competing women's associations and, with considerable ingenuity, eliminate her ambitious rivals. With an appeal for support from the New Voluntary Labor Service, she strengthened her position and became "leader of the women's labor service." The RADwJ (Reich Labor Service for Young Women) provided training in National Socialist doctrine and prepared young women for service in the "national community." In contrast to the "working men" who were urged to "work with their hands," young women were encouraged to pursue "education and reflection on the great roles of housewife and mother, [and to fortify] body and soul."[5] They would learn home economics and agriculture as well as ethnology and genetics.

The Reich Women's Leader addressing foreign journalists

"The German women's labor service [must] further the adaptation of the German woman's professional role to tasks [based on] the family and the soil—settlement above all," Scholtz-Klink told young women. But response was poor, and because the labor service was voluntary, only five percent of girls applied despite powerful slogans such as "Labor service is honorable service." As a result, it became compulsory for all young Germans to join the Reich Labor Service for six months.

By February 24, 1934, Scholtz-Klink had reached her goal. As Reich Women's Leader, she had total control over all NS women's organizations and was responsible for German women of all ages.

Her title sounded impressive, and Nazi propaganda presented Scholtz-Klink, especially abroad, as a leading personality in the party hierarchy. However, according to Hitler's orders, she had the rank of an office manager, with no direct representation in the party leadership, and was subject to the strict scrutiny of NS Welfare, whose control had been entrusted to a local politician, Erich Hilgenfeldt.

Whenever there were conflicts over jurisdiction, it became very clear what little political power she had. She always lost out. For example, the leader of the German Labor Front, Robert Ley, insisted on organizing all working women; Walther Darré claimed peasant women for his own

"Reich food preparation class," and Baldur von Schirach refused to relinquish control of the "Federation of German Girls."

However, Scholtz-Klink was determined, and despite these difficulties immediately began to implement the party ideology. For all girls finishing school, she introduced a compulsory "household" year which, together with the "marriage loan" introduced in 1933, was meant to motivate them to leave professional life. The household year was also a prerequisite for university study. The idea was to convince girls, with the help of skillful propaganda, of the absurdity of their academic aspirations and to keep them away from the universities. Scholtz-Klink fed them the anti-academic slogans of the NSDAP. They proclaimed that theoretical, abstract and purely intellectual work—predominant before the Nazis took power— was lifeless, removed from reality, and in the realm of the conceptual rather than the actual. "Brainwork" and scholarship were masculine pursuits, and women should study in exceptional cases only, for example, if they were destined by "heredity" or "character" to do so.

One female astronomer, who had been passed over for a chair, appeared to meet those criteria, and Scholtz-Klink intervened on the young scholar's behalf, appealing to Martin Bormann, head of the Party Chancellery. "The case of Dr. G. is surely unique, and I support her so strongly because I believe it irresponsible not to promote extraordinary hereditary artistic and scientific talent, but to handicap it, simply because it is a woman who possesses this talent."[6] But the appeal to Bormann went unheeded.

Scholtz-Klink was loyal to the party and worshipped Hitler like a god. She considered *Mein Kampf* gospel, and every word the leader said was a revelation to her. "... and then as human beings and comrades we want to become still better Germans, who dedicate their mortal lives to the service of our great age, so that the Fuehrer can create an eternal Germany out of our discipline and our loyalty," is just one example of her pretentious and zealous style.[7] She believed Hitler understood the "racial soul" of the German people. Even his person "embodied a promise." Scholtz-Klink studied *The Myth of the Twentieth Century* by Nazi ideologue Alfred Rosenberg, with whom she also corresponded. She eagerly absorbed the goals and programs of the National Socialist state. She became a mouthpiece for the philosophy of her male counterparts, who were largely disdainful of women. She constantly urged the observance of German morals, traditions and customs. Scholtz-Klink wanted to maintain high moral standards in the sexual and social spheres. She faithfully repeated the Party line about the "raising of the level of all women" through "service and duty to the German nation." She wanted to communicate to other women her fervent conviction that fulfilling one's duty—quietly in the background and without demanding recognition—was an essential part of the female psyche.

"For mothers it is true that they come to a very quiet and understated power through service, whose sole purpose for ever and ever remains service."[8]

Scholtz-Klink, of course, never served quietly, but traveled constantly from one congress to the next, giving speeches and putting her simple ideas down on paper. In 1938, when her husband started complaining about her numerous party duties, she divorced him.

But Scholtz-Klink wanted German women to fight using "different weapons" and at home, because in public service she saw a blurring of the line between the sexes. "Besides, her [the German woman's] instincts should tell her that by entering parliament, she has only two possible ways to go: Either she takes up men's weapons and maintains the image of the parliamentary woman, which damages the public image of women more than furthering it … or she maintains her womanhood, sits quietly and never achieves a hair's breadth …"[9] She believed that women had no place in politics because "those who have once heard the screaming of Communist and Social Democratic women in the streets, in parliament … know that a truly German woman will not lend herself to that." Just as futile and unnatural was the fight for equality, according to Scholtz-Klink.

One's private life in the Third Reich had to be kept secret because the regime didn't hesitate to invade its citizens' personal realm. It sounded like a threat when Scholtz-Klink said in a cultivated voice, "You, my dear German women, will therefore in future learn through the newspapers and radio … how the money that you hold must be used. For the money that your husbands, or you yourselves, earn does not belong to you alone, it belongs to the German nation."[10]

Naturally, as women's leader, Scholtz-Klink was at the forefront of the NSDAP's campaign against Jews. In her speeches, she cautioned

Gertrud Scholtz-Klink with Gau subleaders of the BdM (Federation of German Girls)

against "raceless talk of humanity," demanded "racial purity" and warned against any disturbance of the "natural order." But that was not all. On the Nazi women's group posters, she offered practical advice: "For fourteen years, you, party comrades, have fought side by side with the Brown Front against the Jews, the mortal enemy of the German nation, have unmasked Jewish lies and avoided Jewish businesses. Not a penny more to a Jewish store, no Jewish doctor, no Jewish lawyer for the German woman or German family! Women, do not underestimate the terrible gravity of this struggle. The Jew wants to lead it until the German nation has been destroyed. We will lead it until Judaism has been destroyed."[11]

Scholtz-Klink attended every party congress. She marched in with her regional leaders, looking like boarding school students in their severe, deliberately unattractive uniforms. Her appearances right after the Fuehrer resembled some kind of stage act, as she faithfully echoed Hitler's statements—as prescribed in his Nazi Women's Book.[12]

In 1934 in Nuremberg, she told the crowd, "The German woman, as we see her, must, if the people's situation demands it, be able to do without luxury and enjoyment; she must be mentally and physically sound; she must be able to make from the hard life we have to lead today a beautiful life ..."

On September 13, 1936—in the midst of peacetime—German women, much to their surprise, heard Hitler say, "As long as we have a healthy male sex—and we National Socialists will see to that—no female hand grenade section or female sharpshooter corps will be formed in Germany."[13]

This was as much a glimpse into the future as the implementaion of the "four-year plan" of 1936, which was intended to adapt Germany's economy to war conditions. Gertrud Scholtz-Klink made her contribution: "If the Fuehrer says, 'We do not have the foreign currency to import all the additional meat that we need,' then we housewives, could give proof of our good professional education by simply saying: We have bread, enough potatoes, and adequate stocks of milk and sugar. I am telling you this to demonstrate how the German woman in the final analysis could be the best economic minister ..."[14]

For appearances' sake, Scholtz-Klink was treated as one of the party cadre, even though the role of Nazi women had been clearly defined in 1921. At that time, a general assembly of all members had decided that women would not be accepted into the party leadership or executive committees. As a result, severe limitations were placed on the ambitious Scholtz-Klink's aspirations. She suddenly looked like a victim of the Nazi anti-women policy that she passionately preached to others but was reluctant to accept for herself. Even praise from her revered Fuehrer was small consolation, since Hitler had claimed in a speech at his headquarters, "I have had four women for show—Mrs. Troost, Mrs. Wagner, Leni Riefenstahl and Mrs. Scholtz-Klink."[15]

But while Hitler sought the company of the other "women for show" and liked to spend time with them privately, he would avoid Scholtz-Klink whenever possible. In 1938, at the height of her modest power, she complained, "I have not yet succeeded in discussing the scope of women's duties with the Fuehrer in person."[16] She could never get close to Hitler, and the entire Nazi elite kept its distance from her as well. The drab Reich women's leader was ignored. No one wanted to meet her socially and she was never invited to the splendid receptions and parties of the Third Reich.

The fact that the wives of party functionaries could not relate to her speeches and avoided them, not reading her publications either, was embarrassing, especially since Scholtz-Klink wrote constantly and published more than fifty books and pamphlets between 1933 and 1944.[17]

Despite all the effort and propaganda, the number of women who voluntarily joined the Nazi German Women's Project amounted to a mere six percent of the membership. The impressive total of four million members was the result of simply incorporating women's associations into the Nazi organization—and canceling one's membership had undesirable consequences.

The compulsory members quietly rebelled, and the "new German woman" stayed away from courses in "ideological schooling," in whatever guise they were offered. However, there was huge interest in baby care and cooking. Courses for mothers created by Scholtz-Klink were a remarkable success, and between 1934 and 1937, more than a million women attended the fifty-four thousand courses offered.

The prevailing atmosphere in the Nazi women's groups is characterized by a telegram Scholtz-Klink received from Vienna on March 14, 1938, shortly after the German Wehrmacht invaded Austria: "On the day of the Fuehrer's arrival in Vienna, the women of Austria sympathetic to Germany, who have longed since the end of the war for Austria's return to the German Reich and have worked for it, welcome the Reich women's leader wholeheartedly and request you to visit the women of Austria soon."[18] Scholtz-Klink gladly complied with this request and undertook an impressive speaking tour through the "Ostmark" to promote the "German Women's Project" and to introduce the "Nazi Women's Association."

In 1940, Scholtz-Klink married for the third time, this time to the SS group leader August Heissmeyer, who brought with him six children from his first marriage. The couple's combined flock of children offered envious party comrades the opportunity to criticize the unpopular Scholtz-Klink for neglecting her official duties. Others, however, felt she was barely spending time with her family.

During the war, the absurdly irrational intellectual world of the Nazi regime lost more and more of its powers of persuasion, and the ideals promulgated by the Nazi Women's leader in her prolix speeches fell victim to reality. Scholtz-Klink revised her views on marriage: the "gainful female professions" that saw "Mistress in your own House!" as a goal were forgot-

State visit in Rome

ten. Merely keeping a home had suddenly ceased to be meaningful. The question of men and women was no longer an issue and there was no more talk of "back to the soil." On the contrary, Scholtz-Klink proclaimed, "We often hear from women the most diverse arguments against work in the arms industry. The question [as to] whether this kind of work should be expected of [any] woman is probably out-of-date today."[19] She even outdid her esteemed Fuehrer, who had long forbidden forced female labor in the arms industry. When at last in January 1943, all women between the ages of seventeen and forty-five were conscripted, Scholtz-Klink welcomed it: "The women trained by the Women's Association and made available to the Wehrmacht are not only to be secretaries and workers, but soldiers of the Fuehrer."[20]

In 1943, Scholtz-Klink offered advice for a "Wartime Christmas." In 1944, she claimed: "Mothers, you [are bearers of] the fatherland." But in 1945, she and her husband went into hiding. The couple took a false name, were denazified and lived in the American occupation zone for three years without being recognized. In February 1948, the former Reich women's leader was arrested and sentenced to eighteen months in jail for misleading the authorities. A further denazification trial classified Scholtz-Klink as merely "incriminated." As a result of massive protests, a second trial was held with a charge of "major offender." The judges found mitigating circumstances in Scholtz-Klink's role and sentenced her to the relatively mild punishment of eighteen months, which she was already considered to have served. The Political Purging Commission of the Federal Republic of Germany prohibited her from engaging in any political action and issued a ban on the exercise of a profession.[21]

Scholtz-Klink remained a true believer in National Socialism. As late as 1974 she held the view that Parliament was the most unsuitable place for expressing the wishes and opinions of a people. "We [the National Socialist women] were one step ahead," she said proudly. In 1978, as a response to critical articles regarding her role during the Nazi period, Scholtz- Klink wrote the book, *Die Frau im Dritten Reich* [Woman in the Third Reich], containing speeches and publications from her glory days.

In her book, Scholtz-Klink reveals no remorse or regret. Instead, she praises the Third Reich and glorifies the Fuehrer: "One day the name of Adolf Hitler entered our consciousness—a combat soldier who woke up our nation, showed us the light, where we only saw darkness before, and held us in his hand ..."[22]

GELI RAUBAL

Adolf's Niece

June 4, 1908 – September 18, 1931

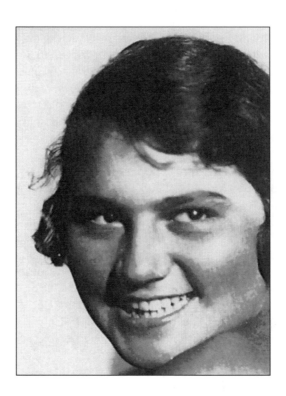

❝ … one thing we need to be clear about: Uncle Adolf wants us to wait two years. Think about it, Emil, two whole years during which we may kiss each other only every now and then, and always under the watchful eyes of Uncle Adolf …," Angela "Geli" Raubal, Adolf Hitler's niece, wrote to her lover and secret fiancé, Emil Maurice.

This letter, written on Christmas Eve, 1927 was put up for sale at the reputable auction house Hermann Historica in Munich in 1933.[1] The document reveals details of the relationship between Hitler and Geli Raubal, who committed suicide in 1931.

None of the women in the sphere of the Nazi elite has intrigued historians as much as Hitler's niece. Historians, journalists and psychologists examining the memoirs of party members, have endlessly speculated on the Raubal case. Most of the conjecture touches on Hitler's sex life. Was Geli Hitler's mistress? Was her death really suicide? Was it murder?

Angela "Geli" Maria Raubal was born in Linz, Austria, on June 4, 1908, a few months after the twenty-year-old Hitler moved to Vienna to retake the arts academy entrance exam. Her mother, Angela Raubal, née Hitler, was the daughter of Hitler's father from his second marriage to Franziska Matzelsberger. Of all the members of his family, Hitler was closest to his half-sister, who was six years older than him. In his youth, he had read his plays to her.[2]

Angela Hitler had left her family home in Leonding in Upper Austria to get married on September 14, 1903, shortly after her father died. Three children—Leo, Angela "Geli" and Elfriede—were born during the marriage to a tax official named Leo Raubal.[3] But Raubal died in 1910, leaving the young widow with three small children and a precarious financial situation. Angela Raubal sought and found help from her husband's family. Her sister-in-law, Maria Raubal, an unmarried elementary school teacher, proved very supportive. In 1913, while living in Peilstein, a small town near Linz where she taught at the elementary school, she took Leo in. Geli joined them in 1915 and entered Maria Raubal's first-grade class at the Peilsteiner elementary school.

A photograph of Maria Raubal in the classroom shows a short woman with a determined expression, her students all sitting on their wooden benches with their arms obediently folded. She has placed her niece Geli, a pretty girl with delicate features, in front in the first row where she can keep an eye on her.[4] A former classmate still remembers the 1915 school year. "[Geli] was a pretty girl with a zest for life. During a school trip to Plöckensteiner Lake, she was the only one to jump in the water, and we stood there and watched in amazement."[5]

While Geli lived with her aunt and learned her ABC's, her mother went to Vienna to look for work. In October, 1915, Angela Raubal took a job as supervisor of a home for female novices and augmented her meager civil servant's pension with the salary.[6] The effects of World War I were being felt in the capital of the Austro-Hungarian empire.

Angela Raubal (1st row, 3rd from the left) in first grade. To the left, in the front, her aunt and teacher Maria Raubal

Uprooted and impoverished people were seen in the streets. There was a great shortage of housing and Angela Raubal thought herself lucky to find an apartment on the second floor of a beautiful art-nouveau building on Gumpendorfer Strasse in Vienna's sixth district.

In October 1917, there were strikes and demonstrations protesting food shortages. Angela Raubal sent for the nine-year-old Geli who stayed with her mother in Vienna for five years, witnessing the end of the war, the disintegration of the Hapsburg empire, the collapse of the economy and the poverty resulting from the galloping inflation that marked the post-war years. Nevertheless, Geli and her mother would always have fond memories of the city on the Danube.

After five years of elementary school, Geli, an average student, took the entrance examination for the Mariahilf Girls High School at #4 Rahlgasse. In 1918, the number of girls attending secondary schools was still low. Attending an intermediate school was a privilege reserved for those of distinguished family background and social status, whether or not they had money.

The Raubal-Hitler family attached great value to education as was apparent from the course they made Geli follow. Angela Raubal—with

Hitler's support—set extremely high standards for her daughter and was very strict. Geli's grades in her first year of high school were not good and her mother, rather than let her attend a municipal school where the courses were easier, enrolled her daughter in another secondary school before the Christmas of 1919. At this school, at #6 Amerlingstrasse in Vienna's sixth district, Geli repeated her first year. She managed to make it to third year, but a mark of "Insufficient" in Latin, Greek, Geography and Mathematics, meant she would have to repeat the year. Her mother again removed Geli from school before the end of term.[7] At a family meeting, a decision was made about Geli's future. Maria Raubal, Geli's aunt, had retired after thirty-four years of teaching and moved into a small house at #43 Dinghoferstrasse in Linz. She took Geli under her wing and tackled the problem of the girl's schooling.

The secondary school for girls founded in Linz in 1889 was not cosidered good enough by Geli's ambitious mother. Angela and Maria Raubal decided on the Academic Secondary School on the Spittelwiese, the most reputable school in Linz. The school was about to break with a time-honored tradition and admit girls for the first time. Geli's mother and aunt persisted, and she was finally accepted, despite her poor grades.[8] Under the strict supervision of her aunt, who was also looking after Geli's brother Leo, her grades improved and she finished the school year on a positive note. In her fourth year, Geli again had problems with Classical Greek, and repeated the exam in the fall. The tiresome study routine ruined her summer and proved to be a turning point—thereafter she had only minor problems at school, which could easily be overcome with the tutelage of a classmate.[9]

Geli was pressured by her family to do well in school. Certain parallels exist to the school experience of her uncle. Hitler, like his niece, had to repeat the first year of secondary school and frequently changed schools and repeated examinations. Hitler ended his inglorious school career by dropping out at the age of sixteen without graduating. His niece would no doubt gladly have done the same. But she bowed to the wishes of her mother and aunt and stuck it out until graduation.

During her time in Linz, Geli got to see her mother only during the holidays. Angela Raubal had changed jobs as well as apartments and from 1919 on, was "Kitchen Supervisor" at the Jewish University cafeteria in Vienna. Ernst Hanfstaengl, chief foreign press officer of the

NSDAP, claims to have visited Hitler's half-sister in Vienna in 1923. "... I found her on the fourth or fifth floor of a rundown tenement. When I rang the doorbell, she opened the door only a crack. That was enough for me to see in the background mattresses lying on the floor of the shabby room."[10]

In fact, Angela Raubal was living at that time in the elegant middle-class neighborhood of Vienna's fourth district where, between 1920 and 1927, she rented a comfortable four-room apartment with a balcony in a well-maintained leasehold building.[11] When she moved to Bavaria, she rented a smaller apartment in the same building—for occasional visits to Vienna. [12]

Hanfstaengl recalled that Geli was a "strapping farmer's girl and full-figured blonde typical of the sweet Viennese girl." Photographs, however, show the person thus described as a sturdy, black-haired girl with a thick neck, thin lips, big, dark eyes and an alert air. In Linz, people liked Geli for her "nice personality,"[13] and her classmates admired her self-confident bearing. One day she raised her hand in religion class, stood up and, to the laughter of the class, said to the teacher, "Professor, your fly is open."[14] Geli Raubal was a classmate of Alfred Maleta, later the president of the Austrian National Council (lower house of parliament), who in school was connected to the Christian Social Party, belonged to the Christian German students' association, as well as the "Nibelungia" fraternity. For many years, he walked Geli to and from school. "I would very humbly walk her home and deliver her to her strict mother [in fact, her aunt, Maria Raubal] who would always look me up and down very critically," Maleta recalled. He remembered Geli very fondly.

"We did not only walk to and from school, but we also went for walks or on little excursions during the holidays. She [Geli] was not really a great love of my youth, but I did have a very romantic crush on her for quite some time. Yes, romantic is probably the best word to describe our relationship, which none of our classmates had any idea about. One day, we walked through the Kürnberger Forest near Linz. Far below is the Danube Valley, surrounded by forests, almost like it was long ago, when the Nibelungs rode in, with the beautiful Kriemhild and the dark Hagen ... Suddenly, [there was] rolling thunder in the distance, ragged gray clouds, the first raindrops ... we ran ... [and] soaked to the skin, I held her protectively in my arms."[15] Geli also accompanied Alfred to the evening social gatherings of the

"Nibelungia" and went with him to the class balls in the dance hall of the Linz clubhouse.

The National Socialist Party and Adolf Hitler were names well known among secondary-school students in Linz. Her classmates listened in awe when Geli told them about her visit, with her mother and brother Leo on June 17, 1924, to her uncle who had been jailed at the Landsberg fortress after his failed putsch.[16] But when she boasted that her uncle—who was living in a small furnished room at the time—had given her a villa in Munich, her classmates had a hard time believing her. After all, Geli Raubal had been exempted from tuition fees since she was six because her family had no money.[17]

Unlike her brother Leo, who had graduated from teachers' college and was a dyed-in-the-wool Social Democrat, Geli had no interest in politics and no personal opinion about Hitler's political ambitions. It did not bother her at all when her friend Maleta criticized the NSDAP. "Strangely enough, it was I who talked to her for hours about Hitler's theories and his political movement, of course in a very negative way ... But I believe that she, as an apolitical woman, did not pick that up at all. To her, Hitler was her dear Uncle who just happened to be a famous politician ..."[18]

Geli's history teacher was Hermann Foppa, a politician and party chairman of the "Pan-German National Party," which had twenty representatives in Parliament in 1921 and was pushing for Austria's union with Germany.[19] The Pan-Germans made up the "nationalist camp" in Austria, and, after a major defeat, were predominantly under the influence of the Nazis. Foppa saw in Hitler the man of the future, and that was what he taught his students.

In 1927, Geli Raubal and her class were preparing for the year-end exams. They were also planning a trip to celebrate the end of their high school days. Foppa thought of Hitler and suggested they go to Munich. They would meet this interesting man from Upper Austria and at the same time go sightseeing in the city.[20] He wondered if Miss Raubal could possibly arrange for class 8A to meet her uncle. Foppa prepared his class with relevant material for the trip and for the subsequent discussions. Maleta claims that he had read *Mein Kampf, The Myth of the Twentieth Century*, but also issues of Lanz von Liebenfels's periodical, *Ostara*. The purpose was—according to

In 1927, Geli Raubal (on the left) took her final examinations at the Academic Secondary School in Linz. (2nd row, 3rd from the left: Alfred Maleta, who later become a member of the Austrian People's Party)

Maleta—to find out why National Socialism, which had only a few supporters in Austria at the time, was so popular in the Reich.[21] In fact, the NSDAP was in crisis at the time and was on the brink of sinking into insignificance. Hitler had been banned from speaking in public until March 1927.[22]

When Hitler agreed to the meeting, the entire class, including Michael Watschinger, the German teacher, and Foppa, the history teacher, traveled to Munich for eight days. While the students were put up at various guest houses, Geli and Maleta stayed in the sumptuous mansion of the Bruckmann family. It was in these luxurious surroundings that the students were introduced to Hitler and his staff at afternoon tea. Maleta reports that Hitler appeared in full Nazi uniform in brown shirt, breeches and jackboots. The class lined up before him, and he greeted each one individually with a firm handshake and a penetrating look. As he spoke to them in his booming voice, the students listened, electrified. When they left, the history teacher—who became regional school inspector after the annexation of Austria—prophesied to his students that Hitler would shape their future with his views, whether they liked it or not. At the end of their stay in Munich, Geli invited her friend Maleta to a brief and private meeting with her uncle at the café "Heck," a simply furnished place with wooden chairs and iron tables, which the Fuehrer frequented with his comrades.

On June 24, 1927, Geli Raubal became one of the first girls to pass final exams at the Academic Secondary School in Linz. Of the three topics she had to choose from in German, she selected "God gave us three graces in this world of need: ideals, love and death."[23] The class photo shows that, besides Geli, only one other girl had been in the class.[24]

In the fall of 1927, Geli moved to Munich, where she enrolled in medical school.[25] But she was not serious about her studies.[26] Rather, it was an excuse for her to be close to Emil Maurice, whom Geli had known for many years as her uncle's driver and aide. In the summer of 1926, love had grown out of the friendship. At the time, Goebbels noted in his diary: "Maurice is here. He tells me of his unhappy love."[27]

Emil Maurice (1897–1979) was the son of a family from Schleswig-Holstein that had originally immigrated from France. The professional clockmaker was a co-founder of the "Department for Physical Education and Sports," the later SA, and was a member of the innermost circle of the NSDAP. "Maurizl," as Hitler laughingly referred to him, was a particular favorite of his idol, whom he followed like a shadow. They were on a first name basis, which was regarded as a special privilege, given the Fuehrer's aloofness. Emil Maurice could boast in the 1920s, of being Hitler's best friend. Not even the consistently recurring rumor, even within the Maurice family, that the dark-haired "Maurizl" had Jewish ancestry, could cast a shadow over their friendship.[28] Maurice regularly served as Hitler's chauffeur between 1921 and 1927. For his participation in the Munich putsch, he was sentenced to nine months and actually served more time than Hitler. In 1925 he joined the recently founded party as Member No. 39, and was appointed by Hitler as inspector of the newly formed SS.[29]

The attractive Maurice, with his small beard and romantic good looks, had always been there even when Hitler took his niece Geli to the Chiem sea to have a picnic and swim. On those occasions, he would drive Hitler's big, open Mercedes. Geli and Henriette Hoffmann, the party photographer's daughter who was Hitler's secretary, sat in the back seat. "We had checkered wool blankets with us. Everything you needed for a picnic ... packed in wicker picnic baskets with lids... Maurice got his guitar from the trunk and sang Irish folk songs ... we girls withdrew to a bathing spot hidden behind bushes ... we swam naked and let ourselves be dried by the sun. Once, a swarm of butter-

Picnic with Hitler at Chiemsee. In the background: Emil Maurice, Hitler's driver and Geli's great love.

flies descended on the naked Geli ...," Henriette recalled.[30]

Maurice fell in love with Hitler's niece, and she returned the feelings of the handsome young man whom she had often met in the company of her uncle. Even years later, Maurice would still speak of her admiringly: "She was a princess who turned heads when she walked by ... her big eyes were poems ... she had wonderfully beautiful, black hair, which she was very proud of ...."[31]

Hitler, who had no idea of Maurice's intentions, often acted as matchmaker and didn't spare "Maurizl" from questions as to when the latter planned to get married, saying, "When you marry, I'm coming by for dinner every day."[32] Wrongly assuming that he was being encouraged, the loyal Maurice acted shortly before Christmas in 1927. "I complied with his wish and asked Geli—only she mattered to me—to become my wife ... and she gladly accepted."[33] Then he asked her uncle for Geli's hand. A terrible scene followed and Hitler harangued the baffled Maurice with reproaches and threats.

On Christmas Eve, 1927, Geli wrote to Maurice: "My dear Emil! The mailman has already brought me three letters from you, but I've never been as pleased as over the last one. Maybe there is a reason for all the suffering we have endured in the last few days. I have suffered in these two days more than ever before. But it had to happen, and it was certainly good for both of us. I now have the feeling that these days have bonded us together forever. One thing we must be clear about: Uncle Adolf wants us to wait for two years. Think about it, Emil, two whole years, during which we may kiss each other only now and then, and always under the watchful eye of Uncle Adolf. You must work to make a living for both of us and we can only see each other in the presence of others, and besides... [34] I will give you my love and be faithful to you unconditionally ... I love you so much! ... Uncle Adolf wants me to continue my studies ... Uncle A. is now very nice. I would like to give him great pleasure, but do not know with what ... But Uncle A. says our love must be kept a complete secret ... I believe I will be totally happy. Whether we only meet in the evening at the Christmas tree or perhaps in the course of the afternoon. Dear, dear Emil, I am so happy to be able to stay with you. We will see each other often, and be alone, too. Uncle A. has promised me. He is so sweet. Just imagine if I were sitting in Vienna now. I could never have been away from you for too long. I felt so alone in Vienna, although my mother is there. You would have stayed here in Munich. And that I owe mostly to Mrs. Hess [wife of Hitler's private secretary at the time].[35] At first I did not want her to come to me. But when she was here, she was so nice, she was the only person who believed that you really love me and for that reason I came to like her. I hope you receive this letter tonight. Many kisses from your Geli. I'm looking to the future!"[36]

The letter affords insights into Hitler's psyche and refutes the rumour about the love affair between Hitler and his step-niece. Geli was not in love with her uncle. Rather, she was hoping to marry Emil Maurice. Hitler, however, to whose care she had been entrusted, was playing the role of a strict guardian. The girl's mother never entered the picture while he determined the future of the nineteen-year-old student and her almost thirty-year-old boyfriend. Neither Geli nor Emil Maurice ever thought of standing up to Hitler and taking matters into their own hands. After long arguments, they bowed to the wishes of Uncle Adolf and accepted his terms. Hitler dominated and manipulated his family as well as his party followers.

Hitler imposed a two-year waiting period on Geli's wedding plans, and until she reached the age of majority, insisted that Maurice build "a life" for himself. He wanted his niece to continue her studies. He engaged Mrs.

Geli Raubal's love letter to Emil Maurice

Hess to prevent secret rendezvous, forbade their engagement and convinced the young couple that "their love had to be kept secret." In Geli's eyes, Uncle Adolf was still "sweet" because he was permitting her to stay in Munich—instead of Vienna or Linz. But Hitler wanted only to terminate the unacceptable affair as quickly as possible. At the end of 1927, he fired Emil Maurice as his driver, stripped him of all party offices and banned him from his circle. Maurice believed that Hitler had fallen in love with his niece and that jealousy was the real motive behind his actions.

The Maurice affair did not lead to a break between Hitler and his niece. Instead, Geli became her uncle's permanent escort early in 1928. She joined him for his regular nightly meetings at the Café Heck and was not excluded whenever Hitler discussed party matters, unusual in the NSDAP. Uncle and niece often frequented the Nazi elite's favorite restaurant, the Osteria Bavaria. The circle around Hitler found Geli's Austrian accent charming and complimented her good looks, which did not at all resemble the ideal of the Nordic-Germanic woman.

"Whenever Geli was at the table, everything revolved around her, and Hitler never tried to monopolize the conversation. Geli was an enchantress. In her natural way, free of all coquetry, she put everyone around her in a good mood through her mere presence. Everyone loved her," Heinrich Hoffmann reported.[37] Joseph Goebbels also met Geli. "Still in Munich, that delightful city. Yesterday I met with Hitler; he invited me to dinner right away—a charming young lady was there…" Hitler did not like to let his niece out of his sight. "Hitler accompanied Geli when she went shopping. He followed her into a hat shop and watched patiently as she tried on all the hats and finally decided on a beret …," wrote Geli's girlfriend, Henriette Hoffmann, who was five years younger and would later marry Baldur von Schirach.[38]

In the summer of 1928, Hitler took Geli, her mother, and Joseph Goebbels on vacation to Heligoland.[39] There was never any mention of Emil Maurice. Privately, however, the Raubal-Maurice affair was not over yet. The rumors were flying within the party and Goebbels noted in his diary following a confidential conversation with fellow member and subsequent regional leader Karl Kaufmann: "He tells me crazy things about the boss [Hitler]. He and his niece Geli and Maurice. The tragedy of women. Are we then to despair? Why must we suffer so from 'woman?' I firmly believe in Hitler. I understand everything. Truth and untruth."[40]

Maurice, calm but determined, was no match for Hitler's intrigues and finally resigned himself. But he did not accept his dismissal lying down. He brought a suit against his employer, the NSDAP, and was awarded compensation from the labor court.[41] Later, the former clockmaker set himself up in business selling electrical equipment.

After that, the rumours about Geli Raubal and Emil Maurice stopped. Uncle Adolf had won.

Some in Hitler's inner circle formed their own opinions as to why Adolf Hitler thwarted the marriage of his step-niece to a young party comrade and valued close friend. "He wanted to prevent her from falling into the hands of someone unworthy," said Heinrich Hoffmann.[42] "It was something like a father's love for his daughter," commented Anni Winter, Hitler's housekeeper. Emil Maurice, who probably knew best, declared after many long years of silence: "He loved her, but it was a strange, unconfessed love!"[43]

In 1929, after breaking off her studies in medical school, Geli decided to take voice training to become a stage actress. At that, Uncle Adolf engaged the bandmaster Adolf Vogel, and Hans Streck to give her pri-

vate singing lessons. Apart from that, Geli indulged in idleness. "...
hairdresser, clothes, dancing and theater can divert her from any serious activity. She only likes to read newspapers and novels. And yet Geli
can read the serialized novels in twelve magazines and newspapers,
one or two instalments a day, and she always knows which goes with
which, and she even notices if an installment is missing," Hitler said of
his niece's lifestyle.[44]

By 1928, Hitler was living in more comfortable surroundings. Mein
Kampf had become a bestseller and was bringing in royalties. Between
1925 and 1929, Hitler's annual income ranged between eleven thousand and fifteen thousand, nine hundred Reich marks, and party
members were bending over backwards to fulfil their Fuehrer's every
wish. Hitler had a car and driver, a private secretary and a bodyguard.
At the end of 1928, Hitler left his small furnished room on
Thierschstrasse and moved, with the financial support of an admirer,
wealthy publisher Hugo Bruckmann, into a large apartment more befitting his station. It was on the third floor of the imposing building at #16
Prinzregentenplatz and consisted of two separate suites with a total of
nine rooms.[45] His staff included the Winters, a housekeeping couple,
and Anna Kirmaier, a cleaning woman. His former landlady from
Thierschstrasse, Mrs. Reichert, and her mother moved into the new
apartment as subtenants.

On October 5, 1929, Geli left her room at the Klein guest house at #43
Königinstrasse and moved in with her uncle, who registered her as the
subtenant of his subtenant. The best corner room of Hitler's apartment
was decorated and furnished according to her wishes. Geli selected
rustic antique furniture from Salzburg—painted armoires, chests and
dressers—and chose light-green wallpaper to compliment the furniture. On the wall hung a watercolor, a gift from her uncle, which Hitler
had painted in Belgium during World War I.[46]

On November 22, Goebbels arrived in Munich. "Geli [in] Munich. With
the boss until two in the morning. He now has a spacious apartment.
Geli, Else Müller and Hoffmann are here. We talk and laugh. Lunch with
him and Geli at noon," Goebbels wrote in his diary.[47]

In 1928, Hitler rented a country house called "Wachenfeld" on the
Bavarian Obersalzberg, where he had vacationed since 1923. His benefactors, Mr. and Mrs. Bechstein, paid the rent "I phoned my sister

[Angela Raubal] in Vienna immediately: 'I have rented a house; do you want to manage my household?'"[48] At the time, Germany and Austria were feeling the effects of the Great Depression and the unemployment rate was rising steadily. In this climate of economic uncertainty, the offer from her successful half-brother was most opportune, and Angela Raubal gladly accepted. Raubal kept an apartment on Schönburgstrasse in Vienna for occasional visits and moved to Bavaria. She was registered as the official tenant of the Wachenfeld house, and she worked as cook and housekeeper on the Obersalzberg until 1935, even though she hated the climate and was homesick for Vienna. Albert Speer described Hitler's estate as follows: "... a small, comfortable wooden house with a peaked roof and modest rooms [including] a dining room, a small living room, three bedrooms. The rustic furniture gave the apartment a comfortable lower middle-class character... a gilded cage with a canary, a cactus... heightened this impression. There were swastikas on all the knick-knacks ..."[49]

Geli spent many weekends at Hitler's refuge and, as photos show, also celebrated Christmas (in 1928 with Goebbels), and birthdays there. On Geli's twenty-first birthday, one of the jackdaws indigenous to the Bavarian mountains sat on the table right next to the cake lit with candles. Geli, who loved animals, had found the injured bird, nurtured it back to health and trained it.

Geli had—in Munich at least—no opportunity to meet men. But she traveled quite often to Vienna to see her girlfriends and escape her uncle's watchful eye.

Hitler pampered his niece, but kept her away from other people her age. She was only allowed to attend a ball at the Deutsches Theater under the supervision of two older party members (Max Amann and Heinrich Hoffmann). "She is my most valuable possession," Hitler told Hoffmann, when he voiced gentle criticism.[50]

The unusual relationship between uncle and niece did not go unnoticed. "'Geli Raubal,' according to his old comrades, 'has always been his love,'" said Albert Speer, repeating rumors that were circulating about them.[51] Uncle and niece would attend every single opera performance in Munich together. "The boss is here accompanied by his beautiful niece, with whom one could almost fall in love. With him, seeing Rheingold," gushed Goebbels, who also attended the Passion plays in Oberammergau with

Geli celebrating her 21st birthday at "Uncle Adolf's" house at Obersalzberg

Geli and Hitler in July of 1930. "Off to Murnau. Lodging in Seehausen. Boss, Geli, Mrs. Raubal and I. First, a lot of people, then completely to ourselves. Walk during the quiet evening. Boss talks about the war. Early to bed. Up in the morning at six. Spent a beautiful morning going up the mountain roads to Oberammergau. The Passion plays begin at eight ... I am most pleasantly [surprised]. A natural stage. Colors, [the] magnificent voices of the people. Christ and Mary Magdalene great. St. John full of charm. Sometimes a bit kitschy ... swarming with party comrades. Thunderstorm in Starnberg and return home," Goebbels reported in his diary on July 21.[52] On January 14, 1931, Goebbels went to Munich, where he gave a speech at the Bürgerbräu [a brew pub]. "The evening with Hitler and Geli. Talked and laughed a lot." The next day, the pair invited him to lunch. "Lunch with Hitler. Geli, Hess and wife. It is very cozy. The boss as paterfamilias ...," noted Goebbels.[53]

The year 1931 was a turbulent one for the NSDAP, whose political agitation had reached a fever pitch. Of the four thousand political rallies held in Hesse-Nassau, for example, two thousand were organized by the National Socialists alone. Hitler rushed from one commitment to the next.

On Friday, September 18, 1931, shortly before three in the afternoon, he set off on a series of party rallies in Northern Germany with photographer Heinrich Hoffmann and his driver Julius Schreck.[54] That day, they drove to Nuremberg and spent the night at the Deutscher Hof. On September 19, Hitler and his entourage were leaving the city heading for Bayreuth, when a taxi carrying a hotel employee caught up with them. Hitler should call Munich urgently. It was very important. On the phone Hitler learned that his niece had had an accident. On the way back to Munich, Hitler ordered his chauffeur to drive at top speed.[55] In Ebenhausen in the district of Ingolstadt, they were going fifty-five and a half kilometers an hour through the town, twice the speed limit, and were stopped by the police, who issued a speeding ticket.[56]

When Hitler arrived at Prinzregentenplatz that afternoon, his niece was dead.

Police captains Sauer and Forster were entrusted with the investigation. The police doctor, Müller, had gone to Hitler's apartment after Georg Winter telephoned the police at ten-fifteen on the morning of September 19. At the apartment were Georg Winter, Anna Winter, Marie Reichert, Anna Kirmair and Franz Xaver Schwarz, the treasurer of the NSDAP.

They made the following statements:
1) Georg Winter: "I am employed in Hitler's household as housekeeper. This morning, at nine-thirty, my wife told me that something must have happened to Raubal, because the door to her room was locked and Hitler's pistol that was kept in the side room in an unlocked cabinet was no longer there. I knocked on her door repeatedly, but got no answer. I became suspicions and, at ten o'clock, I took a screwdriver and opened the closed two-winged door by force. It was locked from the inside, and the key was still in the keyhole. When I opened the door, my wife, Mrs. Reichert and Anna Kirmair were present. After I had opened the door, I entered the room and found Raubal there, lying dead on the floor. She had shot herself. I can give no reason why she shot herself."

2) Mrs. Maria Reichert: "On September 18, 1931, at around three in the afternoon, I heard Raubal's door being locked… A short while later, I heard a small noise coming from Raubal's room, as if something had been knocked over. I paid no particular attention to it. At around ten in the evening, I wanted to prepare Raubal's bed, but found the door to her room still locked. Upon knocking, I received no answer, and I

thought Raubal had gone out ... for what reason she took her life, I cannot state."

3) Anna Winter: At around three in the afternoon, on September 18, 1931, I saw Miss Raubal go into Hitler's room greatly upset, and then hurry back to her own room. I thought it strange. Now I think that she fetched the gun from Hitler's room ... why Raubal took her own life, I do not know."

4) Anna Kirmair: "... Why Raubal took her own life, I do not know."

The unanimity, similarity and brevity of the statements of the witnesses—who in later years became very talkative—are striking. They suggest that party comrade Schwarz had instructed the witnesses beforehand. The household staff was aware of the goings-on in Hitler's household and formed their own opinions, but out of loyalty to Hitler, they remained silent. Mrs. Reichert claims she did not even hear the shot.[57]

The police report further stated that "The body lay in the room, which had only one entrance and a window looking down on Prinzregentenplatz, face down on the floor, in front of the sofa, upon which we found a 6.35-mm Walther pistol. Police doctor Müller determined that death had been caused by a punctured lung, and based on the stage of rigor mortis, had occurred a number of hours before [seventeen or eighteen]. It was a close shot, placed directly against the skin in the dress opening and penetrating the body above the heart, which was not damaged. The bullet had not left the body, but was to be felt under the skin on the left side of the back, somewhere above the hip level."

According to Dr. Müller, Geli took her own life at around five o'clock in the afternoon on September 18. Since the bullet missed her heart, Geli's death must have been very painful. Lying on her face, helpless, she had slowly suffocated. The police found no farewell note in the room. According to the police report, there was only a letter that she had started to write to a girlfriend in Vienna, "in which nothing at all about being tired of living was mentioned."

On September 19, at around three in the afternoon, Hitler sent a messenger to the duty room of police headquarters, informing them that he would be available for an interview in his apartment. He told Captain

Sauer, who arrived at half past three, that "his niece had been enrolled in medical school, but then had lost interest and began to study singing. She had been about to perform somewhere soon, but felt she was not quite ready and wanted to take additional lessons with a professor in Vienna. He had agreed to it, provided that her mother, who was living in Berchtesgaden, joined her in Vienna and when she did not want to do that, he had jettisoned the Vienna plan. She must have been angry at that, but did not appear particularly upset when he left on his trip Friday afternoon, and had quite calmly said goodbye to him. She once said, after participating in a séance that involved the levitation of a table, that she would probably not die a natural death ...".[58]

According to the findings of the police doctor, it was clearly a case of suicide.[59] The body was placed in a wooden coffin and sent to the Ostfriedhof, the Eastern Cemetery. The legal autopsy was not applied for and did not take place. [60] On Monday, September 21, 1931, the office of the public prosecutor of Munich released the body for burial.[61]

On September 21, 1931, the newspaper *Münchner Neueste Nachrichten* printed the following in its local news section: "Suicides—The police report advises: A 23-year-old female private student committed suicide in an apartment in Bogenhausen—the unfortunate young woman—Angela Raubal—was the daughter of Adolf Hitler's stepsister ... there is no information as to her motive. One interpretation is that Miss Raubal met a singer in Vienna, but her uncle prohibited her from returning there. Other sources claim that the unhappy young woman killed herself because she was scheduled to appear soon in public as a singer, but did not yet feel ready."

The *Münchner Post*, a Social Democratic newspaper and opponent of the National Socialists, knew more on September 23. Under the headline, "Mysterious Affair: Suicide of Hitler's Niece," it said, "... On Friday, September 18, Mr. Hitler and his niece had another very heated argument. What was the reason? The vivacious 23-year-old music student Geli wanted to go to Vienna. She wanted to get engaged. Hitler was strongly against it. The two had repeated arguments over that. After a violent scene, Hitler left his apartment ... On Saturday, it was reported that Miss Geli had been found shot in the apartment. She had Hitler's pistol in her hand ... The deceased's nose was broken ... and the body also showed other injuries ... gentlemen from the Brown House [headquarters of the NSDAP, Barlow Palace] were deliberating [after the body had been found] as to what should be published about the motive for the deed. They agreed that Geli's death should be attributed to her frustrated artistic aspirations."

Based on the report in the *Münchner Post*, the public prosecutor prevailed upon Dr. Müller to be more precise in his findings. "On the face, especially on the nose, no injuries linked with pronounced dark-livid death spots were found, nor were any signs of bleeding ascertainable. Raubal died face down and she remained lying in that position for seventeen to eighteen hours. The fact that the tip of her nose was slightly flattened is simply a result of her being face down on the ground for hours. The intense discoloration of the death spots on the face is likely due to the fact that death was caused by suffocation, as a result of a punctured lung."[62]

The two municipal morticians also made recorded statements. Maria Fischbauer said: "At two in the afternoon, on September 19, 1931, I washed and clothed the body in the apartment ... except for the bullet wound opening, I did not notice any wound. I also did not notice that the nasal bone was ... broken." Rosina Zweckl stated: "Between eleven and twelve, on Sunday, September 20, 1931, at the Eastern Cemetery, I transferred the body of Angela Raubal ... to a zinc coffin. While doing so, I took a close look at the body because I had heard that the deceased was the niece of Hitler. She was very blue in the face ... nothing struck me as being suspicious about the nose."[63]

Hitler, however, demanded a rectification according to Section Eleven of the Press Act, which was promptly published by the *Münchner Post*. It stated:
1. It is incorrect to say that I "constantly quarreled" with my niece Angelika Raubal or had a heated argument on Friday, September 18, 1931 or earlier. The truth is that I had no kind of quarrel or dispute with my niece.

2. It is incorrect to say that I was "against" my niece's traveling to Vienna. The truth is that I was never opposed to my niece's planned trip to Vienna.

3. It is untrue that my niece was planning to get engaged in Vienna or that I had any objection to the engagement of my niece. It is true that my niece, agonizing over not being talented enough for a public per-

formance, wanted to go to Vienna to have a leading speech therapist test her voice more thoroughly.

4. It is untrue to say that I left my apartment on September 18, 1931, "following a heated argument." There had been no scene and no disturbance when I left my apartment that day. Munich, September 21, 1931."[64]

Although the police ruled out any third-party responsibility, various versions of the story were often repeated at social gatherings and in the history books: Hitler as an enraged murderer; SS members as murderers; Himmler cleaning up a messy situation for the party; Geli pregnant, alternatively by Hitler, a Jewish music teacher or an artist from Linz. Geli was depicted as desperate for a number of reasons—version one: the victim of Hitler's perversions; version two: crazed with jealousy over Eva Braun; version three: Geli physically abused with a broken nose and serious injuries.[65]

All these rumors have one thing in common: they lack concrete evidence. According to the statements of contemporary witnesses, evidence had indeed existed, but had been destroyed.

The allegations appear unlikey. Moreover, the final police report exists. As the intact forensic files show, no autopsy was done on Angela Raubal. The report could therefore not have been secretly removed.[66] Even the speeding ticket that Hitler got while rushing back to the scene was unearthed. It proves that he was out of Munich on September 19, 1931.[67] Research in the suicide log of the city of Munich has, uncovered a file number[68] proving there really was an investigation by the Munich public prosecutor's office which was very quickly quashed on September 19, 1931. There are no existing documents. The hasty breaking off of the investigation must have been a preventive measure by the Bavarian minister of justice, Franz Gürtner, who was instrumental in furthering Hitler's career.[69] It was Gürtner who had arranged to have Hitler's trial after the putsch heard in Munich, and not in Leipzig, where the revolutionaries would have faced capital punishment. And in 1927 he had a judicial inquiry on Hitler stayed.[70]
s

Gürtner's intervention and the unusually quick release of the body aroused suspicions in 1931—justly or unjustly—of a coverup. According to party comrades, Hitler displayed "deep shock" after Geli's sui-

cide. The report notes of Captain Sauer paint a different picture: "He said that her death had deeply shaken him; she had been the only close relative he had and now this had to happen to *him*." According to the report, Hitler showed no compassion for the dead girl immediately after the tragedy, but thought only of himself and the possible consequences for his career. The exploitation of the suicide of his niece for propaganda purposes came later.

Hitler did not withdraw from public life "for weeks" after Geli's death, either, but spent the three days between September 19 and 23 at a friend's house, because he did not want to stay overnight at the scene of the tragedy.

At the request of Mrs. Raubal, Geli's body was shipped to Vienna. The funeral took place on the afternoon of September 23, 1931, at the Vienna Central Cemetery. Geli was buried in an Emergency Crypt, Left Arcade No. 9, opposite the Karl Lueger Memorial Church.[71] An "emergency crypt" is a burial place in Vienna that may be rented for temporary burial should a permanent grave not yet be available.

Hitler did not attend Geli's funeral because, according to Geli's brother Leo, he was "physically and emotionally not in a condition to do so."[72] In fact, he did not want to cancel a party rally. On the day of the funeral he went to Hamburg and the next day felt physically and emotionally well enough to deliver an inflammatory speech before ten thousand supporters.

The rumor that Hitler suddenly became a vegetarian out of a sense of piety is also exaggerated. He was not eating meat as early as 1924, and the reasons for that were very practical. "As long as I ate meat, I would sweat profusely at rallies. I would drink four pints of beer and lose nine pounds. When I became a vegetarian, I just needed a sip of water every now and then."[73]

Geli's room remained unchanged and unused. It is not true that Hitler turned it into a shrine to his niece. In fact, at the beginning of 1932, Hitler made Geli's room available to Henriette von Schirach, who wanted to change after her wedding dinner in Hitler's apartment. The widespread tale that the Fuehrer retreated to the dead girl's room every year at Christmas in order to honor Geli and his mother, is based solely on the memoirs of Hitler's servant Krause, who often stretched the truth.[74]

Hitler, who always had excellent relationships with his staff, once said of him, "… Krause had a pathological inclination to tell tales. He was not suited to be a servant. He lied unnecessarily …"[75]

In his will, dated May 2, 1938, Hitler made an express reference to the furniture in Geli's room: "The furniture in the room in my apartment in Munich, in which my niece Geli Raubal used to live, is to be given to my sister Angela."

Following Geli's tragic death in 1931, Hitler sent cash to her brother Leo as a Christmas present and attached a note: "Dear Leo! For this year's sad Christmas celebration, the most cordial compliments of the season to you and Aunt Marie … Your Uncle Adolf."[76]

On the first anniversary of Geli's death, Hitler went to visit her grave. "The Fuehrer has gone to Vienna for a private visit. Nobody knows about it, so as to avoid any crowds of people," Goebbels wrote in his diary on Sunday, September 19, 1932, on the way to Vienna.

Hitler's aide-de-camp, Julius Schaub, had gone ahead with Angela Raubal. Goebbels met them in Vienna. "Schaub is here, under the name of Huber. He is arranging accommodation for the boss, who wants to visit Geli's grave on Monday… Mrs. Raubal … bless her heart, came to see me at the hotel and had a good cry. I consoled her, as best I could. Poor, dear Geli. It has been a year now … Hitler is in Vienna …," Goebbels noted.

The sculptor Ferdinand Liebermann was commissioned to make a bust of Geli, which was put in the New Reich Chancellery. The naturalist painter Adolf Ziegler, a favorite of Hitler's, made a painting of the Fuehrer's niece from a photograph. It was hung in a place of honor at the Berghof and was always decorated with flowers.

In November 1933, Hitler was attending the celebration of the tenth anniversary of the Munich Putsch and ran by chance into the "old fighter" and comrade Emil Maurice, who had become a Munich city councillor. They did not speak of Geli, and the two renewed their friendship. Maurice introduced his girlfriend, whom he had met at the Munich Carnival, to Hitler on his birthday on April 20, 1934. The couple arrived at Hitler's apartment with flowers to wish him well. Emil's future wife, Dr. Hedwig Maurice, later recalled that Hitler behaved cordially, congenially and was full of "Austrian charm." When he heard of "Maurizl's" plan to marry the future doctor, Hitler spontaneously assured the couple: "I will take care of the wedding!" The wedding was not held in Hitler's apartment, which was being renovated, but at a first-class restaurant, "Die Vier Jahreszeiten" [Four Seasons] and "all of Munich sent presents."[77]

The whole world heard how Hitler mourned his niece. What Geli had really meant to her uncle can be gleaned from the facts. The Fuehrer and Reich Chancellor did not think it necessary to give his beloved Geli a sanctified burial, to buy a gravesite or to have a headstone erected. The coffin with the mortal remains of Angela Raubal stayed in the municipality of Vienna's emergency crypt for years. At first, payment for the use of the temporary facility was sent each year, but after January of 1938 it was discontinued.[78]

The Raubal family exonerated Hitler of guilt in Geli's death. Leo Raubal, Geli's brother, made statements to this effect,[79] and her mother must have concurred. Nothing about Hitler's relationship with his sister was changed by Geli's suicide—Angela remained close to him. "Sat with Hitler and Mrs. Raubal" is a frequent entry in Goebbels's diary. Angela Raubal was also on hand when her brother's appointement as Reich Chancellor was celebrated by an intimate circle of friends on February 1, 1933. She came to the wedding when the "Reich reporter" and close friend of Hitler's, Heinrich Hoffmann, married for the second time, and was often a visitor at the home of propaganda minister Joseph Goebbels. Quarrels with Hitler occurred only when Angela Raubal behaved like the mistress of Wachenfeld and upset Eva Braun. Hitler subsequently banished his sister from the Obersalzberg and hired a couple to replace her.

"She tells me her tale of woe … It would be good if the Fuehrer took care of her again …," Goebbels wrote in November, 1935.[80] When Angela Raubal married a professor of architecture named Hammitzsch in 1936 and moved to Dresden, she and Hitler were reconciled. From then on, Hitler had his sister represent him at family reunions of his Waldviertel [a region in Lower Austria] relatives. The Fuehrer had no interest in spending time with his country relatives, whom he had visited only once in his youth in 1908. He was not ashamed of his origins— as he often pointed out in *Mein Kampf*—but was afraid of being asked for favors by them. Angela had attended the funeral of Hitler's aunt,

Theresia Schmidt, in August, 1938 and gave a small gift of money from the Fuehrer, who wanted to avoid any personal contact with his cousins.[81] In 1945, the Schmidts, who lived in the zone of the Waldviertel occupied by the Soviets, were arrested (as well as their in-laws) and found guilty by association. The contribution to the funeral costs was seen as evidence of their closeness to the Fuehrer. Only one of Hitler's relatives would survive Russian imprisonment.

The fate of Geli's brother, a Social Democrat, would become a matter of concern for Hitler. Leo, an engineer-lieutenant, was taken prisoner by the Russians after the fall of Stalingrad. Hitler, at the time, considered exchanging him for Stalin's son Jakob, who had been captured by the Germans in 1941. Stalin considered the offer, but then rejected it saying, "War is war."[82]

In the Third Reich, any discussion of the suicide of the Fuehrer's niece was considered taboo. Even the cemetery authorities in Vienna did not raise the subject of Geli Raubal, even though she was still buried in the emergency crypt in violation of the law. Hitler continued to exploit his niece's death for propaganda purposes. He intimated that Geli was the only woman that he had ever loved and that he considered himself married to Germany.

In May 1945, when American soldiers forced their way into Hitler's apartment on Prinzregentenplatz, they found Geli's room the way it had been left in 1931 after her suicide. [83]

On March 11, 1946, Geli was exhumed "according to regulations" from the emergency crypt at the Vienna Central Cemetery and buried in one of a row of common graves.[84] A journalist, "in search of traces of Geli Raubal" found the headstone in 1967, erected in 1946, with the inscription, "Here rests in eternal peace our beloved daughter Geli. She was our sunshine. Born on June 4, 1908–died on September 18, 1931. The Raubal Family."[85]

The debate over Geli's suicide, continued for decades after the war. In 1985, a Viennese funiture restorer, Hans Horvath, was so interested in having the case cleared up that he began looking into the matter. At his own expense, he requested forensic opinions, acquired a substitute grave with a stone cross and a memorial plaque, and applied for Geli Raubal to be exhumed "because the public has a right to have historical events fully accounted for." The project, undertaken with great commitment, was ultimately frustrated by bureaucratic regulations. "This grave [of Angela Raubal] was intended, like all other common graves, to be used for only ten years, and has subsequently been leveled and redeveloped. It is no longer possible to determine the exact location of the gravesite."[86]

EVA BRAUN

The Hidden Love

February 7, 1912 – April 30, 1945

" **T**he Fuehrer has no private life," was the official line disseminated by propaganda minister Goebbels. "He devotes himself to the German people day and night."

Hitler had erected a wall of silence around his long-term partner. Only a small group of people knew of the Fuehrer's affair with the young blonde woman who was assigned to the staff of the Berghof on the Obersalzberg as his private secretary. That was how she was officially registered. Her salary was paid from party coffers.

There were rumors in the Third Reich that "Hitler was living with a woman at the Berghof," but details were not available and the name of the mysterious woman only came to light at the end of the war. The measures taken to keep things secret and the censorship of the press were so efficient, that during the Nazi era only one photograph of Eva Braun was released for publication—by mistake.

It was taken at the Olympic Winter Games in Garmisch-Partenkirchen in 1936. In it, Hitler is sitting in the front row, while his mistress is sitting just behind him with her sister Gretl.

Eva Braun was born on February 7, 1912, at #45 Isabellastrasse in Munich, the daughter of a teacher, Friedrich Braun and his wife Franziska, née Kronberger, a seamstress.[1] The couple already had one girl, four-year-old Ilse, and Friedrich's secret hope for a son was revealed in an error in the birth notice: Eva Anna Paula Braun is privileged to announce his successful arrival upon this earth.[2] Three years later, another girl, Margarete (Gretl) was to follow. The girls were baptized and educated as Catholics and went to their first communion and confirmation, as their Protestant father had promised when he married Franziska, a Catholic. The Brauns led a much better life during the hard postwar years than the average German family. In 1925 they moved into a large, comfortable apartment at #93 Hohenzollernstrasse, had a maid and, with the money from an inheritance, allowed themselves the luxury of a family car, almost unheard of in those days. Eva Braun's parents, with their conservative monarchist-nationalist views, were typical of the lower middle class, from which Hitler had also come. He chose his long-term companion from the familiar milieu to which he had remained closely connected.

The schooling of the three Braun daughters was planned with an eye to future professional work. Eva graduated from the convent elementary school in the country town of Beilngries and the lyceum located on Tengstrasse in Munich with excellent marks, though her teachers frequently complained about the "wild, unruly and lazy child." Her circle of friends viewed her differently. They admired the adventurous Eva, always up to tricks. Drawing and music classes, which her father considered essential, bored Eva. She preferred sports. In this, she resembled her mother, who in 1905 had been a champion skier. As a dedicated member of the Schwabinger gym club, Eva pursued track and field and body building for many years. Her remarkable agility on

The only official photo (released by mistake) that shows Hitler and Eva Braun together at the Olympic Winter Games in Garmisch-Partenkirchen, February 1936 (Braun with her sister Gretl in the 2nd row).

the horizontal bar can be seen in an amateur film shot on the Obersalzberg in 1940.[3]

She enjoyed reading the novels of Karl May, an interest she shared with Hitler, who saw "Winnetou as [the perfect] model of a company commander."[4] Later, at the Berghof, Eva read the works of Oscar Wilde which had been banned in the Third Reich. But above all, she enjoyed movie magazines and sentimental romance novels about women who sacrificed themselves for their husbands—a foreshadowing of her own fate. Eva was especially fond of listening to American musicals and jazz.

"A visit to a dance bar appealed to her more than going to the theater," her boss of many years, Heinrich Hoffmann, reported.[5] Like other young girls, she worshipped movie stars, collected pictures of John Gilbert, Greta Garbo's co-star, and dreamed of a career as a dancer or movie actress.

Her parents, however, enrolled Eva in the Institute of English Ladies in Simbach on the Bavarian-Austrian border to complete her education. Eva remained there until July, 1929. She learned French, typing, book-keeping and home economics. Following that, she returned to the family home and started looking for a job in Munich.

Freidrich Braun happened to hear that a photo shop at 50 Schellingstrasse was hiring people since receiving large orders from the NSDAP. Eva applied to the studio of Heinrich Hoffmann[6] in September, 1929, and was accepted as an apprentice, a salesclerk and girl Friday. She worked there for many years.

She enjoyed the life and bustling activity in the Hoffman studio, which reminded her, in a romantic way, of the world of the cinema. No longer a teenager, she still dreamed of one day becoming a movie star, and this dream stayed with her throughout her life. Later, on the Obersalz-berg, she daydreamed about playing a leading role in a big Hollywood production—after the final victory of National Socialism—and how the whole world would discover her relationship with Hitler.[7] But in 1929 these dreams were well in the future. In the meantime, Eva learned about photography and how to develop film and it soon became her hobby. Eva Braun's first job set the course for her life. In October 1929, she met Adolf Hitler.

"I had stayed at the shop after closing-time to file some papers, and was just climbing a ladder, because the files were up on the cabinet, when the boss came in with a gentleman of a certain age with a funny mustache, in a light-colored English coat, [holding] a big felt hat in his hand. The two of them sat down in the far corner of the room oppo-site me. I stole a glance at them without turning around and saw that the man was looking at my legs. I had just shortened my skirt that day and did not feel entirely comfortable, because I was not sure if I had managed to get the hemline right ... I climbed down and Hoffmann introduced us: 'Mr. Wolf—our good little Miss Braun [will] go and get us some beer and [sausage] from the pub on the corner.'"[8]

After Eva's return, "Mr. Wolf" (Hitler's pseudonym) complimented her, and the two chatted about music and the most recent performance at the Munich City Theater. Eva, having recently left a sheltered Catholic school, did not realize that "the old Mr. Wolf with the slouch-hat and the whip" was the forty-year-old chairman of the NSDAP, even though

Eva Braun (on the right) with her parents and her sisters Ilse and Gretl.

selling postcards with portraits of Hitler was part of her job.

Only her sisters had been privy to Eva's secret—and for a long time, platonic—relationship with Hitler. Whenever he came by Hoffmann's, he brought Eva flowers or a box of candy, gallantly kissed her hand and made charming compliments. For Christmas 1929 he gave her a signed photo. The first photo of the two, taken at that time, shows a smiling Hitler gallantly raising his hat to a radiant Eva Braun. She stuck the photo in her album and wrote one of Hitler's comments underneath: "… I know her quite well, in fact."

At Foto Hoffmann everything revolved around Hitler and the NSDAP. All the party's activities were indefatigably documented, books of photos of the Reich party conventions were published, and pamphlets like *Germany's Awakening—in Word and Image* were produced. The boss was Hitler's "personal photographer" and at the same time "commercial photographer" of the entire Nazi elite—for both their official and private occasions.

In the back of the building at #50 Schellingstrasse were the offices of the Reich party leadership of the NSDAP, and quite close by, at #41, were the office and printing house of the *Völkischer Beobachter*, the party's main newspaper, with Hitler as editor-in-chief. The party leaders regularly visited the Osteria Bavaria, a pub on the corner of Schellingstrasse and Schraudolphstrasse, where members of the SS frequently handed out flyers.[9] Eva Braun soon knew the entire leadership of the party, and there are no indications that her boss's associates made her feel uncomfortable. She quickly acquainted herself with the people around Hoffmann, and soon her entire circle of friends came from the NSDAP's sphere of influence.

Heinrich Hoffmann, in whose home Hitler had been a guest since the beginning of the thirties, witnessed the affair between Hitler and Eva Braun from beginning to end. As go-between, the photographer handled all major financial transactions concerning Eva. As may clearly be seen from his notes, he did not hold her in particularly high esteem: "… with her blue eyes, she could certainly have been called pretty, even though she looked like a doll. An average beauty like those in common advertising photos …"[10]

Later on, Hoffmann would use photos of the couple from which—following instructions—he had removed Eva Braun. The youth brochure "Hitler in his Mountains" showed the solitary Fuehrer in a rural, idyllic setting "on the Gschwander farmer's land." Eva Braun, who had been sitting beside him, was excised by Hoffmann's scissors.[11]

In early November of 1929, the photo shop moved to larger premises. Eva Braun's new workplace was now on the second floor, above the Café Stefanie on the corner of Theresienstrasse and Amalienstrasse. The *Völkische Beobachter* provided a description of the premises and concluded: "The support staff, too, at Hoffmann's are skilled …"[12] A payroll from the year 1932 shows the young Eva Braun, who worked behind the counter serving customers, among the seventeen employees. Baldur von Schirach, the Reich Youth leader of the NSDAP, saw her in action: "She took care of Hoffmann's Nazi postcards later, too, when she was the Reich Chancellor's mistress. She regularly had to report to Hitler which postcards were most in demand. For him it was a kind of "Gallup poll," with which he tested the popularity of his associates."[13]

Even as a working person, Eva Braun lived with her parents under the strict watch of Friedrich Braun, who protected and controlled his three daughters. He checked phone calls, read their mail and kept a close eye on the people they associated with. At ten o'clock in the evening he would switch off their bedroom light. Little did he imagine what undesireable men his daughter Eva was meeting at her workplace.

Hitler invited Hoffman's young employee to the opera, to the movies, to the Osteria Bavaria, or he would take her on a picnic in the beautiful countryside around Munich. The imperial motorcade of Mercedes cars, with fawning drivers and aides-de-camp who catered to Hitler's every whim, did not fail to impress the young Eva. Her parents knew nothing of these escapades. For them, Eva transformed the exciting pleasure trips into boring overtime.

After only a brief acquaintanceship, Hitler had already checked out Eva's ancestry. He, who in his youth in Vienna had never had a problem with Jews, did not want, as Leader of a radically anti-Semitic party, to associate with "non-Aryans." In 1930, Martin Bormann, later in charge of the party's main office, checked out the background of the Braun family to see if there was any Jewish ancestry.[14]

Eva Braun savored the prominent position of her admirer, who was the subject of radio and newspaper reports. The young woman was flattered to have caught the attention of such a famous man. And soon her bewildered parents noticed that their daughter, who had so far shown no interest in politics, was initiating heated political debates within the family. While Eva found a kindred spirit in her mother, her father and her sister Ilse remained skeptical and disapproved of National Socialist ideas. But none of them had any anti-Semitic sentiment. At that time, one of Eva's friends was a Jewish medical student,[15] and her sister Ilse had worked for a Jewish medical specialist, Dr. Martin Marx, for years. Despite massive smear campaigns against Jewish fellow citizens, she continued working as his receptionist, her employment ending when Marx emigrated to America in the summer of 1938.

Attacks by the SA and SS on Social Democrats, Communists, political foes and Jews were commonplace at the time. Members of the SA prevented the population from entering Jewish shops and harassed people who went to see Jewish doctors or lawyers. Eva Braun witnessed this every day but considered the brutality an aberration and assumed that it took place without Hitler's knowledge. In the company of women, Hitler was always the perfect gentleman.

In 1930, the relationship between Hitler and Eva Braun was still platonic and their meetings always took place during the day. Eva wrote

Hitler little letters and put them in the pockets of his trench coat, which often hung on the coat rack of Hoffmann's photo studio. Her boss observed his employee's deeds. "… neither I nor anyone else noticed particular interest by him [Hitler] … [but] Eva was a different story … she told her girlfriends that Hitler had fallen in love with her and that she would definitely succeed in getting him to marry her…"[16]

At the beginning of 1932, Eva became Hitler's mistress. It happened at his apartment on Prinzregentenplatz and did not go unnoticed by the housekeeper, Mrs. Winter.[17] Eva hinted at the affair to her sister: "If he knew the history of that sofa!" she said with a giggle, when she saw a picture of British prime minister Chamberlain having breakfast in Hitler's apartment.

Hitler, from the very beginning, dictated the ground rules of the affair, stipulating that it be kept secret and that they exercise the utmost discretion. Politics—and many other things—had absolute priority, and the hours he spent with his lover were sporadic and sparingly measured. His idea was to have a limited relationship with no strings attached. When asked by Fritz Wiedemann, his aide-de-camp, about possible marriage plans, Hitler replied, "As for love, I am keeping a girl for myself in Munich."[18]

Hitler was not looking for a partner in Eva Braun, whom he called "Hascherl" (poor creature), nor a political comrade-in-arms. Instead, he said in her presence, "Very intelligent men should take a primitive and [subservient] wife. Imagine, if I had a wife now who wanted to tell me how to do my work! In my spare time, I want my peace and quiet … I could never marry!"[19]

Eva Braun spent a large part of her life waiting for Hitler. In 1932 she still lived with her parents, shared a room with her sisters and went to work at Foto Hoffmann every day to earn her living. The financial advantages from her relationship with Hitler were slight: a little jewelry, an occasional envelope with money for clothes, and her own phone (officially for business). If it rang, Eva took the call in bed under the covers, so as not to be disturbed.

But Hitler rarely called. Germany at the time was in the midst of dramatic upheaval. Hitler was traveling all over Germany and spoke in fifty towns between July 15 and 30, 1932. Within one year there were five elections—in a chaotic atmosphere marked by violence. With the Reichstag election scheduled for November 6, 1932, there was no way for Eva to get hold of Hitler during the last phase of the campaign.

Eva Braun endured it all patiently, preferring to die rather than accept separation from Hitler. Finally, tired of the eternal waiting, she wrote him a farewell letter on November 1, 1932, then shot herself in the neck with her father's loaded army pistol of. The bullet just missed the carotid artery. In spite of losing a lot of blood, she was able to call a doctor herself, carefully choosing Dr. Plate, Heinrich Hoffmann's brother-in-law. This way Eva could be sure that Hitler would be informed quickly. The doctor had her admitted to a hospital and the bullet was removed.

Eva Braun's gamble paid off. Hitler came to see her immediately after receiving her letter and demanded to know whether it had been a serious attempt at suicide. "She aimed for her heart," the doctor told him, "but we were able to save her in time."[20]

Eva told her worried parents that it was an accident that had happened while she was carelessly handling the gun. Hitler was moved by Eva's apparent devotion and gave up any intention of leaving her. On January 1, 1933, he invited her to a performance of Richard Wagner's opera *Die Meistersinger*, conducted by Hans Knappertsbusch at the National Theater in Munich. To keep up appearances, they were accompanied by Heinrich Hoffmann and Sofie Spork, to whom Hoffmann had become engaged after the death of his first wife,[21] Rudolf Hess and his wife Ilse, as well as Hitler's aides-de-camp Schaub and Brückner. After the performance, they went for coffee at the apartment of Ernst (Putzi) Hanfstaengl, chief foreign press officer of the NSDAP.[22] It was Eva Braun's first visit to Hanfstaengl's splendid apartment. It was a jovial gathering, and they all had a good time because Hitler, whose mood always set the tone, was in a very high spirits after the opera. "Putzi" played Wagner tunes.

In his memoirs, Hanfstaengl wrote of Eva Braun: "That was not the first time I had seen her. She was a pretty, blonde girl, well-developed, with blue eyes, and a modest, almost timid charm. I had noticed her, several months before, at Hoffmann's photo shop ..."[23]

Three days after the cozy evening at Hanfstaengl's, on January 4, the historic meeting of Hitler and Franz von Papen took place at the house of the Cologne banker von Schroeder, at which they planned the overthrow of the acting Reich Chancellor.

Hitler's appointment as Reich Chancellor on January 30, 1933, greatly concerned Eva Braun, because her lover would now spend a lot of time in Berlin, the home turf of her hated rival for his attention, Magda Goebbels. Eva would not be invited to Berlin until 1935. But she considered 1934 a successful year because Hitler spent a lot of time with her. Significant events such as his appointment as "Fuehrer and Reich Chancellor" and the "Röhm Putsch" did not matter to her. She continued working as a sales clerk and, as the powerful Reich Chancellor's mistress, made fairly modest demands. For example, she urged Hitler, who did not like small dogs, "to give her a puppy."

The Hoffmann studio had expanded into a conglomerate and Eva's boss bought himself a luxurious villa and filled it with art treasures. Goebbels referred to it as "a small museum."[24] Eva was not envious of her boss's wealth, even though she frequently was in debt. "I save [and] accumulate. I am getting on everyone's nerves because I am always trying to sell things. From the suit or the camera to the theater ticket … well, things will get better again, the debts are not that great …"[25]

For Eva, the only thing that counted was that her boss had a direct line to Hitler. For that reason she attached herself to the Hoffmann family, even to the extent of imposing on them. Likewise, she pestered Mrs. Annie Winter, Hitler's housekeeper at his Prinzregentenplatz apartment, for information about Hitler, who always kept his travel plans secret for security reasons. The Hoffmanns were caught between a rock and a hard place. On the one hand, Eva was the mistress of their hero, to whom they owed everything. On the other hand, however, she was their employee. So they vacillated between patronizing affection toward Eva—"Mrs. Hoffmann gave me a theater ticket today …"—and moralizing contempt. They took every opportunity to point out to her the precarious insecurity of her situation. While Heinrich Hoffmann and Goebbels arranged secret dates for Hitler,[26] Sofie, Hoffman's second wife, dropped hints to Eva. "As Mrs. Hoffmann sweetly, and just as tactlessly, told me, he now has a replacement for me …"[27]

But Eva persisted. "I was sitting at Hoffmann's on tenterhooks, and thought every minute, he should be coming now," Eva noted on March

4, 1935, and on April 1: "Why doesn't he go to Hoffmann's for dinner, then I would at least get a few minutes with him?"

Her diary entries for May 28, 1935, are worth noting. Eva, who never became a party member, judged some of the most dramatic events in world history in light of whether or not they left her lover enough free time for her. No politically indocrinated National Socialist woman would have made such naïve claims as, "Goodness, his head was full of political problems all the time, but isn't there a relaxation of tension now? And how were things in the past year? Röhm and Italy caused him a lot of headaches, [but] in spite of all that, he found time for me." Eva is referring to the dramatic events of the Röhm Putsch of June 30, 1934, when Hitler had the chief of staff of the SA, Ernst Röhm, "who aggravated him a lot," murdered.

At the beginning of 1935, Eva tried to talk Hitler into improving her situation. "... he has so little understanding in the presence of strangers [at the shop] that he still has me bow and scrape ..." In February, 1935, she thought she had succeeded in her wishes. On February 18, she wrote, "... but the most beautiful thing was that he is considering taking me out of the shop ... but I had better not celebrate just yet, to give me a little house. I simply must not think about it, it would be so wonderful. I would not have to open the door for our 'honorable customers' anymore and act the shop girl. Dear God, let it be true and become a reality in the foreseeable future ..."

But time passed and nothing happened. In March, as part of a huge crowd, she managed to catch a glimpse of Hitler. "I waited in front of the Carlton for three hours and had to watch as he bought flowers for Ondra [Anny Ondra, wife of the world boxing champion Max Schmeling] and invited her to dinner ..." On May 10, 1935, Eva was sounding desperate. "... after all, he should know me well enough [to realize] that I would never put anything in his way if he were suddenly to discover [he loved] someone else. Whatever becomes of me, [should not concern] him..."

On May 28, Eva Braun decided for the second time to take her own life. She wrote a "final" letter to Hitler. When no answer came, she bought a box of sleeping pills (Vanodorm). Apparently, no one had apprised her of Hitler's heavy schedule. On May 19, he inaugurated the motorway in Frankfurt am Main and traveled to Berlin; he then took part in the "Day

of German Seafaring" festivities in Hamburg on May 25 and 26 and subsequently visited the "Regional Convention" in Mecklenburg which was
followed by "Reich Executive Conferences" in Munich.

"Dear God, help me to be able to speak to him today, tomorrow [will
be] too late. I have decided on thirty-five pills this time, it is to be really an 'absolutely certain affair.' If he would at least have someone call
me," reads her last diary entry for May 28.

Late that evening, Ilse Braun came by to return a dress she had borrowed for a dance competition. She found her sister deeply uncon-
scious, administered first aid and called a doctor. As it turned out, Eva
had taken twenty sleeping pills. Beside her lay the open diary. Ilse
removed the pages covering the period from February 6 to May 28,
1935, and kept them. She later returned the twenty-two pages to Eva,
who took them with her to the Obersalzberg.

These twenty-two pages are, despite their brevity, very revealing of Eva
Braun's psyche. Without punctuation, awkward in expression, and with
the vocabulary of a teenager, the 23-year-old Eva writes about her
minor everyday worries, but also about her great love for Hitler. They
are the notes of a simple, naïve girl, who proudly claims, "I am the
beloved of the greatest man in Germany and the earth." She laments,
"He only needs me for certain purposes." This comment refutes the
frequent rumours that Hitler was totally incapable of sexual relations.
Adolf Hitler and Eva Braun were quite obviously lovers. Dr. Morell, the
Fuehrer's personal doctor, stated for the record during questioning
before a U.S. tribunal after the war, that Eva Braun had often asked
him to prescribe stimulants to increase Hitler's sexual desire because
his libido had diminished in the last years of his life.[28]

After her second attempt at suicide, her parents' hurtful disapproval
devastated Eva and made it impossible for her to remain at home. It
was not Hitler's policies that bothered her father, but the fact that there
was no prospect of legitimizing the relationship. He tormented his
daughter with disparaging remarks about her "life as a courtesan." Eva
and her sister Gretl finally moved into a place of their own on
Widenmayerstrasse, close to Hitler's apartment. It was a comfortable,
three-room apartment with contemporary furniture and central heating. Their mother contributed linens and dishes. Hitler asked his friend
Hoffmann to pay the rent and the wages of the Hungarian maid.

Eva's father, Friedrich Braun, could not accept the humiliation he believed his daughter had brought upon the family. When his reproaches fell on deaf ears and his wife sided with Eva, he decided on a direct appeal to Hitler. He gave a letter to Hoffmann to be passed on. Hoffman gave it to Eva, who destroyed it. A draft of the father's plea survives, and reveals how he timidly hints at the possibility of marriage.

"Dear Reich Chancellor. It is quite unpleasant for me to have to bother you with a private matter, that is, with my grief as father of a family. You, the Fuehrer of the German nation, certainly have quite different worries, certainly greater ones … My family has now been torn apart because my two daughters, Eva and Gretl, have moved into an apartment provided by you, and I, as head of the family, [have] been confronted with a fait accompli. Of course, I frequently protested when Eva came home substantially later than store closing time, because I believe that a young person, who has put in eight hours of intensive professional work, then requires relaxation in the family circle in order to stay healthy. In addition, I take the perhaps old-fashioned moral point of view: the children are only taken from the custody of their parents and from the common home upon marriage. This is my definition of honor. Quite apart from the fact that I miss my children very much. I would be exceedingly obliged to you, dear Reich Chancellor, for your understanding in this matter, and add to it the request not to support my daughter Eva's desire for independence—she is indeed an adult now—but to prevail upon her to return to the family."[29]

In the fall of 1935, Hitler permitted his mistress to take part in the seventh Reich party congress of the NSDAP in Nuremberg which established the laws for "the protection of German blood and German honor" (Nuremberg laws). The ban on marrying Jews was instituted and the new law stipulated "Aryan" descent as a prerequisite for employment in the public service. Eva was among the Fuehrer's guests and sat on the VIP stand.

Ernst Hanfstaengl gave an account of the events and described Eva Braun's "disgraceful role [as equivalent to a] white harem slave." "At least Hitler rewarded her for her constant presence with his protection. She came unobtrusively to the party congress in 1935, but wore an expensive fur. Magda Goebbels, however, who thought herself the only woman to whom Hitler should devote his attention, was unwise enough to make contemptuous remarks about Eva. Hitler was enraged …"[30]

Eva stopped working in 1935, and her great wish for a house of her own was fulfilled. Acting on Hitler's behalf, Hoffmann found a suitable property. It was not a luxurious house, and no love nest, but a simple, single-family home built in 1925—one of a complex of six identical houses—at #12 Wasserburger Strasse (now #12 Delpstrasse) in Bogenhausen. This district of Munich was at that time almost at the city limits, but had the advantage of being within walking distance of Hitler's apartment on the Prinzregentenplatz. The purchase price was thirty thousand Reich marks, and the bill of sale was in the name of the faithful Hoffmann. It was not until 1938 that ownership was officially transferred to "secretary" Eva Braun. A large walled-in garden, about 800 square meters in size, was part of the—still existing—building.

The art deco style house, like many built after World War I, had very small rooms. On the ground floor there was a tiny vestibule with built-in closets, an equally small kitchen and a combined living and dining room. The upper floor, reached via a narrow staircase, had two bedrooms and a bathroom. A small attic served as a guest room and secret "smoking room," since no one was allowed to smoke in Hitler's presence. The furniture was of excellent quality—Hitler took care of that. The dining room set, made of exotic woods and capable of seating twelve people, was designed by Paul Ludwig Troost, the architect of the "Brown House."[31]

The rooms gradually filled with gifts from Hitler. There was an Aubusson Gobelin tapestry, valuable carpets, including an old Samarkand rug, beautiful furniture and lots of silverware—frames, cutlery, dishes—most engraved with Hitler's monogram. A number of rather mediocre paintings adorned the walls, many painted by Hitler. Among them were architectural sketches and drawings as well as watercolors of cityscapes that he had copied from postcards. One of these, *Asamkircherl* (Little Asam Church), was Eva's favorite picture.

In addition to Hitler's own artwork, oil paintings of his portrait adorned the walls dominated by the life-sized portrait in uniform by Heinrich Knirr. Painted in 1933–34, it shows Hitler in martial pose on a mountain peak, coat flapping in the wind, fixed gaze focused on the distance.[32] It was copied in inexpensive prints that proved to be best-sellers, and were put on the market by the millions. Everyone was expected to own a picture of the Fuehrer. But it was necessary to be careful in dealing with this "icon of the people." Any misuse was severly punished "for undermining the people's trust in their political leadership."[33] The first trials took place in 1936. Individuals who destroyed pictures of the Fuehrer, refused to display them, or made disparaging comments when looking at them were sentenced to a few years in jail.[34] During the war, when criticism of the regime was growing, many were sent to concentration camps.

For Eva Braun, her "dear little house" was a status symbol. It raised her self-confidence and gave her great joy. She shared it with her younger sister Gretl. Two Scotch terriers, Stasi and Negus, gifts from Hitler, kept them company, but their barking annoyed the neighbors, so it became necessary to build a wall around the property. Another gift from Hitler was a television set—one of the first in Germany. This was a marvel of technology at the time, as the medium was still in its infancy. Trial broadcasts had begun in 1929, and the first major broadcasts were of the Berlin Olympic Games in 1936.

For her twenty-seventh birthday, Eva Braun received, slightly late, a car that looked like a beetle and whose development had been of special concern to Hitler. It was the prototype of the Volkswagen which the designing engineer, Ferdinand Porsche had given to Hitler for his birthday in 1938.[35] But Eva hardly ever drove the remarkable automobile.

Eva Braun had a fun-loving circle of friends—as is apparent from her home movies. A series of family parties also took place at #12 Wasserburger Strasse, since father and daughter had not only reconciled, but were now on very good terms—the reason being that Friedrich Braun had become an admirer and follower of Hitler's and had joined the NSDAP. On November 8, 1939, Braun attended his first party rally in the Munich Bürgerbräukeller. Unlike Hitler, who left early, Braun dutifully stayed until the very end. As a result, shrapnel from a bomb intended for Hitler hit him, and Eva'a father was among the sixty-three injured in Georg Elser's bomb attack.

After the end of the war, illustrated magazines turned the simple family parties at Eva's house into orgies of excess, while Eva was made out to be a slave. "Hermann Esser[36] told me about Eva Braun, who was a school friend of his second wife. According to her impression, Eva Braun was nothing more than window-dressing in the fantasy world into which Hitler was [rapidly spiralling]. She was not allowed to leave Munich without Hitler's or Bormann's permission. One day at Mrs.

Esser's she even burst into tears about her slave-like existence. 'I am nothing more than his prisoner,' she sobbed. 'As a woman I have nothing at all from Hitler.'"[37]

Such sensational inventions did not correspond with the facts and completely distorted the image of Eva Braun. Talk of a slave-like existence was completely untrue. Eva often had lunch in restaurants with her friend Herta Ostermayr, and was constantly seen with her mother, girlfriends and male friends. Once—following a visit by Hitler—she went to a ball at midnight organized by the City of Munich. She was frequently seen at the movies or the theater and had a passion for dancing. Existing amateur film documents happy outings to the Bavarian lakes. Her own Mercedes and chauffeur ensured Eva's mobility. Eva Braun liked to travel and frequently did so. In March 1938, she journeyed incognito with Hitler to Vienna and stayed at the Hotel Imperial, separated from her lover by one floor. Franziska Braun accompanied her daughter on that occasion and was filmed by Eva on a shopping spree through the city.

At the beginning of 1939, she flew with her mother and sister in Hitler's private airplane to Hamburg, boarded the ship "Robert Ley" there, and took the pleasure cruise Kraft durch Freude, or "Power through Joy," through the fjords of Norway.[38] Private photos show Eva Braun happily playing tennis on deck. She usually spent several weeks in Italy every year and in August, 1939 went to the Venice film festival. As "Hitler's private secretary," she had unobtrusively joined his entourage on a state visit to Italy from May 3 to 9, 1938. Unencumbered by the constraints of official protocol, she explored Rome, Capri, and Ravenna, filming the whole trip. In the fall, she proudly showed her films in the hall of the Berghof: "Now you can see the real Italy," she said to Hitler.[39]

But Hanfstaengl's observation that Hitler never gave his mistress the slightest attention in public is correct. Eva grew angry whenever she heard Hitler's tirades against marriage, but accepted this as an unavoidable consequence of his role as Leader of the German people. She comforted herself with dreams of the future when Hitler would live with her in Linz. "I will take no one with me, except for Miss Braun; Miss Braun and my dog...," Hitler often said in his nightly monologues.[40] Meanwhile, Eva Braun enjoyed her status among the small circle of the initiated, registered with pleasure her lover's growing affection for her and, in high spirits, would even refer to herself as "first lady." Since her first suicide attempt, Hitler had felt responsible for his "Hascherl." He protected her from the imperious National Socialist society women, and even banished Magda Goebbels from his home for a while.

Their relationship grew stronger during the war. Hitler's sociable meetings with young female artists ceased, and he called Eva from his command centers near the front every night at ten o'clock.

The fact that Eva Braun had become a fixture in his life by 1938 is borne out by Hitler's last will and testament, dated May 2 of that year, which he drafted after the invasion of Austria and prior to his departure for Rome, and deposited with minister Heinrich Lammers at the Reich Chancellery.[41] According to it, all his assets were to go to the party, and provisions for his funeral were also made. Following that, he names Eva Braun as first among the beneficiaries. She was to be paid a monthly pension of one thousand Reich marks from the party coffers.[42] Only then would his sister Paula, half-sister Angela and the other relatives in Spital in Lower Austria benefit.[43]

Further evidence of Hitler's attachment to Eva that also revealed his political intentions was the renovation done in the summer of 1938 to the cellar in her house, transforming it into an air-raid shelter equipped with every comfort. There were fans, an air-pressure pump, and an armored door that opened into a subterranean hallway of reinforced concrete which ended in the garden. The plans for the facility were personally drafted by Hitler.[44]

Hitler's visits to the apartment on Widenmayerstrasse had always attracted a crowd of people. The party wanted to avoid anything similar in the new house and took measures to protect Eva Braun's anonymity.[45] The couple preferred to meet at the apartment on Prinzregentenplatz, where Eva Braun could watch Hitler in his bedroom in the morning training with a chest-expander at the open window. This habit, which he kept up for many years, was necessary so that he could keep his right arm outstretched for hours at a time while giving the Nazi salute.[46] Another of their meeting places was the Obersalzberg near Berchtesgaden. Hitler had loved and frequented that region since 1923, and finally bought the "Wachenfeld" house there. Eva's visits to the country house always followed the same pattern. Albert Speer described it: "... after a couple of hours [Hitler went on ahead] and a closed Mercedes followed with the two secretaries; in their company was a simple girl from Munich. She was nice and fresh, rather than beautiful, and had a modest air. It was said that she was the mistress of the leader: Eva Braun. This Mercedes was never allowed in the official motorcade ... the secretaries [were] to provide a cover for the mistress. It surprised me that Hitler and she avoided everything that pointed to an intimate relationship—then withdrew to the upper bedrooms late at night ..."[47]

In 1933, the party began the purchase and rigorous expropriation of the entire Obersalzberg—first through Hess, then through Bormann and his "Adolf Hitler Industry Fund," created for this purpose. The high valley was surrounded by double barbed-wire fences and declared "Fuehrer's territory," where Goering, Bormann and Speer had their own houses built. Guest houses, barracks for the SS guards, a self-sufficient farm, a hospital, a theater, as well as a teahouse attainable only by elevator, were also built. "Wachenfeld" was absorbed into this complex and renamed "Berghof." It had thirty rooms, among them the famous conference room with huge adjustable windows that opened onto a gigantic terrace and offered a magnificent panoramic view of the Untersberg mountain. The steps to the entrance were guarded day and night by two SS officers in steel helmets, who stood as still as statues.[48]

The Obersalzberg was a world all its own, where Eva Braun was to spend two-thirds of her time between 1936 and 1945. She was regarded as mistress of the Berghof without any specified duties. Traudl Junge, Hitler's private secretary, got to know Eva Braun there. She wrote: "She was no mannequin from a fashion magazine. Her elegance did not reflect wealth, but good taste, although she had lightened her naturally blond hair. She used a lot of cosmetics, but her make-up was skillful and enhanced her beauty. She had a graceful walk."[49]

Eva Braun showed the secretary through the house on her fist visit. "From my room under the roof of the former 'Wachenfeld House' a spiral staircase led down to the glass-walled vestibule, which opened on one side to the yard, and on the opposite side to a huge parlor with a splendid faience fireplace. [From there] I continued along the wide hallway with its huge windows, through which one could see the Untersberg ... the dining room was very long and spacious, with a table for twenty-four in the middle ... the main hall was very impressive and I admired the tapestries. Eva Braun, who always liked to give the impression that she was artistically [knowledgeable], told me that these were genuine Gobelin Aubusson tapestries. When films were shown, the tapestries rose automatically, a screen came down, and on the opposite side the paneling opened up to reveal the projector. The hall was furnished in the Gothic style. I admired the mosaic tables, which according to Eva, were a gift from Mussolini ... there were more rooms upstairs." Later, Traudl Junge explored the private area of the house. "... but I was really dying to walk up the wide, velvet-covered stairs to the second floor, where the Fuehrer resided ... There was absolute silence in the corridor. I had been asked to take off my shoes. In front of one door lay two Scotch terriers, as if made of stone ... they were Stasi and Negus, guarding the bedroom of their mistress Eva. Next door was Hitler's bedroom. Between the two rooms was a large bathroom with a marble basin and gilded faucets. The bathroom had no door to the corridor. Adjacent to Hitler's bedroom was his large study ... the small room [for] Eva's maid was located quite close to the staircase ..."[50]

The "Turkish room," as Eva Braun called her own bedroom because of the rugs, appeared quite modest. The only peculiarity was a nude painting, which Hitler had painted of his lover. Eva kept herself busy at Berghof. She drafted letters to Hitler and friends and carefully copied them into a book provided for the purpose. Besides that, one of her hobbies was to keep a "wardrobe file." "I was disappointed," reported Henriette von Schirach. "The furniture was like that of an average bed-and-breakfast ... armoires painted with gentian ... entire volumes of movie magazines ... But what was in the many files on the shelf? Eva worked like an archivist. She opened a file on every single dress, every coat, noting where it was bought, what the price was and including a sketch of the garment as well as a comment on shoes, purse, jewelry that were worn with it ... an unbelievable, senseless piece of diligent work ..."[51]

Those who frequented the Berghof belonged to Hitler's entourage, a clique that was not entirely identical to the top leaders of the Third Reich. It included the permanently resident families of Albert Speer, Rudolf Hess and Martin Bormann, the director of the Reich Chancery, administrator and actual head of the Obersalzberg. Hermann Goering was rarely present. His wife Emmy once committed the gaffe of inviting Eva Braun and the household staff of the Berghof to tea. Hitler vetoed it, and the ladies never met. Joseph Goebbels and Heinrich Hoffmann were frequent guests. Always present and included in the social gathering were Hitler's personal doctors, Dr. Brandt and Dr.

Morell, his aides-de-camp Brückner, Wiedemann and Schaub as well as all of his private secretaries. Heinrich Himmler and Reinhard Heydrich came extremely rarely, high-ranking military officers almost never. Artists and movie actors were always welcome at Berghof, but scholars were not.

Eva Braun liked to invite her best girlfriends, Herta Ostermayr (Hitler's first secretary) and Marion Schönemann, née Theissen, and their children. But—as observers noted with envy—the Braun family literally took over the Obersalzberg and settled in there for long stays. Eva's parents no longer had a problem with the "immoral lifestyle" of their daughter. They were proud of their "quasi son-in-law," who treated them formally, yet with respect. Since the attack at the Bürgerbräukeller, Friedrich Braun had been regarded as "acceptable" and basked in the reflection of the Nazi notables. Gretl Braun, on the other hand, followed her sister Eva like a shadow. In 1944 she married Hermann Fegelein, the much sought-after SS group leader and Himmler's deputy. Only Ilse Braun kept her distance and rejected the secretarial position offered by Albert Speer.

Albert Speer has described the scenario as a guest at Hitler's residence in the Bavarian mountains: "We were standing around informally on the terrace, while the ladies lay on wicker deck chairs with dark red, checkered, rustic cushions. They sunned themselves as if at a resort hotel, for [it was fashionable to be tanned]. Liveried servants, SS selected from Sepp Dietrich's bodyguard, offered drinks with perfect, almost too familiar, manners: champagne, vermouth soda or fruit juices ... at the news that Hitler would soon arrive, the noise of conversation became more subdued, the sporadic laughter died away entirely. The ladies chatted about clothes and trips in an undertone. Eva Braun fetched her movie camera from the deck chair, accompanied by Negus. She got ready to film the appearance... everyone present is in suspense ... yet Hitler wants a casual atmosphere that must not appear subservient, emphasizing that they are his guests here, which makes everyone forget that the same people, in Berlin, will immediately fall back into obsequious submission ... After another half hour, the guests are invited to the dinner table; Hitler going ahead alone, Bormann with Eva Braun behind ..."[52]

A day at the Berghof started late, as Hitler liked to sleep in, and the daily routine was always the same.[53] After a simple lunch, which lasted about an hour, they went for a walk in summer, and in winter sat around the fireplace. The Berghof meals were not gourmet fare. According to the menu on August 9, 1937, before the war, there was barley soup, pork sausage, sauerkraut, mashed potatoes and green salad. Hitler, who was a vegetarian, had semolina noodles with egg. On June 7, 1943, they drank orange juice, ate linseed porridge, rice pudding with herbal sauce, crispbread with butter, and a Nuxo paste, [a mixture of sugar, soybeans and cornstarch].

Eva Braun was respectfully addressed by the men as "Gnädiges Fraülein" and by the ladies as "Fraülein Braun." Guests noticed that Eva would freely criticize her lover in their presence if his tie did not match his suit. She also dared to joke about his headgear: "You and your mailman's caps."[54]

Like everyone else, she addressed him as "My Fuehrer," which in conjunction with the familiar pronoun "Du" sounded odd. In his absence, Hitler was "the boss" or "the Fuehrer." Hitler called her "Evchen" or "Tschapperl." The staff always referred to Eva Braun as their "boss," and avoided any mention of her name in public. Therese Link, the cook at the Obersalzberg guest house, wrote in her memoirs: "I often saw Hitler's girlfriend and sometimes made her some lemonade. She was a sweet, refined girl ..."[55]

After supper, Hitler would leave his guests and withdraw for political and military deliberations. If he came back, a movie was usually shown in the presence of the entire staff. Hitler would sit in the front row beside Eva. She was responsible for selecting the movie and would take into consideration Hitler's preference for light entertainment such as adventure movies and westerns. Her personal favourite was *Gone With The Wind*. But most of the viewers preferred the American movies that Goebbels had banned and declared "harmful for the people." Afterward, they would listen to recordings of Johann Strauss, Franz Lehár and Richard Wagner, and engage in subdued conversation over champagne and sweets. If Hitler began to speak, those present prepared themselves for monologues that would go on until the early hours of the morning.

The political activity around her never concerned Eva. She was never a member of the Nazi Party, hated political conversations and debates, and treated all her associations with National Socialists as personal friendships. That was how she viewed Albert Speer, the architect and later Reich minister for arms and ammunition, Franz Xaver Schwartz, the Reich treasurer, and many others.

In later years, when her position was well-established, Eva Braun's interest in Hitler's eloquence faded, and she revealed to her sister Margarete that his utterances bored her terribly. She soon forgot the political pretensions of her younger days, and made no effort to hide her abhorrence of all political discussions. She despised the contemporary publications intended for women such as NS Frauenbuch and NS Frauenwarthe. The publicized image of the German woman also left her cold. She spoke up only once, in January 1943, upset over learning that perms were to be banned and that cosmetics would no longer be manufactured.[56]

Eva Braun's avoidance of politics was the cornerstone of her relationship with Hitler and insured its survival. She knew better than to test the limits of her options with her lover. She exerted no influence on him—good or bad. If someone told her a tragic story to get her support, she would "put her finger to her lips, like the archangel, to indicate that she wanted to know nothing."[57] On one occasion, Ilse, who never held back her criticism even when at the Berghof, was warned by her sister, "If the Fuehrer puts you in a concentration camp, I will not come to get you out!"[58]

During her sixteen years with Hitler, Eva Braun intervened only once. This took place on behalf of a Jewish doctor named Bloch from Linz, who had treated Hitler's severely ailing mother and cared for her until her death. He escaped being sent to a concentration camp and was permitted to emigrate, leaving behind his modest assets.[59]

In everyday matters, Hitler appreciated his companion's healthy common sense and listened to her advice. Eva recommended his personal physician to him, and was thus able to intervene in the life and health of the hypochondriac dictator—and perhaps the course of world history. "Morell will be eternally grateful to me...," she commented in a letter in 1937.

It was discovered after the war that the fashionable physician, Dr. Theo Morell, had cured Heinrich Hoffmann of a "dangerous condition"[60]— gonorrhea—and had also successfully treated Franziska Braun. The

Braun family were keen supporters of Dr. Morell and Eva invited the miracle doctor to the Berghof, later becoming friends with his wife. Hitler, whose intestinal problems he alleviated, was referred to as "Patient A" in Dr. Morell's files and came to trust the doctor completely. Morell prescribed regular courses of treatment by injection and a handful of tablets to be taken daily. Hitler believed he was mortally ill and that he had only a little time left to realize his plans, so he faithfully followed the doctor's instructions. Krause, his valet, described the situation: "All the injections that he gave Hitler almost every day must wear a person out... Hitler took sheer masses of pills..."[61]

Eva Braun cut a fashionable, elegant figure. Her suits came from the best tailors in Berlin, her furs and gowns from Paris, and she would buy her shoes from Ferragamo in Florence. She had a predilection for expensive jewelry, eventually owning a large collection. Photos always show her wearing matching jewelry and a diamond watch. Hitler's mistress lived in extravagent style where her toilet was concerned—she would change clothes up to seven times a day. Eva Braun had a personal maid at her disposal and a hairdresser (Milla Schellmoser), and her hair was always perfectly done. She used only the most expensive French perfumes and made herself up carefully. She was a heavy smoker and was thus delinquent in her "duty as a German woman," to use the expression of the police chief of Erfurt, who had every woman who smoked in public stopped and cited. Hitler also took part in the anti-smoking campaign directed solely against women and warned the ladies at the Berghof of the noxious nicotine. Undisturbed, Eva Braun would whistle the popular tune "Smoke Gets in Your Eyes." But she never smoked in Hitler's presence.

Until the outbreak of war, Hitler spent many weekends at the Berghof, traveling from Berlin by train or plane on Friday afternoon and returning on Monday. Karl Wilhelm Krause, who was Hitler's valet from 1934 to 1939 and from 1940 to 1943 and who always went with him on these trips, knew Eva Braun very well. In his memoirs, he writes, "I do not want to express an opinion about her, because it would undoubtedly be biased. E.B. and I got along no better than—as people would say—a dog and a cat. We once had a [strong difference] of opinionon on a personal matter, in the winter of 1935–36 and since then were through with each other and only exchanged greetings."[62] The "personal" matter, according to the Braun family, was a trivial one. Rumor had it that Eva Braun, who was well-versed in fashion and particular about clothing, forced the valet—a carpenter by trade, and later a sailor—to press Hitler's pants daily. Krause never forgave her for that.

Krause was in a position to report on Hitler's mistress: "... Eva Braun was not called in for official receptions ... Hitler regarded her as his bethrothed, but he was not jealous. After the renovation of the Berghof there was a connecting door between the two bedrooms. Without any doubt, Eva Braun was personally supported by Hitler."[63]

"Not called on for official receptions" was applied so rigorously at the Berghof that it resembled conditions in an Oriental harem. Whenever there were political or military conferences, Eva Braun was banned from the great hall and if high-ranking visitors came, she was not allowed to leave her room. If the guests stayed longer, she had to move to Martin Bormann's house. This happened during visits by American ex-president Hoover, Admiral Horthy, Arthur Chamberlain, King Boris of Bulgaria, Aga Khan, Cardinal Pacelli, later Pope Pius XII, and many more. What hurt Eva most was that she was never introduced to the Duke and Duchess of Windsor, whose love story had touched her deeply.

On May 22, 1939, the Italian foreign minister and son-in-law of Mussolini, the attractive Count Galeazzo Ciano, came to the Berghof to sign the "Steel Pact"—the military alliance between Germany and Italy. As usual, Eva Braun was confined to her room, but photographed his arrival from her window. Ciano noticed it and immediately inquired who the pretty blonde was. He was given an evasive answer, and Hitler ordered Eva to close her window immediately. She continued shooting, however, using her telephoto lens and labeled the photos with: "Orders: window closed! And what can be made of that."

Eva Braun was passionate about photography and filming. She owned expensive equipment: several cameras, among them an Agfa and a Leica, as well as a sixteen-millimeter Siemens movie camera with interchangeable lenses, and an Agfa Movector film projector. Of the innumerable photo albums that Eva Braun always kept up-to-date and carefully inscribed, thirty-three survived. At the end of the war they were found by the American security service and are now located in the National Archives in Washington. Eva's photos of Hitler with children were more animated than those by Hoffmann, who—as a result of gentle pressure—bought them from her. But as a photographer, Eva failed when it came to Martin Bormann's severe face —"Unfortunately, attempt did not end in satisfaction," is written beneath it. Braun's movies about daily life on the Obersalzberg are among the first color films taken in Germany and are important records of the period.

Eva Braun had had her own apartment in the Berlin Reich Chancellery since the beginning of 1939. Hitler had reserved Hindenburg's former bedroom for her, which was next to his own rooms. But there, too, she was not allowed to move about freely. She had to use the staff entrance and eat her meals alone in her room Cinderella-style, while immediately next door, her lover gave the most lavish receptions in the style of the Bismarck era. Eva turned to her hobby and took some very interesting photographs during her stay at the end of August 1939—unique records from the days before the outbreak of World War II.

She labeled this amazing series of photos "… and then Ribbentrop went to Moscow." In contrast to the posed propaganda pictures, six photographs show Hitler nervously awaiting news from foreign minister Ribbentrop in Moscow. His relief, when he learns by phone of the conclusion of the non-aggression pact with Stalin on August 23, 1939, is so great that he hugs Goebbels and Bormann. Four additional photos "… and the Fuehrer hears the report on the radio," reflect the relaxed atmosphere during the radio broadcast.

In the following days, Eva heard and believed that Hitler wanted to avoid war with Poland—which would trigger World War II—"at all costs." "But Poland will not negotiate," is Eva's caption under a photo that shows Hitler during his alleged efforts to salvage peace. Eva also attended the Reichstag session on September 1, 1939, in which the bellowing Hitler declared that they would "shoot back," after he had given the order to attack the day before. He also announced: "… that the outcome of this war will be the annihilation of Jewry. For the first time, the genuinely ancient Jewish law will be applied: an eye for an eye, a tooth for a tooth."

When the war began to go badly for Germany, it meant the end of the idyllic life on the Obersalzberg. As of 1942, the Berghof was declared the Fuehrer's main command center.

By 1944, it was clear that the situation for Germany was hopeless. The time of lightning warfare ("blitzkrieg") victories was past, and

"Operation Barbarossa," the "Germanic march on the East" to over-throw the Soviet Union—conceived as a summer campaign—had degenerated into a bloody war. Not even the National Socialist propaganda machine could continue to falsify the disastrous reports that were arriving from all fronts. In early 1944, the Russians crossed the former eastern border of Poland, and German forces were no match for their attacks at the beginning of June. By July, the Red Army was approaching East Prussia. The civilian population, whose despair and deprivation were growing daily, suffered under the extensive bombing of German cities, with Berlin under constant air attack.

On July 20, 1944, a bomb went off at the Fuehrer's Wolfsschanze headquarters near Rastenburg in East Prussia. It was the desperate attempt of German officers and politicians to eliminate Hitler, topple his dictatorship and bring about an end to World War II. But the attack, carried out by the German officer and resistance fighter Claus Count Schenk von Stauffenberg, failed. Hitler suffered only minor injuries, and was able to receive Mussolini shortly after.[64]

Hitler wrote to Eva not long after the attack: "My dear Tschapperl. I am all right, do not worry. I [am just] a bit tired. I hope to come home soon and take a rest in your arms. I have a great need of rest, but my duty toward the German people stands above all else ... I have sent you the uniform of the disastrous day. It is the proof that providence is protecting me and that we no longer need to fear our enemies. With my whole heart, your A. H."[65]

Enclosed with the letter was a pencil sketch. It showed the destroyed barracks in the Wolfsschanze, where during a briefing, the explosive smuggled in by Count Stauffenberg in a briefcase, exploded. Hitler interpreted his survival as a sign that he should pursue his mission and he considered the uniform worn on July 20, 1944 to be a historic relic, which was to be preserved for future generations.[66] That was why he sent the stained and torn garment to Eva.[67]

The news of the attempted assassination reached Eva on a swimming trip to Lake König with her friend Herta Ostermayr.[68] She called the Fuehrer's command center as soon as contact could be established and also replied immediately to his letter: "Darling, I am beside myself. I am dying of fear, I feel close to losing my mind. The weather here is gorgeous, everything seems so peaceful that I feel ashamed... You know, I have always told you, that I will die if anything happens to you. From the day we first met, I vowed to follow you everywhere, even into death. You know that I only live for your love, Your Eva."[69]

As instructed, Eva Braun painstakingly took care of Hitler's uniform. It was found among her belongings in the home of a souvenir hunter in Schladming, Austria and confiscated by the Allies after the war.

From mid-1944 on, the "Alpine stronghold" came under intensive bombardment, but the Fuehrer's estate was spared for a long time. Whenever the air raid siren sounded, all buildings were shrouded in an artificial mist, and the inhabitants escaped down a staircase into the gigantic air raid shelter via 65 steps cut into the mountain. There, Eva had her own room with bath.

In 1944, no one could believe any longer in a victory for Hitler. Not even Eva Braun, who was more often in Munich, having been "conscripted for wartime service" at Foto Hoffmann. Her home town lay in ruins after the night bombing raids of April 24 and 25, 1944 that left 140 dead, 4,000 wounded, and 70,000 homeless. But Eva Braun suffered more because her lover, to whom she had committed herself for better or for worse, was displaying signs of physical decline.

The future appeared so gloomy to Eva Braun that she drafted her will on October 26, 1944, at the age of thirty-two.[70] She planned to leave her Mercedes convertible to her father, half of her fur coats, rugs, cash and the large painting of Hitler by Knirr to her mother. The house on Wasserburger Strasse along with the furniture and her Volkswagen were to go to her sister Ilse. Gretl Fegelein, her other sister, was to receive all of her books and diaries. She divided her valuable jewelry equally among her sisters and girlfriends.

On February 9, 1945, Eva belatedly celebrated her birthday, postponed because of the air raids, at her house in Munich, and it also became a farewell party for all her relatives and friends. Shortly after, she had the Daimler-Benz company paint her car in dark green camouflage. At the end of March she set out across Germany, which lay in ruins, to be with Hitler in Berlin.

The Wilhelmplatz was a vast, bombed-out expanse, and only the façade of the Reich Chancellery was still standing after a direct hit. Hitler's headquarters were located in the "Fuehrer bunker" in the garden of the Reich Chancellery.[71] Here, sixteen metres underground, sur-rounded by concrete walls several meters thick, Eva Braun willingly spent the last weeks of her life. Hitler appeared happy that she had come, even though he had ordered her not to leave the Berghof.

As the Eastern front was daily drawing nearer and artillery fire could be heard, various rescue scenarios were considered and rejected. On April 22, Hitler decided to stay in the Reich capital.[72] On April 13, Eva Braun asked lieutenant general Gerhard Engel for instructions on how to shoot herself. According to the numerous eyewitness reports, she handled the situation with complete calm. She sent a letter to the staff of the Berghof giving them a leave of absence: "But, please, for a lim-ited time only. I'm thinking of two weeks or so ..." Eva Braun could easily have saved herself, but she did not want to leave Hitler: "I am very happy to be with him just now."[73] She refused to let herself be flown out.

Eva's letters to her sisters and girlfriends are marked by a strangely removed sense of reality; in the face of death, she writes of mundane matters: "... imagine, the tailoress wants thirty marks for my blouse, she is totally crazy, how dare she charge me thirty marks for this bit of nothing..."[74] and she sends them photos of Hitler's German shepherd, Blondi, which has just had pups. On April 22, she bids her best friend, Herta Ostermayr, farewell: "... we will fight here to the last, but I am afraid the end is drawing threateningly closer and closer. Words cannot describe how I am suffering personally for the Fuehrer ... I cannot understand why it has come to this, but one doubts the existence of God ..."

Her sister Gretl, Herman Fegelein's wife, received Eva's final instruc-tions: "Destroy all my private correspondence, especially the business matters ... also destroy an envelope which is addressed to the Fuehrer and is to be found in the safe in the shelter (at the Berghof). Please pack the letters from the Fuehrer and my draft replies (blue leather book), in waterproofing and bury them or something. Please do not destroy them ..." The letter ends with the assurance that her sister Gretl, who was pregnant at the time, would see her husband again.

The orderly officer Gerhard Bolt met Eva Braun for the first time on April 27, 1945, and wrote this about her: "She was sitting at the table in the vestibule with Hitler and several men of his entourage, having a lively discussion. Hitler was listening. She had crossed her legs and looked everyone she was talking to directly in the eye. At first glance I was especially struck by her oval face, sparkling eyes, classical nose and blond, beautiful hair. She wore a close-fitting gray suit, which revealed the [figure] of a very [shapely] woman, tasteful shoes and on her slender wrist a pretty, diamond-studded watch. Without any doubt, a truly beautiful woman. But her behavior was somewhat affected and theatrical."[75]

On April 28, shortly before midnight, Eva Braun's lifelong wish came true—Adolf Hitler married her. Goebbels and Bormann acted as witnesses. Eva wore a long, high-necked dress of silk taffeta and her finest jewelry. While signing the marriage certificate, she made a mistake. She began with "B," crossed it out and, for the first and last time in her life, wrote "Eva Hitler."

The wedding celebration in the den of the bunker was still going on when Hitler began dictating his private will in the morning hours of April 29, 1945: "Since I believed in the years of the struggle that getting married would be irresponsible, I have now, before ending this earthly existence, decided to take as my wife the girl who, after long years of loyal friendship, has voluntarily returned to the almost besieged city in order to share her fate with mine. It is her wish to join me in death as my wife. This will compensate her for what was taken from both of us by my work in the service of my people ... I myself and my wife choose death to avoid the shame of removal from office or capitulation ..."[76]

The couple withdrew for their wedding night around four o'clock in the morning. At that time, quite close by in the yard of the decimated Reich Chancellery, an execution was being carried out. Hitler had ordered his brother-in-law, Hermann Fegelein, the husband of Eva's pregnant sister Gretl, executed for attempting to escape. Eva knew about it. She loved her "little sister very much, too." Still, she accepted Hitler's final, senseless act of cruelty without visible emotion or objection. The knowledge of her own fate and impending death had destroyed her capacity to feel anything.

On the morning of April 29, the maid (Liesl Ostertag) congratulated Eva on her marriage. "Feel free to call me Mrs. Hitler," Eva tells her. Later, she gives the girl her wedding band and the dress from the night before, instructing her to give both to her friend Herta Ostermayr as keepsakes.

In the early afternoon of April 30, 1945, with the Red Army only 500 metres from the bunker of the Reich Chancellery Adolf and Eva Hitler committed suicide. The valet Linge and an SS man carried Hitler's body outside wrapped in a blanket. Martin Bormann followed with Eva Braun's body, and entrusted it to Kempka, Hitler's driver who said later that he had seen no traces of blood whatever on her body. Kempka poured gasoline on the corpses and set them on fire.[77]

The population learns "that our Fuehrer, Adolf Hitler, fighting to his last breath," is dead on May 1, 1945. A Hamburg radio announcer reading the report, hesitates, incredulous at the news that "Hitler and his wife" are dead.

Eva Braun's life became more fascinating in death than it had been in life. It was then that all the fantastic rumors arose, which were never contradicted by those who knew better. Those who had enjoyed the limelight in the company of Eva Braun preferred quiet anonymity after the war. Classified as "extremely incriminated by the Nazi regime," they were either interned or charged. Friends had to undergo denazification trials before a tribunal that would determine their future. Those who did not lie or deny, remained silent. Heinrich Hoffmann, the photographer, who had known Eva Braun as boss and friend for sixteen years, claimed in 1945 to have forgotten almost everything from that period.

Luis Trenker, the actor and director who had been part of Hitler's inner circle, retired to Italy at the end of the war. There he wrote *Diary of Eva Braun*, proclaiming the authenticity of the astonishing book. In it, "Eva Braun" depicts cruel rituals of animal torture on the Obersalzberg. Bulls were denied water for long stretches of time and then made to drink until they burst—much to the enjoyment of Himmler and Hitler who watched from behind protective barriers. But Trenker also plagiarized whenever his own rich imagination failed him. The dubious 1913 memoir of Countess Larisch-Wallersee in which she writes about the Empress Elisabeth, often provided him with material.

"The creams that he [Hitler] sent me seem to be good—I put raw veal on my face twice a week, and once a week I take a bath in warm olive oil. I have really had a hard time getting used to the leather underwear that he [Hitler] wants [me to wear] ...," are the words that Trenker puts in Eva Braun's mouth.[78] Trenker's fictionalized diary received a sensational, but short-lived success in France and Italy. The manuscript, consisting of ninety-six photocopied pages that Trenker claimed Eva had personally given him in Kitzbuehel, contained no indication whatever of Eva's authorship. The Braun family initiated a libel suit, and the court determined the book to be a clumsy forgery. Further distribution of the "diary" was prohibited.[79] Luis Trenker himself stayed away from Germany for five years, only to reappear with an article entitled, "My Heart Always Beat for Tyrol."[80]

But the "Diary Case" did not end with the trial, not by a long shot. Writer Hans Habe also entered the fray. After seeing a few handwritten letters of Eva Braun's, he felt he was a handwriting expert and guaranteed the authenticity of the falsified diary. He claimed phrases such as, "Adi never notices my clothes," and "Lacks the courtesy to send flowers," were proof of the document's authenticity. He wanted it published immediately because, "anyone who reads just one page of it [will know] exactly when Germany's deepest humiliation began."[81] In 1954, Habe did an about-face and pretended in an interview with the paper *Wiener Samstag* that he had discovered the forgery. "... [in 1948] I strongly advised against publication ... The comparison of the letters ... with the manuscript lent force to the assumption that it was a forgery. I felt it was my duty [at that time] to expose the fraud."[82]

Other shocking reports were also proven untrue. There were many rumors that Hitler and Eva were not dead at all. An informer stated that they had reached Argentina in a submarine, and were living in a sanitarium. [83]

Eva's real diary survived the chaos in the aftermath of the war, even though she had asked her sister Gretl to destroy the manuscript. The Braun family did not comply with her wish, and at the end of the war gave it to Hermann Fegelein's mother, who hid it in the park at Fischhorn Castle in Zell am See. Officers of the secret service of the Third U.S. Army, who had infiltrated prominent families of the Nazi regime, found the manuscript. It was seized and, by a roundabout route, ended up in the National Archives in Washington.

In September 1945, an undercover agent (Walter Hirschfeld) visited Eva's sister Gretl and Herta Ostermayr and discovered the hiding place of Eva's jewelry.[84] Letters, films, photo albums, sketches and note-books of Hitler and Eva Braun were found at the house of an SS lieu-tenant colonel, who had not destroyed the material—as ordered—but had kept it, along with the uniform Hitler had worn on July 20, 1944, as a keepsake, hiding it in Schladming.[85]

After the war ended, the Braun family fought not only to salvage Eva's reputation, but also for her estate, which was threatened with confis-cation. On December 31, 1947, Friedrich Braun turned to the State Ministry for Special Tasks in Munich with the request that no trial be ini-tiated against his deceased daughter. Since she had no political posi-tion whatever and had never played a role militarily, he applied for the release of her property. He also claimed that she had not left a will, although he knew better.[86]

Research has gradually shed some light on the mystery surrounding Eva Braun. But the public's curiosity about Hitler's mistress was not satisfied with the details of her real, and rather mundane life story. When scholars failed to come up with the expected revelations, historian Hugh Trevor-Roper said, "Eva Braun is a disappointment to history."

HENRIETTE VON SCHIRACH

The Fuehrer's Disciple

February 3, 1913 – January 27, 1992

When Henriette von Schirach published her book *Anekdoten um Hitler* (Hitler Anecdotes) in 1980,[1] she earned little recognition and no sympathy for it. The news magazine *Der Spiegel* reported: "The Fuehrer as no one knows him. An odd book that has just been published, wants at last—publisher's text—to show the other Hitler, the cheerful, sociable Austrian, the inspired artist, the fellow human being, the clever person full of ideas."

The magazine observed sarcastically that Mrs. von Schirach had delved into her little sewing basket of memories and written a collection of gems about her "brown friend of the family." And a publishing house specializing in treasures from the Third Reich had published it.[2]

In contrast to many women within the sphere of influence of the Nazi elite, Henriette von Schirach did not shy away from the limelight even after the collapse of the thousand-year Reich, which she characterized as the "price of glory." Instead, with missionary zeal, she tried, unfailingly, to interpret for the public her personal vision of Hitler—Hitler, the kind uncle, the benefactor of her parents.

Henriette von Schirach was the only person who had been indoctrinated by Hitler in person from childhood on. It was then that her National Socialist mindset had been irrevocably formed. It overtook all subsequent insights and could be shaken neither by facts nor by logical arguments. Apart from a few observations and half-hearted concessions to the zeitgeist, or temper of the times, Henriette von Schirach never distanced herself from Hitler. He was, and remained for her, not the feared dictator, but the fatherly master of her early years. Henriette von Schirach grew up in the National Socialist world. "My father was a photographer and my mother an angel," was how she described her parents. In fact, her mother was a professional actress and appeared in revues where she sang popular songs. Her father, Heinrich Hoffmann, was the official photo reporter of the Third Reich, Hitler's personal photographer, and an "artful, and dangerous party comrade from Day One."[3]

In 1911, Hoffmann counted among his clients the Bavarian royal family, the Russian czar and artists like Roda Roda, Joachim Ringelnatz and Marcel Duchamp. Avant-garde artists thought highly of his creative portraits, which resembled engravings. One day, the young actress Therese "Nelly" Baumann visited his studio to have her picture taken in a grand gown and a lavish flowered hat, with her eyes modestly lowered. After the photo session, Hoffmann got to know his model better. They were married that same year.

On February 3, 1913, their daughter Henriette "Henny" was born, followed by a son, Heinrich, on October 24, 1916. The family lived in the Schwabing district of Munich, and Hoffmann's photo studio was opened in 1915 at #33 Schellingstrasse in the suburb of Max.[4] Hoffmann had taken it over from Franz Marc, one of the most popular painters of Germany and co-founder of the "Blue Rider" group. Little Henny would often accompany her father to work at the studio.

"The tiny house had great charm. In the room downstairs there was a fireplace, one wall was covered with a Gobelin tapestry that served as background. Delft jugs stood there, and gauze curtains gave soft light. Father's photos showed his model[s] not in the haste of the moment, but revealed [their] spiritual side … a staircase led up to the 'lab,' with the large flat trays full of developer and fixative in the red light. The little house stood against the undeveloped wall of a tall tenement, which was covered with wild vines from top to bottom …"[5]

Henny's childhood was uneventful until she was eight years old and father brought home a new acquaintance, a certain Adolf Hitler.[6] She remembered that first encounter clearly: "After the introduction, Hitler asked: 'What are you reading,' then I immediately went and brought my books … stories about knights and heroes … Then he said: 'You don't know anything at all about the Greeks?'"

Henriette's family home was a haven for the early National Socialist movement. In 1919, Heinrich Hoffmann belonged to the right-wing "Residents' Guard." On April 6, 1920, the conservative, nationalist and anti-Semitic Hoffmann joined the German Workers' Party (DAP) and later the Nazi Party. The stocky, rotund photographer with his alcoholic's red nose was soon a welcome fellow traveler with party comrades.7 Hitler, too, was fond of the "Bohemian" atmosphere, as well as the artistic surroundings at Hoffmann's house, and regarded the jovial photographer who liked to eat and drink, as a "delightful wag" with whom he had found a "second" home.

"Hitler would come to us every afternoon," Henriette reported. "My father was sleeping, he had to get up very early, and I was practicing my piano in the next room. Hitler rang once, and I opened the door for him. He sat down at our gigantic desk and leafed through magazines … I was, meanwhile, practicing on the piano … then he took a stool and played the "Annenpolka" for me. He told me the story of the Nibelungs, the saga of the treasure at the bottom of the Rhine and about the dwarf king Alberich."[8] Over the years Hitler kept a close eye on the intellectual development of the girl and gave her many books, including *The Life of Prince Eugene*, Schwab's *The Finest Sagas of Classical Antiquity*, and Schliemann's work on the discovery of Troy. The adoptive uncle would always check to see if the books had, in fact, been read. Hitler also checked Henriette's homework and gave her drawing lessons. By way of thanks, each week she gave him a homemade scrapbook of pictures and text she had cut out.

Heinrich Hoffmann, a highly talented photographer, was—after his father and his uncle—carrying on the family tradition. Party propaganda would later spread the word that he hailed from an "old dynasty of photographers in Hesse." Hoffmann's official title was "Royal Bavarian Court Photographer."[9]

Hitler would not allow Hoffmann to photograph him for years. The politician believed that this would stimulate the public's interest in him and consoled his party comrade with talk of the future: "In return, you are to be the only man who may photograph me at any time."[10] Hoffmann gave in to the Fuehrer's request and was destined to be richly rewarded for it.

Hitler usurped Hoffmann's family life and daughter. Henriette noticed how submissive her parents became as soon as the Fuehrer of the Nazi Party entered the house. She saw that this man's wishes were the equivalent of orders that absolutely had to be obeyed. She observed the Nibelung-like loyalty of his companions and that the party comrades jokingly proclaimed Therese Hoffmann "Mommy Hitler."

Hitler attended not only to the girl's intellectual education, but was concerned as well with her physical development. He showed her some exercises on the rings that were installed on a doorjamb in the corridor of the Hoffmann apartment. On Sundays, the two visited matinees of art films and Munich museums. Hitler saw to it that Henriette got her first skis, and for her confirmation he gave her a tennis racket.[11] At the age of twelve, the photographer's daughter was allowed to listen to Richard Wagner's operas in Bayreuth at Hitler's side.

Over many years, Mr. Hitler—as he preferred to be called, in spite of all the familiarity—remained a central figure for the girl, in his blue suit with a light trench coat and wide-brimmed velour hat. "Hitler never acted like a father toward me. He treated me like a comrade, absolutely equal and [he was] not at all arrogant. He was a good playmate for me," Henriette declared, looking back.

The Hoffmann couple was flattered that their hero, whose intellectual superiority they recognized and admired, cared for their daughter in such a friendly way. Hitler was fond of saying, "There is nothing more beautiful than educating a human being."

When Therese Hoffmann died in 1928, it was Hitler who took on the task of telling the then fifteen-year-old Henriette about her mother's death: "Hitler sent his driver to pick me up, and then he told me." He also prepared her for the funeral: "I will hold your hand firmly and you will not cry."[12] Afterward, Henriette's brother, Heinrich, was sent to boarding school, and she remained under Hitler's guardianship. The experiences of her early childhood left indelible traces and formed the girl's and later young woman's outlook on life.

Henriette witnessed all the stages of Hitler's career. "But in particular I remember the room on Thierschstrasse. We arrived there one day after a rainstorm, in the open car. The car was never allowed to be closed and Hitler took my father and me upstairs to his room. He gave me a towel so that I could dry my long, wet hair. He prepared some tea on a corner of the desk. He had an old, blue and white teapot, cups from different sets. It was all very primitive, yet he warmed the pot and behaved ceremonially, like a Japanese tea master ... I was allowed to look at all the books that were standing around ... one showed the remains of the palace of Knossos ..."[13]

Starting in 1923, Hitler allowed Hoffmann to photograph him. From then on, Henriette's father thoroughly cashed in on "[being close] to the Fuehrer." He allied himself for good or ill with his subject and set about marketing Hitler's private life. "The personal relationship with the Fuehrer gives him the opportunity to create pictures that afford the German people better insight into the soul of its marvelous leader ...," wrote the chairman of the Reich Guild Association for the photography trade, after grimly noting the monopoly by Hoffmann's company.[14]

As part of the entourage of the Fuehrer, Heinrich Hoffmann grew extremely rich and moved with his family to Trogastrasse in Bogenhausen, a stylish area of Munich.

Even the door-knocker in Henny's family home was a work of art and in the vestibule hung a painting by Breughel. Hoffmann, the organizer of the "Great German Art Exhibition" of 1937 and commissioner in charge of "exploiting the seized works of degenerate art," loved old masters. Hoffmann's dry humor was, however, symbolized by a Flemish picture affixed to the door of the toilet, upon which, it said in Gothic script, "Do not turn me over." If one did so, they would view a naked backside.[15]

Henriette was indoctrinated with Nazi slogans during the most formative phase of her life. She was even taken along to party rallies at the Munich beer hall, Löwenbräu. "Just the entry of the flags and banners into the hall filled with thousands of people was terrifying and exciting, beautiful and daring, but also unpleasant ... then Hitler, who was suddenly no longer the friendly Mr. Hitler, climbed onto the podium made of boards, [and] tried to speak in his hoarse Austrian voice. He relished being interrupted by cheers, rising as if from a sea of humanity that worshipped him and that he could command. He could have said everything more quietly, but he shouted, he shouted and people liked it."[16]

National Socialist life continued to thrive in the small house after an addition to the back at #50 Schellingstrasse, where Hoffmann had moved his photo studio in 1925. Although the locality was cramped, the accommodating Hoffman ceded a part of it to the party leadership, to create within it a Hall of Honor.[17] Thus Henriette witnessed and followed the Nazi Party's development from a splinter group to a mass movement at close quarters. She watched with interest as her father photographed the members of the SA complete with standard in the backyard or had the regional leaders pose for group shots in the Hall of Honor. Heinrich Hoffmann had also secured for himself the lucrative business of distributing busts of Hitler in various sizes.

Henriette knew the most powerful men of the Third Reich from the days of their modest beginnings. The zealous, small-eyed rabbit breeder Heinrich Himmler, who looked like an office manager; the lean lieutenant Rudolf Hess with the fanatical face of a candidate for the teaching profession, whose gaze would be fixed on Hitler as if hypnotized, the bull-necked, stubborn Gregor Strasser; and Julius Streicher, the "sinister one," who wore the figure of a hanged rabbi around his neck as a mascot. The only one who captivated the girl was Hermann Goering, maybe because he gave Henriette a terrier called Wiski and at a photo appointment in the Hoffman studio, invited her to Berlin.

There she witnessed the tumultuous opening of the Reichstag on October 13, 1930, and that same evening, a splendid party at Goering's. Hitler, Goebbels and Hess were there, as well as a dozen aristocrats. Henriette acted as Hitler's secretary, one of those present reported.[18]

In her parent's home, Henriette met not only the party functionaries, who gathered around Hitler as his "royal household," but also the two

The wedding reception of Baldur and Henriette von Schirach at
Hitler's apartment on March 31, 1932.

women who played a prominent role in Hitler's life: Geli Raubal and
Eva Braun. She took to Geli, Hitler's unfortunate niece, and felt sympathy for her. But for Eva Braun—who worked as an apprentice for her
father and liked to pose for pictures—Henny, who liked to put on intellectual airs, had nothing but contempt. To her, Eva seemed stupid.
The deeper reason probably lay in an unadmitted rivalry for Hitler's
attention. But that did not stop the two from enjoying life together.
They engaged in sports, went ice skating and skiing and had a good
time at costume balls during the Munich carnival.

Whether Henriette really entertained hopes for the twenty-four-year-
older Hitler, is unclear. In any event, she often spoke of the politician's
imaginary or actual advances at the beginning of the 1930s. "… it
rings. Out of bed and to the door … it is Mr. Hitler. He stands there in
the hallway, on the red carpet … Mr. Hitler is wearing his English trench
coat and holds his gray velour hat in his hand. And then he says something that doesn't fit him at all and says it quite seriously: 'Will you kiss
me?' He is quite formal about it. Imagine, kissing Mr. Hitler. 'No, not
really, Mr. Hitler; it is impossible!'"

The girl's father attributed the story to his daughter's vivid imagination.
"You're fooling yourself. Now, off to bed."[19]

Hitler turned to Eva Braun after Geli's suicide. And Henriette chose Baldur von Schirach, leader of the Nazi students' association and the youngest in Hitler's entourage. She joined the National Socialist German Students' Association, helped package the students' newspaper *Die Bewegung* (The Movement) and did various office jobs. It was a milieu that she liked and in which she felt comfortable. Whenever they did not have to distribute National Socialist flyers on the steps of the university, the students spent entire nights discussing literature. They recited Stefan Georg and quoted from Ernst Jünger.

In Baldur von Schirach, Henriette was to find a kindred spirit. Both had deep roots in the National Socialist milieu, both were Hitler protégés. They were both interested in art, culture and literature, which made for endless conversations. The student leader later confessed that he had fallen in love with the very lively, enterprising and talkative Henriette on their first evening together. She was attracted to the twenty-three-year-old man with the soft, unremarkable features and stilted, halting diction. Schirach knew Hitler's *Mein Kampf* by heart and had already reorganized his entire life according to the Fuehrer's wishes. Henriette was especially impressed by the numerous poems of homage that the student leader had dedicated to his Fuehrer as "singer of the National Socialist movement." By 1931, Schirach could already point to several small volumes of poetry. In them, for example, one reads: "I was a leaf in an infinite space, now you are my home, my tree …"[20]

Baldur von Schirach, born in Berlin on May 9, 1907, had spent his youth in Weimar, where his father—a former cavalry captain of the Prussian Guard, Cuirassier Regiment—directed the Court Theater. Baldur's mother was an American who, during her entire life hardly ever spoke German, and brought up her four children in her mother tongue. After World War I, his father lost his job and one of Baldur's brothers shot himself because of the "misfortune of Germany." Baldur, in the atmosphere of postwar political and social conditions, grew ripe for the ideas of National Socialism. Instruction at the academy near Bad Berka, and the ideas of the reform headmaster Hermann Lietz—who believed in an educational rather than an instructional school—made Baldur into a "decent anti-Semite" (his own definition). It also provided him with the basic principles with which he later inspired the Hitler Youth. Hans Severus Ziegler, later the deputy regional leader for Thuringia, became Schirach's first National Socialist mentor. The second, however, was Hitler, who took the fifteen-year-old under his wing.

Like Baldur, who, on Hitler's advice, studied English literature, art history and Egyptology in Munich, Henriette enrolled in art history at the university with the vague notion of perhaps one day switching to archaeology.[21]

At the end of 1931, Henriette and Baldur began planning their wedding. By chance, they got hold of a copy of the engagement and marriage order issued by SS Reich leader Heinrich Himmler for SS members. In it there is talk of "German Nordic-defined men," of "the selection and preservation of racially and genetically healthy good blood," as well as the necessity of checking those wishing to marry through the Race Office of the SS.[22] This decree—the forerunner of the later compulsory euthanasia and genocide of "'racially unsound" fellow citizens—initially seemed absurd even to party comrades. The engaged couple—both dark-haired—asked themselves, according to their own account, if they could have passed this marriage test. But then they noticed that not a single one of the SA or SS leaders known to them fitted that Nordic type. Later, Baldur von Schirach wrote in his memoirs that they had dismissed the whole thing as a short-lived New Year's joke.[23]

They were married on March 31, 1932, at the old Registrar's Office in Munich, the "Old Peter." Adolf Hitler and Ernst Röhm, chief of staff of the SA, with a face scarred from dueling, acted as witnesses. The latter excused himself shortly after the ceremony, pleading "urgent business." It was later discovered that the homosexual Röhm was involved in a blackmail affair at the time.[24]

The remainder of the party went to Hitler's apartment on Prinzregentenplatz for the wedding dinner. Hitler only had spaghetti with tomato sauce and an apple. Among the numerous gifts for the young couple's household was a guest book with an extremely topical first entry: "At time's turning point! Adolf Hitler" an allusion to those eleven million electors who had given him their votes in the Reich presidential elections on March 13, 1932. Conversation at the table was monopolized by Hitler. The first commercial flight in Germany was about to take off, and Hitler spoke for hours about the gigantic preparations for the next election campaign. In an innovative plan, the Nazi Party would charter a three-engined plane from Lufthansa in order to attend three mass rallies per day. He also told the newlyweds in detail of his fears, that his stomach might possibly not be able to take the flying around. The father of the bride, Heinrich Hoffmann, had been a fixture in Hitler's entourage for a long time. He was present at all his public appearances and on all the election campaign trips. In 1932, he also took part in these first "German flights." Later he was the only one permitted to interrupt the Reichstag sessions, and he was allowed to move about freely and take photographs unhindered and uncensored.

At the end of the wedding celebration, Hitler gave the newlywed Henriette a note with instructions for his future visits to the Schirach home: "I eat everything that Nature yields of her own accord: fruit, vegetables, vegetable oil. Please, spare me everything that animals give up against their will: meat, milk and cheese. From animals [I eat] only eggs." Hitler's wedding gift came sometime later. It was a young German shepherd that had won first prize at the dog show in Berlin. At the request of the owner, Hitler took the dog that had been so zealously trained it now posed a serious threat because it kept attacking people. Later, every year at Christmas, Hitler would send orchids.

With financial support from their parents, the young couple rented an apartment at #31 Königinstrasse, close to the English Garden which had been built according to the plans of the painter Franz von Defregger, who had lived here until his death.[25] With Henny's dowry, the couple bought a forester's cabin as a weekend retreat in Urfeld, close to the Bavarian Lake Walchen.

Baldur von Schirach married well. With the rise of the Nazi Party, his father-in-law's small business had expanded into a major publishing house and business empire. The publishing house alone employed more than three hundred people in 1943 and had a turnover of fifteen million Reichs marks.[26] At the time, the connection to Heinrich Hoffmann was like marrying into a ruling family. Baldur's father-in-law stood right at the top of the National Socialist hierarchy and always had access to Hitler. Because of that, Baldur von Schirach was also counted as part of the inner "court circle" and, with Henny, was invited to the Obersalzberg. His influential father-in-law served as a sounding board among the Fuehrer's guests and was always ready to intercede. For the ambitious Schirach, who possessed no support within the party and constantly had to strive for the Fuehrer's favour, his father-in-law's position was vital.

On October 30, 1931, Schirach had been appointed Reich Youth leader of the NSDAP. In June 1932, he gave up the leadership of the Nazi Students' Association in order to dedicate himself exclusively to the Hitler Youth. In October 1932 he organized the Reich Youth Conference in Potsdam, in which seventy thousand young people took part. The Hitler Youth membership increased dramatically. By September 1935, the number of members had reached 1.9 million boys and 1.26 million girls.[27]

Soon after her wedding, the nineteen-year-old Henriette joined the NSDAP. She did not have an official function within the party machinery, but alllied herself—with some minor exceptions—entirely with the goals of her husband, who was aiming for nothing less than complete control of the educational system in the German Reich.[28] The "intellectual schooling" of young people was also a great concern of Henriette von Schirach's. Hitler's definition of the Hitler Youth, "agile as greyhounds, hard as Krupp steel and tough as leather," seemed less than complete to her. She felt that the intellectual aspect was being neglected.

At the end of January, 1933, as the party was celebrating Hitler's assumption of power, Henriette von Schirach's first child was born at a Munich clinic. Hitler congratulated her personally with a bouquet of roses. Observing a Schirach family tradition, the baby girl was baptized Angelika Benedikta. Henriette and Baldur would also have three sons, Klaus, Robert and Richard.

The Reich Youth leader had also been a member of the Reichstag since August, 1932. In the spring of 1933, the Schirachs moved to Berlin and rented a house at #28 Bismarckstrasse on the Small Wannsee. There was a fashionable and well-groomed park next door, complete with flamingos, that frequently served as a backdrop for movie scenes depicting the wealthy. The Schirach's property bordered on the lakeshore, and the roomy, luxurious house had a beautiful entrance hall. Supporting this luxury were the Reich Youth leader's poems of homage to Hitler. Shirach's highly regarded poetry launched "Year one of National Socialist literature." People eagerly purchased the poems after Hitler's assumption of power, and they were printed in all the newspapers.

Life in Berlin, however, did not come up to Henny's expectations. She returned to Bavaria in 1934, and lived at the cabin in Urfeld, which had been bought as a weekend getaway. Baldur took a suite in the Hotel Kaiserhof in Berlin and lived the life of a commuter. The lovely house on the Wannsee was sold.

Shortly after, Henriette found an unoccupied house called "Aspenstein." This small, baroque style castle in Kochel near Lake Walchen, at the foot of Kesselbergstrasse, below Urfeld, had eleven rooms and chapel turrets. It had originally housed the abbots of the nearby Benediktbeuern seminary and was "a pleasant place to enjoy the summer." The Schirachs bought the dilapidated building, renovated it and spent a large part of their time there.

Among the many guests that Baldur and Henriette von Schirach invited to their little castle was SS leader Heinrich Himmler, who had participated in the brutal murder of one of the witnesses to their marriage, Ernst Röhm. The Schirachs did not seem to bear him any grudge, but were careful not to joke about Himmler's "engagement and marriage edict."

"He was congenial and quite relaxed," the Youth leader said of their guest. "Himmler enjoyed watching our children playing on the lawn in front of the house, saying, 'There, you see right away the Germanic race, the Nordic element.' When he left he said, 'I would like to give you a Julleuchter (earthenware candlestick holder) for your beautiful house.'"[29]

The Schirachs visited Himmler—who was usually not very sociable and was shunned in Nazi circles—and his wife in their house "Lindenfycht" near Gmund at the northern tip of Lake Tegern. They observed the private life of the feared Reich SS leader, who governed the concentration camps. "We sat down for coffee. Mrs. Himmler, a cool, serious woman, treated her husband badly. I had never seen a man as henpecked as Heinrich Himmler. He overflowed with kindness, but the kinder he was, the worse he was treated. At home, the SS leader was a nobody, always having to give in. Mrs. Himmler always addressed him as 'Heinrich,' in a severe tone. At dinner, he poured himself his customary cup of weak camomile tea ... [he] encouraged his wife to help herself [to this or that], and she would invariably say, 'No, I do not want any of that.'"[30]

Henriette, whom Goebbels had described as very witty, was capable of entertaining an entire table of guests. That evening, she repeatedly tried to inject some life into the party. But Mrs. Himmler nipped any attempts at humour in the bud with her silent disapproval. Later the Schirachs learned that Himmler had a mistress. Knowing his domineering wife, they were surprised that he had mustered the courage.

But the Schirachs socialized with Himmler less for private than for solid political reasons. The Reich SS leader preferred to recruit new SS members from among the Hitler Youth.

On November 10, 1938, the day after the "Kristallnacht" riots in Munich, Henriette called her husband in Berlin and reported that many homes occupied by Jews in the Bogenhausen district had been looted and that one Jewish family had sought refuge with her in her father's house. The looters had known exactly where to find their victims. The Trade Supervisory Office in Munich had had a printed list since February 1938, of all Jewish business owners, including their home addresses. As a member of the Reichstag, Schirach had voted in 1935 for the introduction of the race laws, and later wrote: "I was an anti-Semite, and I believed that it was possible to be an anti-Semite in a decent fashion." He shared that view with his wife. Nevertheless, after "Kristallnacht," he contacted his regional leaders and forbade the Hitler Youth from participating in these "criminal activities."[31]

The war put an end to Schirach's ambitions to achieve complete control over education in the Third Reich. In the winter of 1940 he joined the Wehrmacht as a volunteer and his wife only saw "Private Schirach" at Hotel Kaiserhof on occasional free Saturdays during training. At that time, Hitler decided to replace Schirach, whom he considered incompetent as leader of the Hitler Youth. But he told Henriette that he had other tasks in mind for her husband, "if he survived the French campaign."[32] Henriette hoped that her husband, given his American roots, would be sent to Washington as ambassador. Instead, on August 10, 1940, Hitler decreed in a signed letter: "... assume your new office now today ... your name will forever be linked to this undertaking ..."[33]

The new assignment was in Vienna, and Hitler spent a total of twenty minutes explaining to Schirach the duties of the "Gauleiter" (regional leader), Reich governor and lord mayor of Vienna. Henriette von Schirach recalled that her husband noted down only two sentences during the meeting: "Treat workers and artists equally importantly," and "Vienna is a pearl; I will give it the setting that is worthy of it." Hitler told him that "difficulties had arisen" in the cultural sector. In fact, there was a cultural vacuum in Vienna, which had come about after 1938 because of the emigration and banishment of Jewish artists and dissenters. Schirach was to distract the Viennese from their social problems with cultural activities and convince them of the political significance of the former capital city and court seat, now downgraded to a provincial town. Besides that, the Gauleiter of Vienna was to arrange for and support the evacuation of the immigrant Czechs and the deportation of approximately 60,000 Jews remaining in Vienna.[34]

Schirach's appointment to Vienna looked like an honorable promotion—only the regional administrators of Berlin and Munich ranked higher—but, in fact, he was being sent away to disguise the fact that he had lost his influence over the education of young people.

The prospect of moving with her three children to Vienna, greatly pleased Henriette, who was very zealous in matters of culture. "I admit that I forgot the whole war at the idea of being allowed to live in Vienna," she wrote in her memoirs.[35] The task of choosing a suitable residence was an easy one, for the number of properties at the disposal of the regional administrator was enormous. The city of Vienna hastily offered the Hofburg, the former imperial residence in the city center. Hitler suggested Belvedere Castle, the former summer residence of Prince Eugene. The Schirachs chose a villa in Döbling, at #52–54 Hohe Warte (today, home to the Egyptian embassy), which had already been "Aryanized" and occupied by Schirach's predecessor, Gauleiter Bürckel. The property included a large garden. It bordered on the Rothschild botanical garden, which was deserted by this time. Its owner had emigrated, leaving behind his fortune.

The Vienna edition of the *Völkischer Beobachter* of August 28, 1940, welcomed with pleasure the arrival of the new Gauleiter.[36] Among the population, however, the Schirachs encountered barely concealed hostility and rejection. "It never occurred to us that we were appearing as representatives of the hated Hitler, as usurpers, intruders ...," Henriette said naively.[37] Yet her husband's first official act on August 15, 1940, had been to hand over the "former Parliament, which had served as an ill-conceived representative of the people, to its true and genuine destiny as 'Gauhaus,' or Regional House."[38]

By 1940, the Viennese were extremely dissatisfied. The initial euphoria over Austria's annexation had vanished. "While in the first few days after the union, the Bavarian breakdown train distributed its uneatable gullasch [sic] as alms to the people, at the same time, thousands of cattle from the Alpine regions were shipped off to the Old Reich," an anonymous person wrote to the Reich Governor, and another noted,

"If unemployment has now disappeared because of the war, it must be noted that this solution of the question is not to everyone's taste."[39] Living conditions had not improved, but had in fact worsened. The key positions in the party, administration and business had been filled with Reich-German functionaries, and the feeling of having been downgraded to a provincial town of the Prussian empire was spreading.[40]

In accordance with the Fuehrer's instructions, Schirach dedicated himself to the task of making Vienna a "Jew-free city." Since the union, the Jewish population had been pressured to emigrate through persecution and terror. The aim was to confiscate their property and possessions and force them to leave the country. Desperate, the president of the Jewish congregation, Dr. Löwenherz, urged on by lieutenant colonel Adolf Eichmann, administrator of the Jewish Section, traveled around the world begging for the acceptance of Austrian Jews. Eichmann authorized Dr. Löwenherz to tell the American Joint Distribution Committee that no deportations to Poland would take place if the Committee made foreign currency available and if the "Dejewing of Vienna" could be completed by the end of 1940.[41] Löwenherz also attended the conference in Evian, where thirty-two countries argued about the fate of the refugees and then refused to accept any of them for trivial reasons.[42] Where two hundred thousand Jews had lived in Vienna before the union, at Schirach's assumption of his post, there were only sixty thousand left. When England entered the war, the exodus of Jews from Vienna came to a standstill, and the long threatened deportation began in 1940.[43]

Schirach demanded that the governor general of Poland, Hans Frank, "take the Jews off his hands."[44] In public speeches he mocked the attempts by Dr. Löwenherz to spare the elderly and sick from the deportations.

In January 1941, Eichmann published the first transport lists and by June, ten thousand Jews had been deported to Poland. According to Schirach's letter to the Gestapo of February 7, 1941, he reserved for himself "the proviso on decisions related to Jew measures re stays of deportation."[45] In the fall of 1942, when the number of Jewish residents had dropped to seven thousand, the Gauleiter prided himself on having made his "active contribution to European culture" with the deportations.[46] Later, Schirach partially admitted his guilt, but denied his active role and shifted the blame to Himmler. He also claimed to have believed that the resettled Jews would be employed in Poland as artisans in the textile industry and be able to lead a pleasant life. "I trusted Dr. Frank," he stated for the record.

But Henriette von Schirach—as she later claimed—noticed nothing at all of the general conditions and the atmosphere in Vienna, although one contemporary witness reported: "The removal of Jews to Poland took place in public. The trucks stood before the houses, while the people assigned to this carried out the evacuation. Every passer-by saw this."[47]

The Gauleiter's wife allegedly also did not know that, shortly after taking office, her husband had pressed for the "branding of all Jews and their dwellings without exception" with the Star of David.[48] It also escaped her notice that Baldur von Schirach had forbidden Jews to enter the Vienna Woods, the Frendenau, all public gardens and baths, that they were allowed to use neither streetcars nor municipal trains, could not make calls from public phones or send any mail. By order of the Reich governor, Jews felled timber in the Vienna Woods on Sundays without pay and cleaned the streets of the city. Henriette, who prided herself on her good powers of observation, also didn't notice that Jews were only allowed to shop in certain stores. And the fact that her husband refused any personal conversation with Jews also escaped her notice during their life together.[49]

Henriette was more interested in the cultural offensive initiated by the Fuehrer's headquarters, than in the fate of her fellow human beings. Vienna's arts and culture were in a deep crisis at the time that could no longer be ignored. The decline had already begun with Austria's introduction of the "class state," when the "Austrian Art Office," in charge of censorship and propaganda, had created conditions that drove many artists, especially film directors, out of the country. The union with the German state then set in motion the exodus of the Jewish artists. Those who did not leave the homeland of their own accord were prohibited from working and faced deportation. Life-threatening conditions suffocated all creativity. The Nazi Reich Chamber for Cultural Affairs, with its subsections for pictorial art, music, theater, film, radio, literature and the press, monitored those allowed to practice a profession. The orientation toward Germany, on the other hand, led many renowned artists to move to the vibrant metropolis of Berlin. Vienna's Burgtheater and the State Opera, in particular, suffered from the loss of their best performers. Austria's cultural scene was becoming a wasteland.

Despite the war—related restrictions—the offensive against England was in full swing—the Schirachs attempted to restore the old traditions and were to some extent successful. They defied Goebbel's ban and a performance of the modern opera *Johanna Balk* by Wagner-Régeny was produced. Leading artists like Furtwängler, Knappertsbusch, Clemens Krauss and Karl Böhm received long-term contracts. Honorary rings of the city of Vienna were awarded and tribute was paid to famous artists. The Schirachs celebrated the eightieth birthday of Gerhart Hauptmann in 1942 at their home, and two years later they did the same for eighty-year-old Richard Strauss.

Soon, Vienna's star seemed to be shining more brightly than Berlin's. Meanwhile, Baldur von Schirach, who was so concerned about Austria's cultural heritage, dissolved the venerable Klosterneuburg Canons Monastery.[50] That action was triggered by a secret report by Bormann, head of the Reich Chancellery, claiming that the population would not oppose the removal of monasteries. The transformation into an Adolf Hitler School was already decided on, but because of the war, never came to be. Henriette von Schirach later tried to shift the blame to Bormann and claimed that she had intervened with Hitler for the preservation of the Austrian monasteries.

The Shirachs enjoyed staging public and formal events. In order to avoid any social faux pas, they resorted to court protocol from the time of Emperor Franz Joseph, and staged events in the imperial style. The footmen served in Hapsburg liveries, using china and cutlery from the imperial silverware chamber. In his banquet speeches, Schirach liked to mention the fact that the Empress Maria Theresia had ennobled his ancestors. Like Emperor Franz Joseph, Baldur von Schirach annually sent out invitations to hunt wild boar and fallow deer at the "Lainzer Tiergarten," the former imperial hunting preserve.[51] The princely lifestyle of the Schirachs sparked criticism. One diplomat wrote that "Schirach appears with the daughter of the Reich's foremost drunk, Hoffmann, and [acts like] a sovereign, while his braided adjutant whispers the names of the guests ... Hypocrisy is written on his face, [while] he behaves skilfully and obligingly, [playing] the haughty party bigwig..."[52]

"In Vienna, Henriette and I kept a very hospitable house. At my official villa at #52 Hohe Warte, diplomats and artists were guests almost every evening. Hitler had sent me to Vienna not least because my predecessor Brückel had concerned himself too little with the wishes of the city by the Danube. After the union, Vienna had fallen more and more into the shadow of the theater city of Berlin. I tried to change that," Baldur von Schirach said of his life in Vienna.[53] Hitler came to Vienna on February 28, 1941 on the occasion of Bulgaria's admission to the Three Power pact. Following the ceremony, Hitler invited the Bulgarian foreign minister, Count Ciano, ambassador Oshima and Ribbentrop to breakfast at the Belvedere, Prince Eugene's former luxury castle, which the Gauleiter's wife was also permitted to attend.[54] He then spent the evening with the Schirachs and a few guests on the Hohe Warte. On March 25, Hitler returned to Vienna to celebrate Yugoslavia's entry into the tripartite pact.[55] The Gauleiter gave a dinner, to which Henriette von Schirach invited young Viennese artistic notables. Hitler was in high spirits. But when he began to speak about the city on the Danube, in which he had lived from 1907 to 1913, his good mood darkened. He erupted into vehement criticism and concluded with the words: "In Vienna, everything is sloppy." Then, at midnight, he went on a nostalgic tour through the sleeping city, accompanied by the Schirachs. Full of enthusiasm, he pointed out the Karlskirche, the Parliament, Maria at the Waterside and other sights that he had drawn in his youth.[56] In his monologues at the "Werewolf," the Fuehrer's headquarters in the Ukraine, Hitler talked about this visit to Vienna. After mentioning that the Schirachs had been "completely captivated by the atmosphere of the city," he said, "Now [that] I have been in Vienna again, the filth [the Jewish population] is gone, but it has become a poor city ..."[57]

In the spring of 1943, Henriette von Schirach traveled to the occupied Netherlands, where she witnessed the deportation of Jewish women and children firsthand. "I woke up in the middle of the night—hearing loud screaming and shouting. I rushed to the window ... beneath me, on the street, stood a few hundred women with bundles, clearly hastily rounded up, guarded by men in uniform. One heard crying and then a clear commando voice: 'Aryans stay back!' At that, the procession started to move and disappeared over the bridge in the darkness. The next morning no one would tell me anything about the mysterious line-up ... But my friend Miedl, who came to pick me up, had been informed: 'That's an evacuation of Jewesses!'—'Are the Germans doing this?'—'Who else?'—'Does Hitler know about this?'"[58] Henriette took seriously his sarcastic reply that she should report the incident to Hitler if he really knew nothing about it.

According to her account, her husband was sitting in the dining hall of the Berghof on the evening of Good Friday, 1943, while she confronted Hitler with the incident. He shouted at her, "You are sentimental! What concern of yours are the Jewesses in Holland!" Then, he formed two scales with his hands. "You see, each day ten thousand of my most valuable men die ... the best. The balance is no longer correct, the balance in Europe is out of order. Because those who are inferior don't die in the camps, they survive, and what will Europe look like then in a hundred years? In a thousand? ... I am only bound to my people, no one else ..."

Hitler, according to Henriette, then flew into one of his rages, while the other guests sitting around the fireplace in the great hall fell silent and stared uncomfortably at the floor. Nobody spoke up for her, Henriette wrote accusingly, and finally she and her husband hurriedly left the Obersalzberg. They had shaken with fear of retaliation for a long time. After the controversy at the Berghof, the Gauleiter of Vienna was "politically a dead man."[59]

Goebbels, who had also been present, wrote in his diary that Henny acted like a silly goose and noted cynically that the Schirachs had only discovered their compassion "after almost sixty thousand Jews had been deported from their own doorstep."[60]

A further account accurately details the events of the evening:[61] A briefing on the plan for a new offensive in the Russian campaign with the objective of taking Kursk had tired Hitler and put him in a bad mood. Nonetheless, Schirach made a cautious proposal for more humane treatment of the Russian civilian population, and was abruptly silenced. An attempt to paint a rosy picture of Vienna and the Viennese for the Fuehrer failed miserably. "I know these people," Hitler observed, "They hailed me after the union. That means nothing. They are fickle and have, in the past, cheered even for the most vile of characters, because they are racially inferior, a hodgepodge of many different peoples and races." At that, Henriette von Schirach requested that her husband be transferred to Munich. The atmosphere was already quite tense when she started talking about the Dutch Jewesses. Hitler allegedly reacted coolly, but remained calm.

In the course of an interview that Jochen von Lang conducted with the Schirachs, he drew their attention to the measures for the creation of a "Jew-free" Vienna carried out between 1940 and 1943. It seems that it was only the manner of the evacuation that had outraged them, the police screaming and kicking the slow ones, and the wailing of the victims. The interview contradicted their belief that the Germans had handled the Jews strictly, but always fairly.[62]

They were not banished from Hitler's entourage. At the end of June, 1943, Baldur von Schirach was dining on the Obersalzberg again, and arranging a meeting between Hitler and the Norwegian poet Knut Hamsun.

On September 10, 1944, the first heavy American air attack on Vienna took place. It was meant primarily for the northwest part of the city center. On November 4, a bomb landed in the immediate vicinity of the Schirach villa at Hohe Warte. "The doors and windows of our house were torn out, furniture and books lay in an awful jumble ... our kitchen was hurled into a muddled heap of dishes and fragments, the electrical current was interrupted ...," was how Henriette von Schirach described the scene.[63]

From their shelter constructed on the Gallitzinberg, Baldur von Schirach watched the devastation. When his attempt to have Vienna declared an open city was rejected by the Fuehrer's headquarters, he sent Henriette with the children to their country home "Aspenstein" in Bavaria.

At the beginning of April 1945, Schirach left his residence on the Hohe Warte for the shelter beneath the Hofburg. Shortly after, he retreated before the approaching Soviet troops to the west of Austria. He could take very little with him, and packed his most valuable treasures into a trunk. The contents of the "gold trunk," which would continue to be significant in the post-war period, were estimated at 500,000 German marks (1958 rates) and included a painting by Rubens, one by Renoir, several volumes of classic books, as well as original letters from Goethe to his son August. These were part of the estate of Schirach's American mother, who had come from a wealthy family.

After he fled, Austrian freedom fighters broke into the Schirachs' country villa in the Helene Valley near Baden at the end of April, 1945, where they found not only supplies of foodstuffs on an enormous scale, but also a large number of Gobelin tapestries and objects d'art that the governing couple had appropriated from the Schönbrunn Palace, the Klosterneuburg Monastery, as well as various Viennese museums.[64]

Schirach's adjutant Höpke deposited the "gold trunk" at a secluded farm in Pinzgau. Schirach then assumed the name "Dr. Falk," disguising himself with glasses and a beard, and volunteered as an interpreter to the Americans at Schwaz in Tyrol. Only Schirach's wife and Höpke knew the agreed password, "Dr. Faust," that would signal the farmer to hand over the trunk to an envoy.[65]

On June 21, 1945 the couple were reunited, not at the agreed-upon rendezvous at a small, remote hotel in the mountains near Kufstein in Tyrol, but in the Rum internment camp near Innsbruck. Baldur von Schirach had suddenly renounced National Socialism and given himself up to the Americans of his own accord.

Henriette von Schirach could not comprehend her husband's change of heart. "Why didn't you escape? You could have disappeared," she asked him during their brief encounter at the prison camp. No one would have suspected the harmless writer Dr. Richard Falk—the forged papers were first-class. Moreover, Schirach was believed dead, beaten to death by an angry Viennese mob.

Henriette was extremely upset that her husband was showing more loyalty to the Hitler Youth leaders than to his own family. Suddenly left on her own with four small children, she was forced to abandon her hopes for an escape abroad, which a short while ago had seemed within reach.

Baldur von Schirach was flown to Nuremberg on September 10, 1945. Henriette and the children were made to pay the full price for their former glory. In the streets, people reviled them as "Nazis," and old acquaintances avoided them. The anger of the population was directed against Henriette, the wife of a Nazi bigwig and war criminal.

On November 1, 1945, the Viennese *Arbeiter-Zeitung* wrote: "So much honor, so much bad luck! He [Heinrich Hoffmann] is in prison, his son-in-law is in prison ..." Both Henriette's father and husband were being held by the International Military Court in Nuremberg. She was forced to leave Aspenstein and returned to the cabin in Urfeld, which she had bought with her dowry. Pillagers raided Aspenstein and it finally served as command headquarters for the American Tenth Armed Division. On December 24, 1945, Henriette von Schirach was transferred to the women's camp in Tölz. Her four children were taken into care. After three months of internment, she was released in the spring of 1946 without explanation.

The trial of the Allied Military Court of Justice, at which Baldur von Schirach had to testify as one of the main defendants, was already underway. Henriette was trying to get hold of witnesses and material for the defence and frequently came to Nuremberg. There she also saw her father, who, now slim and abstinent, was putting his huge picture archive in order for the Americans. When asked about Hitler, he claimed to have only fleetingly known the man. He had sought him out on assignment for an American photo agency for purely professional reasons. In the fall of 1946, Henriette von Schirach decided it was time to send for the "gold trunk," still in safekeeping in Pinzgau. She sent a female courier, who gave the farmer the proper password and was handed the trunk. It contained only six worthless volumes of classics.

Two weeks before sentencing was handed down by the Nuremberg tribunal, Henriette was allowed to speak to her husband: "There we are in small talking cells, one next to the other. Between the accused and us, a fine-meshed grating is drawn; when I try to push a cigarette through, it gets stuck. May we shake hands? No, that is forbidden," is how Henriette depicted the encounter.[66]

Shortly after Schirach was sentenced to twenty years imprisonment in Spandau, Henriette was again arrested and interned in the Göggingen women's camp near Augsburg. While she waited for a denazification trial, the Schirach children were threatened with assignment to a foster home.

On December 11, 1947, the prosecutor finally preferred charges against Henriette von Schirach and classified her as an old party member in Group II (politically incriminated). At the subsequent hearing, prominent witnesses like Hans Carossa, Kasimir Edschmid and Waldemar Bonsels appeared for the defence. On December 16, 1947,

*"The price of glory" – Henriette von Schirach on her way to the internment camp
(Göggingen near Augsburg), June 1947*

judgment of the Bad Tolz tribunal was handed down: Henriette von Schirach was regarded as a "less incriminated person of the Nazi regime" since, apart from her party membership since 1932 and her marriage to Baldur von Schirach, nothing incriminating could be proven. She was fined 2,000 marks and put on probation for a year.[67]

Once again free, Henriette von Schirach vehemently protested the expropriation of Aspenstein, which had been turned over by the U.S. military government to the SPD (German Socialist Party) as a training facility. She pounded on the door of her former property and demanded the key. When she was threatened with violence, she filed charges of intimidation. But Aspenstein, no matter how hard she tried, remained lost to her. She did get the Urfeld cabin back, because she was able to prove that it had not been acquired with her husband's money.

In the period that followed, Henriette lived from hand to mouth, taking a variety of jobs. As an advertising consultant for the film and theater director Erik Charell she dropped the name Schirach. "In the time that followed, I changed my name, used the first names of my boys and was called Roberts or Richards. Sometimes I mixed them up. When I was working for Erik Charell who needed pictures for his production of *Das weiße Rößl* (The White Horse Inn), I introduced myself as Richards, and later, switched in confusion to Roberts. Charell grew suspicious, now wanting to find out who I really was, and I knew that he wanted nothing to do with Nazis. So, I could only withdraw of my own accord...," Henriette wrote.[68] In Munich, she started a small film distribution business under the name of "Paris Film." Her idea of making a movie about the atempted assassination of Hitler on July 20, 1944, was met with scandalized rejection in the press.[69] In 1949, Henriette von Schirach made headlines when she became involved with the film producer, Peter Jacob, who was embroiled in a casino incident, and filed for divorce from her imprisoned husband.

The press at that time expressed the opinion that it was unreasonable for her to be married to a war criminal. Henriette immediately responded in the daily *Süddeutsche Zeitung* of October 10, 1950. "... he is no criminal, but an idealist, and much too good for politics." Albert Speer, a fellow prisoner of Schirach's in the Spandau jail, noted at the time: "Today ... heard that Mrs. von Schirach has been severing relations with her husband for over a year and has started a new relationship.

But after all, it was a marriage in which she was partly interested in his power and he was partly after her money. The children are said to have taken their father's side ..."[70] Baldur von Schirach agreed to the divorce, and the marriage was dissolved in early November, 1950. His fellow prisoners got the impression that the matter did not affect him very much. He actually wanted to prevent Henriette from publishing memoirs under the name Schirach because he was planning to do so after his release.

Peter Jacob went bankrupt over dubious film deals, which he had financed with what remained of Henriette's money. She remembered the "gold trunk" once again and in January 1956, more than ten years after the end of the war, and six months after the signing of the Austrian State Treaty, went into action. On January 3, she appeared at the Innsbruck police station, and to the amazement of the police made a claim that valuable luggage had been stolen from her in the postwar chaos, and brought charges against persons unknown. "Have the soldiers wrapped their sandwiches in Goethe's letters, sold the souvenirs whose value they did not recognize, for a pack of cigarettes?" speculated the *Frankfurter Allgemeine*.

Henriette von Schirach stated under oath that she had only heard about the trunk in 1955, but this was refuted by witnesses. She was summoned before a lay court, charged with perjury, and fined three hundred marks.[71] The contents of the trunk were not found.

The trial attracted attention and served as publicity for Henriette von Schirach's first book, which she wrote at the suggestion of an American publisher. The unambiguous title of her memoirs, *The Price of Glory*, raised no doubts as to the political views of the author, who—as her ex-husband would also later do—slipped into the role of the innocent, misled young person who learned too late about the Nazi crimes. Henriette was able to finance a modest life with her "postwar creations," as the newspapers referred to her literary production. In 1958, she declared her income to be between five hundred and seven hundred marks a month.

In 1956, the debate about the three Spandau inmates—Hess, Speer and Schirach—flared up again. In view of the long period in prison and the high costs, many argued in the international, and especially the British, press in favor of an early release of the war criminals.

Henriette went to London to present a petition to the British foreign minister for a reduction of her ex-husband's twenty-year sentence. She was unsuccessful.

With the release of a new edition of her book *The Price of Glory*, Austrian television invited Henriette Hoffmann-von Schirach, as she now called herself, to take part in its talk show *Club 2* on October 28, 1976. Henriette dominated the entire program, exhorting the other panelists to be proud of their compatriot, the Austrian Hitler. She also compared the American internment camps to the Nazi concentration camps. The panelists accused her of being an accessory to Nazi crimes. The heated debate continued after the program ended. The *Arbeiter-Zeitung* responded to protests on October 31, 1976, "But it was [an] unmasking, [and] one could not have wished it more dramatic." While the *Wiener Zeitung* had advocated the day before: "… put an end to this once and for all … the prominent [Nazis] should never again be given a platform for agitation."

Henriette von Schirach continued her book production unwearied. *Anekdoten um Hitler* (Hitler Anecdotes) appeared in 1980 and in 1983, *Frauen um Hitler* (Women around Hitler) was published, based on material provided by Henriette Hoffmann-von Schirach. She eagerly gave interviews when asked. But with advancing age, her memory deteriorated. Statements grew vague, facts and figures receded, and she confused fact and fiction. Only her positive attitude toward the Nazi regime remained unchanged.

Henriette Hoffmann-von Schirach died on January 27, 1992.

REFERENCES AND SOURCES

Publisher's note: The sources and references listed here are, in most cases, in German. Even where an English version may exist, the German title has been quoted, because the page numbers cited by the author refer to the German version of the respective reference.

Hitler and the "German Woman"

[1] Sabine Weiberg, *Der Hitler-Putsch.* In: *München - Hauptstadt der Bewegung.* Exhibition catalog. Munich 1993, p.114 f.

[2] Albert Speer, *Spandauer Erinnerungen.* Frankfurt/Main-Berlin-Vienna 1975, p. 122 f.

[3] Alfred Maleta, *Bewältigte Vergangenheit.* Österreich 1932-1945. Graz 1981, p. 52.

[4] Postcard from Elsa Bruckmann, Munich, June 2, 1925, The Azimuth Museum, Independance, Missouri, USA.

[5] Werner Maser, *Die Frühgeschichte der NSDAP Hitlers Weg bis 1924.* Frankfurt/Main - Bonn 1965, p. 409.

[6] Adolf Hitler, Monologe im Führerhauptquartier 1941-1944. Die Aufzeichnungen Heinrich Heims. Edited by Werner Jochmann. Hamburg 1980, p. 259.

[7] *Der Hitler-Putsch.* Bavarian documents regarding November 8/9, 1923. Edited by Ernst Deuerlein. Stuttgart 1962, p. 561.

[8] Gottfried Feder quoted by Ernst Hanfstaengl, 15 *Jahre mit Hitler.* Zwischen Weißem und Braunem Haus. Munich 1980, p. 57.

[9] Hitler, Monologe, p.174.

[10] Alfred Rosenberg, *Der Mythos des XX. Jahrhunderts.* Munich 1930, p. 512.

[11] Engelbert Huber, *Das ist Nationalsozialismus.* Stuttgart 1933, p.121 f.

[12] Hitler, Monologe, p. 235.

[13] Mathilde Ludendorff, *Die Volksseele und ihre Machtgestalter.* Munich 1936.

[14] David Pryce-Jones, *Die Mitfords. Ein Familienroman aus der englischen Aristokratie.* Frankfurt/Main 1990.

[15] This and other entries from Goebbels' diaries are taken from: *Die Tagebücher von Joseph Goebbels.* Edited by Elke Fröhlich. Part I. Aufzeichnungen 1924-1941. Sämtliche Fragmente. 4 vols., Munich 1987. Entry dated January 19, 1931.

[16] Joseph Goebbels, *Deutsches Frauentum*. In *Signale der neuen Zeit*. 25 ausgewählte Reden von Dr. Joseph Goebbels. Munich 1934, p.118.

[17] Joseph Goebbels, *Michael - Ein deutsches Schicksal in Tagebuchblättern*. Munich 1929, p. 41.

[18] Hitler on November 23, 1937. In: *Max Domarus, Hitler. Reden und Proklamationen 1932-1945*. Vol. I, Triumph (1932-1938), Würzburg 1962, p. 452.

[19] Hitler at Fuehrer Headquarters on August 19/20, 1941.

[20] C. Rosen, *Das ABC des Nationalsozialismus*. Berlin 1933, p.199.

[21] Münchner Neueste Nachrichten, No.169. Quoted in Joachim Fest, *Das Gesicht des Dritten Reiches. Profile einer totalitären Herrschaft*. Munich 1980, p. 356.

[22] Carlo Schultheis, *Frauen trugen das Eiserne Kreuz*. In: Das militärische Archiv No. 3/1994, p.12.

[23] Hanna Reitsch, *Das Unzerstörbare in meinem Leben*. Autobiography. Munich 1975.

[24] Hitler, Monologe, p. 201.

[25] Hitler aus nächster Nähe. Aufzeichnungen eines Vertrauten 1929–1932, Edited by H. A. Turner, Berlin 1978. Chapter 12 – Hitlers Privatleben.

[26] Hitler, Monologe, p. 308.

[27] Letter dated January 24, 1944. In: H. Trevor-Roper (Ed.), *The Bormann Letters. The private correspondence between Martin Bormann and his wife from January 1943 to April 1945*. London 1954, p. 42 ff.

[28] Adolf Hitler to Fritz Lauböck, NS 26/ 14. Federal Archives Koblenz.

[29] Letter dated May 28, 1928. In: Werner Maser, *Hitlers Briefe und Notizen. Sein Weltbild in handschriftlichen Dokumenten*. Düsseldorf 1973, p.123 ff

[30] Hitler, Monologe, p.109.

[31] Felix Kersten, *Totenkopf und Treue. Aus den Tagebuchblättern des finnischen Medizinalrats Felix Kersten*. Hamburg (no year), p. 229 ff

[32] Hitler at Reich party congress 1934. Quoted in Domarus, *Hitler*, p. 450.

[33] Albert Speer, *Spandauer Tagebücher*. Frankfurt/ Main-Berlin-Vienna, p. 90.

[34] Hitler, Monologe, on March 1, 1942, p. 309 f.

[35] Trevor-Roper, *The Bormann Letters*, p. 45.

[36] Ernst Kaltenbrunner's testimony before International Military Tribunal (IMT) in Nuremberg. Quoted in Joachim C. Fest, *Das Gesicht des Dritten Reiches. Profile einer totalitären Herrschaft*. Munich 1963, p. 369.

Carin Goering – Nordic Idol and Cult Figure

[1] Fanny Countess Wilamowitz-Moellendorf, née. Baroness Fock, Carin Göring's sister, took part in the funeral procession. In: *Carin Göring.* Berlin 1942, p.156 ff.

[2] Wilamowitz, *Carin Göring*, p. 57.

[3] Björn Fontander, *Göring och Sverige.* Stockholm 1984, p.18 f. Based on a translation, comments and anecdotes of Agneta Newton-Silfverskiöld, to whom I am eternally grateful. Her father, Dr. Nils Silfverskiöld, was, while he was married to Mary von Rosen, a member of Carin Göring's family.

[4] Alfred Kube, *Pour le merite und Hakenkreuz.* Quellen und Darstellungen zur Zeitgeschichte, Vol. 24. Munich 1986, p. 6 ff.

[5] Information according to Curt Riess. Käthe Dorsch left Goering after three years in 1920 to marry the actor Harry Liedtke zu heiraten. But they remained friends.

[6] Based on information provided by Mary von Rosen, who, on February 20, 1920, witnessed the first encounter between Goering and Carin von Kantzow. Based on a conversation with Agneta Newton-Silfverskiöld.

[7] Göring, letter dated February 22, 1924, to his mother-in-law. Quoted in Wilamowitz, *Carin Göring*, p. 92.

[8] Marriage to Nils von Kantzow on July 7, 1910; son Thomas was born on March 1, 1913.

[9] Fontander, *Göring*, p. 27 f.

[10] Biographical information according to Wilamowitz-Moellendorf, *Erinnerungen und Begegnungen.* Berlin 1936, p. 9 ff

[11] Quoted in David Irving, *Göring.* Munich and Hamburg 1986, p. 56.

[12] Leonard Mosley, *Göring. Eine Biographie.* Munich 1975, p. 40.

[13] Fontander, *Göring*, p. 27.

[14] Carin's correspondence was later kept, together with Goering's diaries and notes, at Carinhall. In 1945, when the frontline was closing in, everything was transferred to Berchtesgaden, where it was looted later on. The bulk of the correspondence was sold to private collectors. Some of it ended up in the USA. Copies of 101 letters written by Carin were kept by the family and then published by her sister Fanny Wilamowitz in *Carin Göring*.

[15] Letter dated May 5, 1922. Quoted in *Fontander*.

[16] Alfred Kube, *Hermann Göring - Zweiter Mann im Dritten Reich.* In: *Die braune Elite I*. Darmstadt 1989, p. 71.

[17] Trial records–Nuremberg Trials; Der Prozeß gegen die Hauptkriegsverbrecher vor dem Internationalen Militärgerichtshof. Nuremberg

1947. IX, p. 489.

[18] Adolf Hitler on January, 3/4, 1942 at Wolfsschanze. *Adolf Hitler, Monologe im Führerhauptquartier 1941-1944. Die Aufzeichnungen von Heinrich Heimp.* Edited by Werner Jochmann. Hamburg 1980, p.172.

[19] Marriage certificate issued by Registrar's Office Obermenzing dated February 3, 1923. Institute for Contemporary History, Munich. Private papers of Goering's. ED 180/l.

[20] Fontander, *Göring*, p. 45.

[21] ibid., p. 44.

[22] Letter by Carin Goering to her mother. January 1923. Quoted in Wilamowitz, *Carin Göring*.

[23] Wilamowitz, *Carin Göring*, p. 20.

[24] Letter by Carin Goering after March 15, 1923. Quoted in Wilamowitz, *Carin Göring*.

[25] Report of the 95-year-old widow of officer Fevrel. Quoted in *Fontander*, Göring, p. 44.

[26] Letter. Quoted in Irving, *Göring*, p. 67.

[27] E. Deuerlein (Ed.), *Der Hitler-Putsch: Bavarian documents related to events on November 8/9, 1923.*

[28] Also see: Gerhard Jagschitz, *Die Nationalsozialisten in Österreich*, Graz 1976.

[29] Wilamowitz, *Carin Göring*, p. 68

[30] ibid., p. 92 ff.

[31] Otto Gritschneder, *Bewährungsfrist für den Terroristen Adolf H. Der Hitler-Putsch und die Bayerische Justiz.* Munich 1990.

[32] According to Agneta Newton-Silfverskiöld.

[33] Statement of Anna Törnquist, a nurse. Hermann Göring Collection ED 180 at Institute for Contemporary History, Munich.

[34] Fontander, *Göring*, p.101

[35] Certificate of Professor Olof Kirnberg. Göring Collection ED 180/1 at Institute for Contemporary History, Munich.

[36] Letter dated January 26, 1927. Quoted in Irving, *Göring*, p.124.

[37] Letter dated May 18, 1928. Quoted in Wilamowitz, *Carin Göring*, p.117.

[38] ibid., p.119.

[39] Henriette von Schirach, *Der Preis der Herrlichkeit.* Wiesbaden 1956, p.181.

[40] Letter dated February 28, 1930. Quoted in Wilamowitz, *Carin Göring*, p.126 ff.

[41] Ellen Rydelius, *Leva randigt.* Stockholm 1951, p.197 ff

[42] Göring Collection. ED 180/1 at Institute for Contemporary History,

Munich.

[43] Goebbels' diaries - *Die Tagebücher von Joseph Goebbels. Sämtliche Fragmente.* Edited by Elke Fröhlich, part I, vol. 2. Munich 1987. Entry dated January 4, 1931.

[44] Goebbels, *Tagebücher*. Entry dated January 29, 1933.

[45] According to Agneta Newton-Silfverskiöld, her father was the only one who made a point of remaining seated.

[46] Erich Gritzbach, *Hermann Göring. Werk und Mensch*. Munich 1938.

[47] Hans Schwab, *Das Hohelied der Liebe: Deutsches Werden*. Cologne 1933.

[48] Quoted in Wilamowitz, *Carin Göring*, p.141.

[49] Quoted according to Fontander, *Göring*. p.171.

[50] The Fock family rewarded pastor Jansson upon delivery of the receipt for the cremation with an agate bowl owned by Carin Goering. More information on the transfer of the urn can be found in Fontander, *Göring*, p. 264 ff.

Emmy Goering - The "Grand Lady"

[1] Files of the Ministry for Special Matters (MSO), dossier 1089, testimony of October 24, 1948. Bavarian Main State Archives Munich.
Akten des Ministeriums für Sonderangelegenheiten (MSO) Fasz. 1089, Zeugenaussage vom 24.10.1948. Bavarian Main State Archives Munich.

[2] Denazification trial of Emmy Goering. Indictment of prosecutor Julius Herf. MSO dossier 1089.

[3] According to information received from Barbara Ganzinger, née Rigele, who personally knew "Aunt Emmy," a great aunt of hers by marriage.

[4] Emmy Göring, *An der Seite meines Mannes-Begebenheiten und Bekenntnisse*. Göttingen 1967, p. 97.

[5] ibid., p.100.

[6] Henriette Schirach, *Frauen um Hitler*. Munich 1983, p.118.

[7] Emmy Göring, *An der Seite meines Mannes*. Göttingen 1967, p. 31.

[8] Baldur von Schirach, *Ich glaubte an Hitler*. Hamburg 1967, p.145 f.

[9] Goering's hunting diary dated September 26, 1936 – October 6, 1937. Library of Congress Ac. 9342.

[10] David Irving, *Göring*. Munich-Hamburg 1986, p.150.

[11] At "Kaiserhof," Hitler had an entire suite: a bedroom with bath, a room for his aide-de-camp and a parlor. The parlor was a corner room.

From the window facing west, he could look across Wilhelmsplatz and directly at the Reich Chancellery.

[12] Fritz Tobias, *Der Reichstagsbrand. Legende und Wirklichkeit.* Rastatt/Baden 1962.

[13] Power of attorney dated September 12, 1933.

[14] Letter by Phipps dated March 22, 1935 - FO 371/ 18879, copy at Institute for Contemporary History, Munich.

[15] Irving, *Göring.* p. 232.

[16] E. Göring, *An der Seite*, p. 65 f.

[17] *Die Braune Elite I.* Edited by Ronald Smelser, Rainer Zitelmann. Darmstadt 1992, p. 73.

[18] Contained in a dispatch dated March 10, 1933, of the Swedish Telegram Office TT - Tidningarnas Telegram Byrö.

[19] Louis Lochner. Letter dated April 20, 1935. Quoted in Irving, *Göring*, p. 230.

[20] Letter by Phipps dated April 15, 1935. FO 371/18879. Foreign Office, London.

[21] *Pariser Tageblatt* dated April 21, 1935. Klaus Mann, *Briefe und Antworten 1922-1949.* Reinbek 1991, p. 706.

[22] *Die Tagebücher von Joseph Goebbels. Sämtliche Fragmente.* Edited by Elke Fröhlich, part I, vol. 2. Munich 1987. Diary entry dated November 9, 1935.

[23] Circular issued by Reich ministry of justice to the presidents of regional courts and public prosecutors dated September 25, 1935. R 22/845 and 995. Federal archives in Koblenz.

[24] Klaus Mann, *Briefe und Antworten 1922-1949.* p. 707.

[25] Letter of prosecutor Kempner. RG 153, National Archives, Washington.

[26] Irving, *Göring*, p. 235.

[27] *Madonna ohne Makel.* In: *Spiegel* 1962/8, p. 39 ff.

[28] Documentation on Adolph Hitler 1944-1953. Compiled based on CIC files. F135/4 Minutes of the cross examination of Hitler's dentist Blaschke. Institute for Contemporary History, Munich.

[29] Irving, *Göring*, p. 245.

[30] E. Göring, *An der Seite*, p.130 f.

[31] Hermann Göring; private documents ED 188/4. Institute for Contemporary History, Munich.

[32] Bella Fromm, diary entry dated April 12, 1935, *Als Hitler mir die Hand küßte* (When Hitler Kissed my Hand). Berlin 1993, p. 224.

[33] According to Barbara Ganzinger in May 1998.

[34] Robert M. W Kempner, *Das Dritte Reich im Kreuzverhör.* The unpub-

lished transcripts of the cross examinations of the prosecutor. Munich and Esslingen 1969, p. 172.

[35] Membership approved by Hitler - MA 743, Institute for Contemporary History, Munich.

[36] Lower membership numbers were sought after, because they were more prestigious and showed an early affiliation with the NSDAP.

[37] Excerpt from the indictment before the denazification court of the labor camp Garmisch-Partenkirchen. Gen. Reg. 204/46 dated July 20, 1948, MSO 1048, Bavarian Main State Archives, Munich.

[38] E. Göring, *An der Seite*, p. 72.

[39] More details to be found in Irving, *Göring*, p. 26.

[40] Letter to State Minister for Special Matters, Hagenauer, dated October 31, 1947.

[41] ibid.

[42] Six-page letter, summarizing the events, dated November 4, 1947, MSO, 1244 and 1084,
Bavarian Main State Archives, Munich.

[43] Irving, *Göring*, p. 761.

[44] Henriette von Schirach, *Der Preis der Herrlichkeit*. Wiesbaden 1956, p. 99.

[45] E. Göring, *An der Seite*, p. 305 ff.

[46] Jack Wheelis, who died in 1954. Cf. Irving, *Göring*, p. 767.

[47] Kempner, *Das Dritte Reich*, p.172.

[48] H. Schirach, *Der Preis*, p.149.

[49] Letter by Emmy Goering dated October 31, 1947. EMSo 1048. Bavarian Main State Archives Munich.

[50] Emmy Goering herself claimed that she had not received an increase in pay.

[51] Indictment for denazification trial on July 20, 1948, MSO 1048, Bavarian Main State Archives, Munich. Also see: Klaus Mann, Mephisto (1936), about Gustaf Gründgens' theater career during the NS regime.

[52] Quoted in *Frankenpost* dated July 21, 1948.

[53] MSO, 1048 - Bavarian Main State Archives, Munich.

[54] On July 11, 1949, Emmy Goering applied for a trial under the Liberation Act. M/St. 6205 - 57 MSO 1048 and 1089, Bavarian Main State Archives Munich.

[55] Letter by Dr. Auberbach of the Bavarian Regional Office for Restitution, dated June 30, 1949. MSO 1048, Bavarian Main State Archives, Munich.

[56] *Der Spiegel*, 1962/8, p. 39 ff.

[57] *Wer schrieb Emmy Görings Memoiren?* (Who wrote Emmy

Goering's memoirs?) Z 18 - Institute for Contemporary History, Munich.
58 *Der Spiegel*, 1968l5, p. 45 ff.
59 *Die Zeit*, report of March 30, 1973.

Magda Goebbels – The First Lady of the Third Reich

[1] Biographical information according to Erich Ebermayer / Hans Roos, *Gefährtin des Teufels. Leben und Tod der Magda Goebbels* (The Devil's companion. The life and death of Magda Goebbels). Hamburg 1952. Satirical treatment of Ebermayer's book in Robert Neumann, *Magda Goebbels* in: *Mit fremden Federn. Der Parodien zweiter Band*. Frankfurt/Main 1955, p.133 ff:

[2] Bella Fromm, *Als Hitler mir die Hand küßte*. Berlin 1993, p.130.

[3] Volker Ellis Pilgrim, *Du kannst mich ruhig Frau Hitler nennen. Frauen als Schmuck und Tarnung der NS-Herrschaft*. Hamburg 1994, p. 36.

[4] Curt Riess, *Das war ein Leben. Erinnerungen*. Munich 1986, p. 326.

[5] Chaim *Arlosoroff: Leben und Werk. Ausgewählte Schriften, Reden, Tagebücher und Briefe*. Berlin 1936.

[6] Bella Fromm, *Als Hitler*, p. 79 f.

[7] Shlomo Avineri, *Arlosoroff*. London 1989.

[8] Joachim C. Fest, *Das Gesicht des Dritten Reiches. Profile einer totalitären Herrschaft*. Munich 1980, p.128.

[9] Guido Knopp, *Hitlers Helfer*. :Munich 1996, p. 30.

[10] This and the following records of Joseph Goebbels are taken from: Joseph Goebbels, *Die Tagebücher. Sämtliche Fragmente*. Edited by Elke Fröhlich. Munich-New York-London-Paris 1987, part I, vol. l. Diary entry dated November 7, 1930.

[11] Elke Fröhlich, *Joseph Goebbels - Der Propagandist*. In: *Die Braune Elite I*. Edited by Ronald Smelser and Rainer Zitelmann.1989 Darmstadt, p. 52 ff.

[12] Goebbels, *Tagebücher*. Diary entry dated February 15, 1931.

[13] Dr. Otto Wagener, *Das Erleben einer Zeitenwende*. HS. Manuscript. ED 60.2103/57. Institute for Contemporary History, Munich. Henry Ashby Turner, *Otto Wagener - Der vergessene Vertraute Hitlers*. In: *Die Braune Elite II*. Edited by Ronald Smelser, Enrico Syring, Rainer Zitelmann. Darmstadt 1993, p. 243 ff. Wagener fell out of favor in 1933 and was simply forgotten about.

[14] *Hitler aus nächster Nähe. Aufzeichnungen eines Vertrauten, 1929-1932*. Edited by H. A. Turner. Berlin 1978, p. 376 ff.

[15] Adolf Hitler, *Monologe im Führerhauptquartier 1941-1944. Die*

Aufzeichnungen Heinrich Heims. Edited by Werner Jochmann. Hamburg 1980, p.108.

[16] Leni Riefenstahl, *Memoiren*. Munich-Hamburg 1987, p. 201.

[17] Ernst Hanfstaengl, *15 Jahre mit Hitler. Zwischen Weißem und Braunem Haus*. Munich 1970, p. 284.

[18] Elke Fröhlich, *Braune Elite I*, p. 62.

[19] Leonie Wagner, *Nationalsozialistische Frauenansichten*. Ph.D. thesis at Univ. Kassel 1996, p. 91.

[20] See report in *Vossische Zeitung* dated July 6, 1933.

[21] Ernst Hanfstaengl, *Zwischen Weißem und Braunem Haus*, Munich 1970, p. 319.

[22] Guido Knopp, *Hitlers Helfer*. Munich 1996, p. 51.

[23] ibid., p. 54 ff:

[24] Interview with the daily *Salzburger Nachrichten* dated August 23, 1997.

[25] Lida Baarova, "Úteky" [Flight], Toronto 1983; Interview with the daily *Salzburger Nachrichten* dated August 25, 1997. Lida Baarova lives in Salzburg.

[26] Based on notes by Eleonore Quandt. Quoted in Ebermayer / Roos, p.176.

[27] ibid., p. 325 f.

[28] Pamphlet *Der Panzerbär*, dated April 22, 1945.

[29] Statement of Red-Cross nurse Erna Flegel. Documentation Adolph Hitler 1944 -1953. Compiled on the basis of CIC files. F 135/2. Institute for Contemporary History, Munich.

[30] Gerhard Boldt, *Die letzten Tage in der Reichskanzlei*. Hamburg 1947, p. 61.

[31] Joseph Goebbels, *Tagebücher* 1945. Die letzten Aufzeichnungen. Berlin 1977, p. 457.

[32] ibid., p. 456.

[33] Albert Speer, *Erinnerungen*. Berlin 1969, p. 484 ff:

Leni Riefenstahl – The Amazon Queen

[1] Siegfried Kracauer, From *Caligari to Hitler. A psychological history of the German film*. Princeton 1970, p.110 ff:

[2] Leni Riefenstahl, *Kampf in Schnee und Eis*. Leipzig 1933, p. 13 ff

[3] ibid., p.18 f.

[4] Preface by Paul Ickes for: *Riefenstahl*, Kampf, p. 6.

[5] The French version of her memoirs contains a full chronology of

Riefenstahl's films and projects: Eine Chronologie aller Filme und Projekte Riefenstahls im Anhan der französischen Ausgabe ihrer Memoiren. L. Riefenstahl, *Memoires*. Paris 1997, p. 853 ff.

[6] Leni Riefenstahl, *Memoiren*. Munich and Hamburg 1987, p.154.

[7] Riefenstahl, *Kampf*, p.109.

[8] Joseph Goebbels, *Die Tagebücher. Sämtliche Fragmente*. Edited by Elke Fröhlich. Munich-New York-London-Paris 1987, part I, vol. 2. Diary entry dated December 11, 1932.

[9] Georg Strasser left the party at that time.

[10] Riefenstahl, *Memoiren*, p.186.

[11] Goebbels, *Tagebücher*. Diary entry dated December 8, 1932.

[12] Riefenstahl, *Memoiren*, pp.158 and 291.

[13] Luis Trenker was received by Hitler in August 1933. He held the writer, director and actor in high esteem; Hitler had seen his film *Der Rebell*, a historical drama about the Tyrolean freedom fighters four times. Adolf Hitler, *Monologe im Führerhauptquartier 1941-1944. Die Aufzeichnungen Heinrich Heims*. Edited by Werner Jochmann. Hamburg 1988, p. 467.

[14] Hitler at Obersalzberg on March 13, 1944. Hitler, *Monologe*, p. 406.

[15] The film was long believed to have been lost. It was only in the 1990s that a copy of the film resurfaced. Clips of it can be seen in: *Leni Riefenstahl. Die Macht der Bilder*. A Ray-Müller Film.

[16] Leni Riefenstahl, *Hinter den Kulissen des Reichsparteitagfilms*. Munich 1935

[17] Riefenstahl, *Hinter den Kulissen*, p.13.

[18] ibid.

[19] Goebbels, *Tagebücher*, part I, vol. 3. Diary entry dated November 24, 1937.

[20] ibid. Diary entry dated November 26, 1937.

[21] Riefenstahl, *Memoiren*, p. 304 f. Hitler did not go to Tyrol in March 1938. The story told here actually happened in April.

[22] Original telegram, shown in Ray Müller's film *Leni Riefenstahl. Die Macht der Bilder*.

[23] Transcript of cross examination by Hans Wallenberg and Ernst Langendorf on May 30, 1945. HQ 7th Army, German Intelligence Section. F 135/2. Institute for Contemporary History, Munich.

[24] Rudolf Herz, *Hoffmann & Hitler*. Catalog of eponymous exhibition at the Munich Stadtmuseum. Munich 1994, p. 64 f.

[25] Luis Trenker, *Das Tagbuch der Eva Braun*. A court banned this forgery in 1948.

[26] Leni Riefenstahl, *Die Nuba. Menschen wie von einem anderen*

Stern. Munich 1973.

[28] Ray Müller received the Emmy Award 1993 for this.

Gertrud Scholtz-Klink – The Party Comrade

[1] Biographical information: personnel file Gertrud Scholtz-Klink in BDC, Federal Archives, Berlin. Leonie Wagner, *Nationalsozialistische Frauenansichten. Vorstellungen von Weiblichkeit und Politik führender Frauen im Nationalsozialismus*. Frankfurt/Main 1996, p.192 f.

[2] Gertrud Scholtz-Klink, *Die Frau im Dritten Reich*. Tübingen 1978, p. 28.

[3] Jill Stephenson, *Gertrud Scholtz-Klink - Die NS-Musterfrau*. In: *Die Braune Elite II*. Edited by Ronald Smeler, Enrico Syring, Rainer Zitelmann. Darmstadt 1993, p. 4 ff.

[4] ibid., p. 221.

[5] *Aufbau des deutschen Arbeitsdienstes*. Edited by Gertrud Scholtz-Klink. Leipzig 1934, p.117.

[6] Scholtz-Klink.1978, p. 416.

[7] Scholtz-Klink, *Verpflichtung und Aufgabe der Frau im nationalsozialistischen Staat*. Berlin 1936, p. 23 f.

[8] Lydia Gottschewski, *Männerbund und Frauenfrage. Die Frau im neuen Staat*. Munich 1934, p. 37.

[9] Scholtz-Klink, *Vortrag auf dem Delegiertentag sämtlicher badischer Frauenverbände 1933*. p. 488.

[10] Scholtz-Klink, *Die Frau in der deutschen Volkswirtschaft*. In: *NiedersachsenStürmer* dated August 25, 1934.

[11] *NS-Frauenwarte*, vol. 1 1933, issue 20.

[12] Adolf Hitler, *NS-Frauenbuch*. Munich 1934.

[13] Taken from Hitler's speech addressed to NS women. In: *Völkischer Beobachter* date September 13, 1936.

[14] Scholtz-Klink, *Verpflichtung und Aufgabe der Frau im nationalsozialistischen Staat*. Berlin 1936, p.12 f.

[16] Elke Fröhlich, *Braune Elite*, p. 227.

[17] Werkverzeichnis Scholtz-Klink. In: Wagner, *Nationalsozialistische Frauenansichten*, p. 217 ff

[18] *Völkische Frauenbewegung*. p. 208. Original quotation!

[19] Scholtz-Klink, *NS-Frauenwarte*. Issue 16, p. 489.

[20] Scholtz-Klink, Speech in Bad Schachen. September 1943. ED 34, Nr. 277/52, p.1, Institute for Contemporary History, Munich.

[21] *Die Reichsfrauenführerin im Kreuzverhör*. In: *Dokumentation: Das*

Dritte Reich. Ein Volk, ein Reich, ein Führer. Edited by C. Zentner. Hamburg 1975, p. 262 f.
[22] Scholtz-Klink, *Die Frau im Dritten Reich.* Tübingen 1978, p. 28.

Geli Raubal - Adolf's Niece

[1] Adolf Hitler - Angelika Raubal - Emil Maurice. Nr. 5187/ 1993 in auction catalog 1993 of the auction house HERMAN HISTORICA.
[2] Angela Hitler was born in Vienna on July 28, 1883. Adolf Hitler, Monologe im Führerhauptquartier 1941-1944. Die Aufzeichnungen Heinrich Heims. Edited by Werner Jochmann. Hamburg 1980, p.187.
[3] Leo, born on October 2, 1906; Angela, born June 4, 1908; Elfriede, born January 10, 1910. Biographical information according to registry archives in the city of Linz. The Raubal family is listed in the Linz registry - HS. 2026, 73333; Archives of the city of Linz.
[4] Johann Baumgartner, *Adolf Hitler - seine große Liebe in Peilstein.* In: *Oberösterreichische Heimatblätter,* vol. 48, No. 3, 1994, pp. 281 ff
[5] ibid.
[6] M-1986/98 MA 8. City and Provincial Archives in Vienna.
[7] Report card from the school in Amerlingstrasse dated March 31, 1922. Even in religious instructions, Geli only achieved a "D."
[8] On April 10, 1922, Angela Raubal entered grade 3A. Main catalog. Archives of Academic Secondary School in Linz. Willibald Katzinger - Monika Klepp - Gerhart Marckhgott - Erika Sokolicek, Die Geschichte des Akademischen Gymnasiums Linz. Linz 1998, p.183 ff:
[9] Classmate Alfred Klimesch, who later become director of the first Austrian broadcasting company, RAVAG. Report cards of Angela Raubal 1922-1927. Main catalog. Archives of Academic Secondary School in LinzHauptkatalog.
[10] Ernst Hanfstaengl, *15 Jahre mit Hitler. Zwischen Weißem und Braunem Haus.* Munich 1970,
p.152 f., p. 231 ff. Hanfstaengl, whose Ph.D. thesis on Bavarian history in the 18th century attracted attention because of one-sided accounts and unjust judgments, let his imagination roam freely when writing his memoirs.
[11] Vienna 4, Schönburgstrasse 52/1/9. According to MA 8 - M 1986/98.
[12] Vienna 4, Schönburgstrasse 52/4/15.
[13] Statement of classmate Hermann Pfeifer, who later become a Catholic priest in Linz. Quoted in Werner Maser, *Adolf Hitler. Legende - Mythos - Wirklichkeit.* Munich 1971, p. 62.

[15] ibid., p. 49.

[16] On June 17, 1924, with the mother and brother Leo.

[17] BMfU – Ministerial decree dated November 29, 1924 - Z. 27602/5.

[18] Maleta, *Bewältigte Vergangenheit.* p. 48 f.

[19] Application (February 1921) for organizing a referendum on annexation by Germany. Friedrich Walter, *Österreichische Verfassungs- und Verwaltungsgeschichte von 1500-1955.* Vienna 1972, p. 281 ff.

[20] Hitler was granted a permit for emigration by the provincial government of Upper Austria on April 30, 1925. Until February 25, 1932, he was stateless.

[21] Maleta, *Bewältigte Vergangenheit.* p. 50.

[22] "On the whole, the party has not made a lot of progress ... it failed ... to restore its membership ... to the level of 1923" – report of Reich commissioner for public order on March 28, 1927. Federal Archives in Koblenz, R 134/32.

[23] *Die Geschichte des Akademischen Gymnasiums Linz* (The History of the Academic Secondary School in Linz), p.187.

[24] Angela Raubal on the left. Picture in Geschichte, p.185.

[25] On November 7, 1927. Reg. No. 1947. University archives of Ludwig-Maximilians-University Munich.

[26] In 1928, Angela Raubal was expelled for having failed to pay her tuition fees.

[27] *Die Tagebücher von Joseph Goebbels.* Edited by Elke Fröhlich. Part I. Sämtliche Fragmente. 4 volumes. Munich 1987. Diary entry dated September 24, 1926.

[28] Biographical information acccording to Dr. Hedwig Maurice, Emil Maurice's widow, who suspects that Emil Maurice's grandfather was Jewish.

[29] *Munich–Hauptstadt der Bewegung.* Catalog of eponymous exhibition at Munich Stadtmuseum. Munich 1993, p. 233 f.

[30] Henriette von Schirach interviewed by David Irving on November 27, 1970. Institute for Contemporary History, Munich. Also: Henriette Schirach, *Frauen um Hitler.* Munich 1983, p. 57f

[31] Talking with Nerin Gun 1967. Quoted in Nerin E. Gun, *Eva Braun-Hitler, Leben und Schicksal.* Velbert und Kettwig 1968, p.17 and p. 23.

[32] Emil Maurice talking to Nerin Gun, 1963. Quoted in N. Gun, *Eva Braun-Hitler,* p.17.

[33] Ibid., p. 24.

[34] Of the following two pages, only the summary text of the exhibition catalog is still available.

[35] Ilse Hess. Wife of Hitler's private secretary at the time.

[36] Angela Raubal to Emil Maurice. Letter dated December 24, 1927. Letter from the estate of the Maurice family. Quoted from the facsimile of the auction catalog 1993 of the auction house HERMANN HISTORICA, Munich. At this point, I would like to thank Mr. Ernst-Ludwig Wagner for his assistance.

[37] Heinrich Hoffmann, *Hitler, wie ich ihn sah.* Berlin 1974, p.124.

[38] H. Schirach, *Frauen um Hitler*, p. 51.

[39] Diary entry dated July 13, 1928.

[40] Ibid., diary entry dated October 19, 1928.

[41] *Der Spiegel*, No. 24/1987, p. 94.

[42] Heinrich Hoffmann, *Hitler wie ich ihn sah.* Berlin 1974, p.126.

[43] Emil Maurice interviewed by Nerin Gun. Gun, *Eva Braun-Hitler*, p. 24.

[45] *Hitler aus nächster Nähe. Aufzeichnungen eines Vertrauten 1929-1932.* Edited by H. A. Turner, Frankfurt/Main 1978, p. 98.

[46] *München-Hauptstadt der Bewegung.* 1993, p.125 ff. and p. 169 f.

[46] Description of furnishings according to housekeeper Anni Winter in 1967. Gun, *Eva Braun-Hitler*, p. 20.

[47] Goebbels, . Diary entry dated November 22, 1928.

[48] Hitler, *Monologe*, p. 207.

[49] Albert Speer, *Erinnerungen.* Frankfurt/Main-Berlin 1969, p. 59.

[50] Heinrich Hoffmann, *Hitler.* p.126.

[51] Albert Speer, *Spandauer Tagebücher*, Frankfurt/Main-Berlin-Vienna, p.198.

[52] Goebbels, *Tagebücher*. Diary entry dated July 21, 1930.

[53] Ibid., diary entry dated January 15, 1931

[54] *Münchner Neueste Nachrichten* – weather forecast for September 18, 1931.

[55] Hitler, *Monologe*, p. 226.

[56] Violation of motor vehicles regulations No. 1562 of the Bavarian Police Station Reichertshofen dated September 20, 1931. Facsimile in *Der Spiegel* 1987/24, p. 85.

[57] So far, this has been attributed to the deafness of the "half-blind, old Reichert". In fact, she was 45.

[58] Final police report.

[59] Entry in suicide records of police department of Munich - Pol.Dir. 7856, entry no.193. State Archives in Munich.

[60] Information from Prof. Dr. W. Eisenmenger, Institute for Forensic Medicine at Univ. of Munich, May 13, 1998.

[61] Stamp of Office of Public Prosecutor in Munich I, dept. XVI on the official autopsy report dated September 21, 1931.

[62] Appendix to final police report.

[63] Statements of Maria Fischbauer and Rosina Zweckl in final police report.

[64] Hitler's statement was published in *Münchner Post* and in *Volksboten* dated September 23, 1931. Also in: Hitler, *Reden, Anordnungen, Schriften IV/2 (Februar 1925 bis Januar 1933)*, Munich 1994.

[65] *Der Spiegel* No. 24/1987.

[66] Information received from Prof. Eisenmenger, Institute for Forensic Medicine at Univ. of Munich on May 13, 1998.

[67] Identification of driver by Munich police regarding speeding violation of vehicle II A-19357 (Hitler's Mercedes) on September 19, 1931, at 1:37 pm.

[68] File no. XVI 2304 /31, also on death notice TA 716. State Archives Munich.

[69] Franz Gürtner, Bavarian minister of justice, 1922 – 1932; Reich minister of justice until his death in 1941. Lothar Gruchmann, *Franz Gürtner-Justizminister unter Hitler*. In: Elke Fröhlich, *Die Braune Elite II*, p.128 ff.

[70] Investigation for suspicion of perjury. Clemens Vollnhals, *Der Aufstieg der NSDAP in München 1925 bis 1933: Förderer und Gegner*. In: *München-Hauptstadt der Bewegung*, p.157 ff.

[71] Settlement file No.22936/31-MA 43 – Municipal cemeteries.

[72] Statement of Leo Raubal in 1967 vis-à-vis Werner Maser.

[73] Hitler, *Monologe*, p. 218.

[74] Karl-Wilhelm Krause, *Zehn Jahre Tag und Nacht*, no year, p. 35.

[75] Hitler, *Monologe*, p. 227.

[76] Original letter kept by Leo Raubal (1906-1977). Quoted in Werner Maser, *Adolf Hitler. Legende-Mythos-Wirklichkeit*. Munich 1975, p. 316.

[77] Interview with Dr. Hedwig Maurice in Starnberg in August 1998.

[78] According to MA 43, the "short-term, payable right of use" was paid on January 23, 1938, for the last time.

[79] Interview with Werner Maser in March 1967.

[80] Goebbels, *Tagebücher*. Diary entry dated November 15, 1935.

[81] Funeral of Hitler's aunt Theresia Schmidt in August 1938. Andrej Iwanowski, Michael Siegert, Drei Goldkronen von Adolf. In: *Profil* dated July 27, 1998, No. 31, p. 62 f.

[82] Swetlana Allilujewa, *20 Briefe an einen Freund*. Vienna 1967, p. 232.

[83] *München-Hauptstadt der Bewegung*, photo p. 470.

[84] According to MA 43 - Group 23E, Row 2, No. 73.

[85] Nerin Gun, *Eva Braun-Hitler*, p. 27.

[86] Rolf Rietzler, *Das Grab von Onkel Adolfs Nichte*. In: *Der Spiegel* 1987/24, p. 84 ff.

Eva Braun – The Secret Love

[1] Isabellastrasse 45.

[2] Birth notice (Braun estate).

[3] The amateur movies of Eva Braun. Broadcast by ORF (Austria) on July 23, 1997.

[4] Speer, *Spandauer Tagebücher*. Frankfurt/Main-Berlin-Vienna 1975, p. 523.

[5] Heinrich Hoffmann, *Hitler, wie ich ihn sah*. Berlin 1974, p.132 ff.

[6] Rudolf Herz, *Hoffmann & Hitler*. Fotografie als Medium des Führer-Mythos, Munich 1994, p. 48.

[7] Her sister Ilse interviewed by Nerin Gun. Quoted in Nerin E. Gun, *Eva Braun-Hitler*. Leben und Schicksal. Velbert und Kettwig 1968.

[8] Report based on inteview with Ilse Braun. Quoted in Gun, *Eva Braun*, p. 46.

[9] *München-Hauptstadt der Bewegung*. Exhibition catalog. Munich 1993, photos p.128 and p.174.

[10] Heinrich Hoffmann, *Hitler, wie ich ihn sah*. Berlin 1974, p.135 f.

[11] The original photo was found in an album of Eva Braun's. Contained in N. Gun, *Eva Braun*, after p. 80.

[12] *Völkischer Beobachter*, Munich edition, No. 259, November 8, 1929.

[13] Baldur von Schirach, *Ich glaubte an Hitler*. Hamburg 1967, p.118.

[14] Ilse Braun interviewed by N. Gun. Quoted in N. Gun, *Eva Braun*. 1968.

[15] Photo in N. Gun, *Eva Braun*, after p. 32.

[16] Heinrich Hoffmann, *Hitler*, p.136.

[17] Speer, *Spandauer Tagebücher*, p.140.

[18] Fritz Wiedemann, *Der Mann, der Feldherr werden wollte*. Stories and experiences of Hitler's superior officer during World War I and subsequent personal aide-de-camp. Velbert und Kettwig 1964, p.112 f.

[19] Albert Speer, *Erinnerungen*. Frankfurt/Main and Berlin 1969, p. 06.

[20] These events according to Nerin Gun, who conducted interviews with the Braun family. The same wording can be found in numerous memoirs. For example, Baldur von Schirach, who mentions summer 1932 as the date of the attempted suicide - Schirach, *Ich glaubte an Hitler*. Hamburg 1967, p.137 ff.

[21] Sofie Spork. Hoffmann's first wife had died in 1928.

[22] David G. Marwell, *Ernst Hanfstaengl - Des Führers Klavierspieler*. In: *Die Braune Elite II*. Edited by Ronald Smelser, Enrico Syring, Rainer Zittelmann. Darmstadt 1993, p.137 ff.

[23] Ernst Hanfstaengl,*15 Jahre mit Hitler. Zwischen Weißem und*

Braunem Haus. Munich 1970, p. 287.

[24] Rudolf Herz, *Hoffmann & Hitler*, p. 52 ff.

[25] Tagebuch Eva Braun. Diary entry dated April 29, 1935. Original: National Archives, Washington. Copy under MA 672 - Eva Braun's diary at the Institute for Contemporary History, Munich.

[26] Werner Maser, *Adolf Hitler. Legende - Mythos - Wirklichkeit*. Munich 1975, p. 341.

[27] Diary entry of Eva Braun dated May 10, 1935.

[28] Maser, *Hitler*, p. 320.

[29] The original of the letter is kept by the Braun family. Printed in *Der Spiegel*, 1973/17, p. 130 f.

[30] E. Hanfstaengl,*15 Jahre*, p. 359.

[31] P. L. Toost died in 1934. His wife Gerdy continued to manage the architectural office and was responsible for the complete furnishings of "Berghof."

[32] Shown in: Rudolf Herz, *Hoffmann & Hitler*, p.124. Eva Braun left it to her mother in her last will, because her mother had always admired the painting.

[33] Treachery Act dated December 20, 1934.

[34] Files of special court, Akten des Sondergerichts, Mü 1 No. 8395. Bavarian State Archives, Munich.

[35] *Rund um den deutschen Volkswagen*. In: *Allgemeine Automobilzeitung* No. 6, June 1938, p. 8.

[36] Long-time party comrade, later Bavarian state minister.

[37] E. Hanfstaengl, *15 Jahre*, p. 359.

[38] The leisure-time organization "Kraft durch Freude" of the German Labor Front was the first to develop a system of subsidized tourism. In 1935, the construction of two line ships was started. Those ships had only one class.

[39] Henriette von Schirach, *Frauen um Hitler*. Munich-Berlin 1983, p. 230.

[40] Speer, *Erinnerungen*, p.113.

[41] Maser, *Hitler*, p. 305, as well as Maser, *Hitlers Briefe und Notizen*; facsimile p.157 ff.

[42] That was in line with the income of a Gau leader. In 1938, the Steyr-Daimler-Puch convertible cost 4,900 Reich marks; the Volkswagen was to be priced at 900 Reich marks – a trip to North cost 450 Reich marks – *Allgemeine Automobilzeitung* No. 6, June 1938.

[43] By using the old name, Hitler violated a strict ban, because his home country had been called Gau Lower Danube since the occupation of Austria.

[44] The almost indestructible installation still exists; today, it is used as a

wine cellar.

[45] To varying success; sometimes, desperate people came to the gate to ask for help.

[46] Speer, *Spandauer Tagebücher*, p.140.

[47] Speer, *Erinnerungen*, p. 59.

[48] Descriptions of Obersalzberg. In: *München-Hauptstadt der Bewegung*, p. 394 ff.

[49] Traudl Junge, *Er war mein Chef*. Munich 1965, p.160.

[50] Ibid., p.165 ff.

[51] H. Schirach, *Frauen*, p. 234.

[52] Speer, *Spandauer Tagebücher*, p. 204.

[53] Day-to-day minutes at Obersalzberg kept by Heinz Linge. Copies at the Institute for Contemporary History, Munich.

[54] Speer, *Erinnerungen*, p.114, as well as "Der Spiegel" 1973/21, p. 135.

[55] Notes of Therese Link. ZS 3135 Vol. I. Institute for Contemporary History, Munich.

[56] Speer, *Erinnerungen*, p. 269.

[57] Henriette von Schirach, *Frauen um Hitler*, Munich 1983, p. 220.

[58] Ilse Braun interviewed by Nerin Gun. Quoted in N. Gun, *Eva Braun*.

[59] Handwritten report by Dr. Bloch, Federal Archives in Koblenz, NS 26/65.

[60] Maser, *Hitler*, p.372.

[61] K. Krause, *Zehn Jahre Tag und Nacht. Kammerdiener bei Hitler*. Hamburg 1949, p. 58. Cf. Maser, *Hitler, Kapitel 8: Der kranke Führer*, p. 370. The list of all drugs regularly taken by Hitler, which was compiled after the war, was four pages long.

[62] K. Krause, *Zehn Jahre*, p. 45.

[63] Ibid., p. 45,

[64] John Toland, *Adolf Hitler*. New York 1977. p.1089 ff.

[65] Hitler's letter and Eva Braun's reply are the property of an anonymous collector. Quoted in Nerin E. Gun, *Eva Braun*, p.164.

[66] We listened to our beloved Fuehrer's voice – Providence confirms again Adolf Hitler's mission to free the German people from humiliation and need – *Völkischer Beobachter*, special edition dated July 21, 1944.

[67] Hitler's uniform after the attack. Photo in Federal Archives in Koblenz; in: John Tolland, *Adolf Hitler*. New York 1976.

[68] Interview between Gun and Herta Ostermayr in the summer of 1968.

[69] N. Gun, *Eva Braun*, p.164.

[70] Quoted literally, ibid., p.175 ff.

[71] Percy Ernst Schramm, *Hitler als militärischer Führer. Erkenntnisse*

und *Erfahrungen aus dem Kriegstagebuch des Oberkommandos der Wehrmacht*. Frankfurt/ Main 1962, p.154.

[72] Ein genauer Bericht über das Leben im Bunker. H. R. Trevor-Roper, *Hitlers letzte Tage*. Frankfurt/Main 1965.

[73] Letter to Herta Ostermayr dated April 19, 1945. English translation. Institute for Contemporary History, Munich.

[74] Letter to her sister Gretl dated April 18, 1945.

[75] Gerhard Boldt, *Die letzten Tage der Reichskanzlei*. Reinbek bei Hamburg 1964.

[76] Hitler's political testament dated April 29, 1945. Federal Archives in Koblenz, NS 20/129 f. facsimile in Maser, *Hitlers Briefe*, p. 213.

[77] Interrogation Kempkas on special brief by Major Trevor-Roper on January 12, 1946. Documentation Adolph Hitler 1944-1953. F135/2. Institute for Contemporary History, Munich.

[78] Quoted in: Leni Riefenstahl, *Memoiren*. Munich-Hamburg 1987, p. 461.

[79] Trial of September 10, 1948, before the Bavarian Regional Court, Munich. Dr. Otto Gritschneder represented the Braun family in court.

[80] *Münchner Illustrierte*, October 1953.

[81] *Die Weltwoche*, Zurich, on February 13, 1948.

[82] *Wiener Samstag* of September 11, 1954. Also: *Der Spiegel* 1954/44

[83] February 4, 1946, Intelligence Organization, Allied Commission for Austria – F135/2. Institute for Contemporary History, Munich.

[84] Report of Conversation with Gretl Braun-Fegelein ... September 25, 1945. F 135/3, p. 366. Institute for Contemporary History, Munich.

[85] Statement of lieutenant colonel Franz Konrad on January 6, 7, 8 and 16, 1946. F 135/2, p. 227 ff. as well as p. 306. Institute for Contemporary History, Munich.

[86] Letter dated December 31, 1947. File 1257 – Bavarian Main State Archives, Munich. At the end of 1948, Eva Braun's assets were seized.

Henriette von Schirach – The Fuehrer's Disciple

[1] Henriette von Schirach, *Anekdoten um Hitler*. Starnberg 1980.

[2] NS-Kuriosa - Trunkene Sehnsucht. *Der Spiegel*, 1980/25, p.180.

[3] Reinhard Spitzy, *So haben wir das Reich verspielt*. Vienna-Munich 1986, 2nd edition 1987, p. 211.

[4] They lived at Georgenstrasse 39, then moved to Schnorrstrasse 9.

[5] Henriette von Schirach, *Der Preis der Herrlichkeit*. Wiesbaden 1956, p. 34.

[6] According to photographer Bert Garai, Hitler was part of the inner circle around Hoffmann as early as 1921. Bert Garai, *The man from Keystone*. London 1965, p. 88 ff

[7] Spitzy, *So verspielten wir*, p. 211.

[8] Henriette von Schirach, *Frauen um Hitler*. Munich 1983, p. 240.

[9] Rudolf Herz, *Hoffmann & Hitler*, Fotografie als Medium des Führers-Mythos. Exhibition catalog. Munich 1994, p. 26.

[10] Hitler at Wolfsschanze on April 3, 1942. Roundtable discussions at Fuehrer HQ: *Tischgespräche im Führerhauptquartier 1941 bis 1942*. Edited by Henry Picker. Bonn 1965, p. 243.

[11] Baldur von Schirach, *Ich glaubte an Hitler*. Hamburg 1967, p.122 f.

[12] Interview between David Irving and Henriette Hoffmann-von Schirach on November 27, 1970. File 4770-72, ZS 2238 - Institute for Contemporary History, Munich.

[13] H. Schirach, Frauen, p. 242.

[14] Lorenz Tiedemann. In: *Photographische Chronik*, No. 40, 1937, p. 299.

[15] Spitzy, *So verspielten wir*, p. 211.

[16] H. Schirach, *Der Preis*, p. 225.

[17] *München-Hauptstadt der Bewegung*, photo on p.168.

[18] Diary of Erhard Milch. MTb, October 13, 1930.

[19] H. Schirach, *Der Preis*, p. 85.

[20] Baldur von Schirach, *Die Feier der neuen Front*. Berlin 1929.

[21] Statement of Henriette von Schirach, Club 2. ORF (Austrian broadcasting corporation) on October 28, 1976.

[22] Gudrun Schwarz, *Eine Frau an seiner Seite*. Hamburg 1997, p. 24 ff.

[23] B. Schirach, *Ich glaubte*, p. 212.

[24] Conan Fischer, *Ernst Julius Röhm - Stabschef der SA und unentbehrlicher Außenseiter*. In: *Die Braune Elite I*. Edited by Ronald Smelser and Rainer Zitelmann. Darmstadt 1989, p. 213.

[25] Königinstrasse 31.

[26] Herz, *Hoffmann & Hitler*. Unternehmensgeschichte, p. 53 f.

[27] NS26/395, Federal Archives in Koblenz.

[28] Ministry for special matters, MSO file 1742. Bavarian Main State Archives, Munich.

[29] B. Schirach, *Ich glaubte*, p. 214.

[30] Ibid.

[31] Schirach's testimony before the International Military Court in Nuremberg. In: IMT vol. XV, p. 466.

[32] Statement of Henriette von Schirach, Club 2. ORF broadcast on October 28, 1976.

[33] Jochen von Lang, *Hitler-Junge. Baldur von Schirach. Der Mann, der Deutschlands Jugend erzog.* Munich 1987, p. 270.

[34] Ibid.

[35] H. Schirach, *Der Preis*, p. 203.

[36] *Völkischer Beobachter.* Vienna edition of August 15, 1940, p. 3.

[37] H. Schirach, *Der Preis*, p. 203 f.

[38] *Völkischer Beobachter* dated August 15, 1940.

[39] Anonymous letters from the Austrian population. Briefe aus der österreichischen Bevölkerung. 19400/130. – Documentary Archives of the Austrian Resistance (DÖW).

[40] Michael Wortmann, *Baldur von Schirach - Studentenführer, Hitlerjugendführer, Gauleiter in Wien*, p. 254. In: *Die Braune Elite I.* Edited by Ronald Smelser and Rainer Zitelmann. Darmstadt 1989, p. 254.

[41] DÖW. File 8919 / a, p.11 ff:

[42] *Schuld und Verstrickung.* In: *Neue Zürcher Zeitung* dated May 5, 1998, p. 37

[43] Ibid. On December 27, 1939, Eichmann transferred 300,000 Reich marks to the Israeli community to finance a transport to Palestina. In January 1940, this support of emigration was banned.

[44] Note of Bormann on October 2, 1940. IMT, vol. XXXIX, p. 425.

[45] DÖW. File 19400/65.

[46] Speech of Baldur von Schirach on September 14, 1942. Austrian State Archives – General Administrative Archives. Reich Governor File 1406.

[47] Testimony of Wilhelm Bienenfeld, the deputy leader of the Vienna Jewish community, on April 8, 1946. DÖW File 919/a.

[48] DÖW. File 15858. Circular issued by the Reich governor on November 17, 1940.

[49] Statement of Bienenfeld, ibid.

[50] For lack of other offenses, the prelate of the monastery was accused of insulting his servant and hanging up the Fuehrer's picture only when he expected visitors. DÖW. File 2840 - Document 3927. Report on the seizure of the monastery of Klosterneuburg.

[51] DÖW. File 18869. The last hunt was organized on December 11 – 13, 1943.

[52] Ulrich von Hassel, *Vom anderen Deutschland. Aus den nachgelassenen Tagebüchern 1938-1944.* Frankfurt/Main 1964, p. 293.

[53] B. Schirach, *Ich glaubte*, p. 271.

[54] Nicolaus von Below, *Als Hitlers Adjutant 1937-45.* Mainz 1980. p. 264.

[55] Ibid., p. 265.

[56] Statement of Henriette von Schirach. Club 2, ORF broadcast on October 28, 1976.

[57] *Monologe im Führerhauptquartier 1941-1944*. Edited by Heinrich Heims. Hamburg 1980, p. 380.

[58] H. Schirach, *Der Preis*, p. 220 f.

[59] Statement of Henriette von Schirach im Club 2. ORF broadcast on October 28, 1976. Also quoted in: Joachim C. Fest, *Das Gesicht des Dritten Reiches*. Munich 1970, p. 317. Another report can be found in Nicolaus von Below, *Als Hitlers Adjutant*, p. 340.

[60] Goebbels, *Tagebücher*. Diary entry dated June 24, 1943.

[61] J. von Lang, *Der Hitler-Junge*, p. 338 ff.

[62] Lang, *Der Hitler-Junge*. p. 341.

[63] Ibid., p.124.

[64] Noted down at the end of April 1945. DÖW File 16659.

[65] Report of the daily *Die Presse* on January 4, 1956.

[66] H. Schirach, *Der Preis*, p. 97.

[67] Ministry for special matters, MSO -1742. Bavarian Main State Archives, Munich. Another report in *Süddeutsche Zeitung* on December 20, 1947.

[68] H. Schirach, *Der Preis*, p. 71 ff:

[69] International Biographical Archives - Munzinger-Archives, 31/ 1956.

[70] Albert Speer, *Spandauer Tagebücher*. Frankfurt/Main-Berlin-Vienna 1975, p. 224.

[71] *Frankfurter Allgemeine* on January 17, 1958.

BIBLIOGRAPHY

The author based her research, among other sources, on the following books:

Martin Broszat, *Der Nationalsozialismus. Weltanschauung, Programm und Wirklichkeit.* Stuttgart 1960.

Alan Bullock, *Hitler. Eine Studie über Tyrannei.* Düsseldorf 1959. (Available in English as *Hitler: A Study in Tyranny*)

Walther R. Darré, *Neuadel aus Blut und Boden.* Munich 1935.

Max Domarus, *Hitler. Reden und Proklamationen 1932-1935.* Kommentiert von einem deutschen Zeitgenossen. I. Band, Triumph (1932-1938). Würzburg 1962. (Available in English as *Hitler: Speeches and Proclamations 1932 – 1945*, set of 4 volumes)

Joachim C. Fest, *Das Gesicht des Dritten Reiches. Profile einer totalitären Herrschaft.* Munich 1963. (Available in English as *The Face of the Third Reich: Portraits of the Nazi Leadership*)

André François-Poncet, *Botschafter in Berlin 1931-1938.* Berlin-Mainz 1962. (Available in English as *The Fateful Years: Memoirs of a French Ambassador in Berlin, 1931–1938*; out of print)

Joseph Goebbels, *Michael. Ein deutsches Schicksal in Tagebuchblättern*, Munich 1933. (Available in English as *Michael: A Novel*; out of print. However, there are several English versions of Goebbels' diaries)

Joseph Goebbels, *Die Tagebücher von Joseph Goebbels.* Im Auftrag des Instituts für Zeitgeschichte und in Verbindung mit dem Bundesarchiv. Hrsg .von Elke Fröhlich. Teil I: Aufzeichnungen 1924-1941. Sämtliche Fragmente.4 Bände, Munich 1987 ff. (For English versions, see above)

Joseph Goebbels, *Signale der neuen Zeit. 25 ausgewählte Reden von Dr. Joseph Goebbels.* Munich 1934.

Emmy Göring, *An der Seite meines Mannes*. Göttingen 1967. (Available in English as *My Life with Goering*; out of print)

Nerin E. Gun, *Eva Braun-Hitler. Leben und Schicksal*. Velbert und Kettwig, 1968 (Available in English as *Eva Braun: Hitler's Mistress*; out of print)

Ernst Hanfstaengl, *15 Jahre mit Hitler. Zwischen Weißem und Braunem Haus*, Munich 1970. (Available in English as *Hitler: The Missing Years*)

Rudolf Herz, *Hoffmann & Hitler*. Fotografie als Medium des Führer-Mythos. Katalog der gleichnamigen Ausstellung. Munich 1994. (Exhibition catalogue)

Heinrich Hoffmann, *Hitler, wie ich ihn sah*. Berlin 1974.

Adolf Hitler, *Mein Kampf*. 37. Auflage. Munich 1933. (37th edition)

Adolf Hitler., Monologe im Führerhauptquartier 1941-1944. Die Aufzeichnungen Heinrich Heims. Hrsg. von Werner Jochmann, Hamburg 1980. (Available in English as *Table Talk, Nineteen Forty-One to Nineteen Forty-Four (Studies in Fascism: Ideology and Practice)*)

David Irving, *Göring*. Munich 1987. (Available in English as *Goring: A Biography*; out of print)

Eleonore Kandl, *Hitlers Österreichbild* (Ph.D. thesis). Vienna 1963.

Robert M. W. Kempner, *Das Dritte Reich im Kreuzverhör. Aus den unveröffentlichten Vernehmungsprotokollen des Anklägers*. Munich 1969.

Felix Kersten, *Totenkopf und Treue. Heinrich Himmler ohne Uniform*. Aus den Tagebuchblättern des finnischen Medizinalrats Felix Kersten, Hamburg (no year) (Available in English as *The Kersten Memoirs, 1940 – 1945*; out of print)

Guido Knopp, *Hitlers Helfer*, Munich 1996.

Alfred Kube, *Pour le merite und Hakenkreuz. Hermann Göring im*

Dritten Reich. 2. Auflage. Munich l987.

Jochen v. Lang, *Der Sekretär. Martin Bormann: Der Mann, der Hitler beherrschte*. Munich 1987.

Jochen v. Lang, *Der Hitler-Junge. Baldur von Schirach: Der Mann, der Deutschlands Jugend erzog*. Hamburg 1988.

Werner Maser, *Adolf Hitler. Legende - Mythos - Wirklichkeit*. Munich 1975. (Available in English as *Hitler: Legend, Myth and Reality*; out of print).

Werner Maser, *Hitlers Briefe und Notizen*. Sein Weltbild in hand-schriftlichen Dokumenten. Düsseldorf 1973. (In English: *Hitler's Letters and Notes*)

Werner Maser, *Tribunal der Sieger*. Berlin - Darmstadt - Vienna 1979.

Werner Maser, *Das Regime - Alltag in Deutschland (1933-1945)*, Munich 1983.

Albert Speer, *Spandauer Tagebücher*. Berlin 1975. (In English: *Spandau: The Secret Diaries*)

Albert Speer, *Erinnerungen*. Frankfurt/Main.1969. (In English: *Inside the Third Reich: Memoirs*)

Leni Riefenstnhl, *Memoiren*. Munich 1987. (In English: *Leni Riefen-stahl: A Memoir*)

Alfred Rosenberg, *Der Mythos des 20. Jahrhunderts. Eine Wertung der seelisch-geistigen Gestaltungskämpfe unserer Zeit*. 12. Auflage. Munich 1943. (In English: *The Myth of the Twentieth Century: An Evaluation of the Spiritual-Intellectual Confrontations of Our Age*; out of print)

Baldur v. Schirach, *Die Hitlerjugend. Idee und Gestalt*. Berlin 1934.

Baldur v. Schirach, *Ich glaubte an Hitler*. Hamburg 1967.

Henriette v. Schirach, *Der Preis der Herrlichkeit*. Wiesbaden 1956.

Henriette v. Schirach, *Frauen um Hitler*. München 1983.

Ronald Smelser, Enrico Syring, Rainer Zitelmann (eds.), *Die Braune Elite I und II*. Darmstadt 1993.

Hugh Trevor-Roper, *Hitlers letzte Tage*. Zurich 1948. (In English: *The Last Days of Hitler*)

Hugh Trevor-Roper (ed.), *The Bormann Letters. The Private Correspondence between Martin Bormann and his Wife from January 1943 to April 1945*. London 1954.

Henry Ashby Turner (ed.), *Hitler aus nächster Nähe. Aufzeichnungen eines Vertrauten, 1929-1932*. Frankfurt/Main 1978. (In English: *Hitler – Memoirs of a Confidant*)

Fanny Wilamowitz-Moellendorf, Gräfin v., *Carin Göring*. Berlin 1942.

Leonie Wagner, *Nationalsozialistische Frauenansichten: Vorstellungen von Weiblichkeit und Politik führender Frauen im Nationalsozialismus*. Frankfurt/Main 1996.

Albert Zoller, *Hitler privat*. Düsseldorf 1949.

PHOTOARCHIVES

Archives of Bernd Mayer, Bayreuth:16

Bayerische Staatsbibliothek (Bavarian State Library) Munich: 21, 27, 45, 54, 69, 100, 105, 121, 131, 137, 143, 149, 151, 153, 187, 203

Bildarchiv des Österreichischen Instituts für Zeitgeschichte der Universität Wien (Picture archives of the Austrian Institute of Contemporary History at the University of Vienna): 15, 56, 58, 80, 84, 88, 113, 115, 118

Estate of Michael Watschinger, provided by Prof. Bruno Watschinger, M.D.: 129

Private archives: 25, 125, 133

Ullstein Bilderdienst Berlin: 181

Cover: Archives of Bavarian State Library Munich (photo of Eva Braun, bottom left-hand corner, Magda Goebbels, bottom right-hand corner, Emmy Goering, top left-hand corner) and Austrian Institute of Contemporary History at the University of Vienna (photo of Leni Riefenstahl, top right-hand corner)

ACKNOWLEDGMENTS

In researching this book, the following people have assisted me with valuable information and support. In particular, I am grateful to:

Dr. M. A. Bachmann, State Archives Munich; Johann Baumgartner, Peilstein, Upper Austria; Dr. Friedrich Berg, Vienna; Sylvia Breuer, BG und BRG 2 (high school of 2nd Vienna district), Zirkusgasse, Vienna; Dr. Gerhard Bruner, Vienna; Dr. Ingela Bruner, executive board of DonauUniversität ("Danube University"), Krems; Univ.-Prof. Dr. W. Eisenmenger, head of the Institute for Forensic Medicine at the Univ. of Munich; Barbara Ganzinger, Vienna; Christa Hirschvogl, BG 6 (high school in 6th Vienna district). Rahlgasse, Vienna; Inge Janda, Vienna - Munich; Rudolf John, Vienna; Univ.-Prof. Dr. Walter Koch, Institute for Historical Auxiliary Sciences, Ludwig-Maximilians-University, Munich; Herbert Koch, Vienna City and Provincial Archives; Sonja Lantzberg, BG 6 (high school in 6th Vienna district), Amerlinggasse, Vienna; Roland Leitgeweger, Archives of the City of Linz; Ursula Lochner, University archives in Munich, LudwigMaximilians-University, Munich; Dr. Hedwig Maurice, Starnberg, Bavaria; Dr. Franz Mayr, principal of the Academic Secondary School in Linz; Dr. Naasner, Federal Archives in Berlin (formerly: Berlin Document Center); Agneta Newton-Silfverskiöld, Vienna; Maria Neubacher, Linz; Eva Reichl, principal of BG und BRG 19 (high school in 19th Vienna district), Gymnasiumstrasse, Vienna; Dr. Hermann Rumschöttel, director general of the State Archives of Bavaria, Munich; Dr. Doris Schmitzberger-Natzmer, Vienna; Rainer Schraml, Wilhering Monastery, Upper Austria; Dr. Walter Schuster, Archives of the City of Linz; Werner Steindl, Austrian National Library, Vienna; Leopold Tichatcek, 43rd dept. of the City of Vienna, MA 43, Vienna; Edwin Tobias, Austrian National Library, Vienna; Katharina Voigt, Vienna; Ernst-Ludwig Wagner, HERMANNN HISTORICA, Munich; Dr. Heinrich Walter, Vienna; the employees at the Institute for Contemporary History, Munich; den Mitarbeitern des Instituts für Zeitgeschichte der Universität Vienna; the employees at the Documentary Archives of the Austrian Resistance Movement (DÖW), Vienna.